Gurus, Swamis, and Avataras

GURUS, SWAMIS, AND AVATARAS

Spiritual Masters and Their American Disciples

by
MARVIN HENRY HARPER

THE WESTMINSTER PRESS
Philadelphia

ISBN 0–664–20927–0

Library of Congress Catalog Card No. 76–175547

BOOK DESIGN BY
DOROTHY ALDEN SMITH

Published by The Westminster Press®
Philadelphia, Pennsylvania

PRINTED IN THE UNITED STATES OF AMERICA

CONTENTS

1
WHAT IT IS ALL ABOUT

Hare Krishna, Hare Krishna, Krishna Krishna, Hare Hare,
Hare Rāma, Hare Rāma, Rāma Rāma, Hare Hare.[1]

A group of young people, wearing long pieces of yellow
cloth thrown across one shoulder, chanting *"Hare Krishna,*
Hare Krishna, Hare Hare" to the accompaniment of drum-
beat on a street in Boston; a dozen students on a university campus in Atlanta, sitting on the floor before a
large picture of a man, chanting *"Meher Baba ki jai"*; five
hundred people attending a Spiritual Unity of Nations
Seminar in Detroit; a Spiritual Master holding an audience spellbound in Washington, D.C.; a large Vedanta
publishing house in Hollywood—these are only a few
of the evidences that "Hinduism has invaded America."
American contacts with Hinduism are not new. Since
Swami Vivekananda organized the first Vedanta Societies
in New York and Boston, and Swami Yogananda established the Self-Realization Fellowship in California, there
have been swamis and gurus in our midst. What is new is
the widespread appeal of cults that venerate Hindu personalities.[2] In the past few years many cults have sprung
up in all parts of the country, and literature is appearing
increasingly in bookstores and on newsstands.[3]

How has this come about? What is there about these Hindu cults that makes them so attractive to so many people in this country? Returning to America some years ago, after many years spent in India, I became interested in this phenomenon. Not all the "new religions" that have appeared recently in the United States trace their origins to Hindu influence, of course, but many do. It was with these latter that I became primarily concerned. It soon became clear that the majority had developed around some charismatic personality, either a Hindu Guru, Swami, Avatara, or "Master," or an American who had been strongly influenced by Hindu thought. It is for this reason that I will call them "personality cults." A number of the cults now established in America, such as the Vedanta Society, the Sri Aurobindo Society, the Radhasoami Satsang, the Meher Baba Lovers, the International Society for Krishna Consciousness, and the Sivananda Yoga Center, are branches of personality cults in India. Believing that an introduction to the history, teachings, and practices of these personality cults in contemporary Hinduism would be of interest to those who are members of these Hindu-based movements in the United States, or to those who are curious, I have undertaken this study.

During my years of residence in India as a teacher in a college in Madhya Pradesh (the "Central Provinces"), I became impressed with the significant roles that the various types of religious leaders play in the Hindu community. I became especially interested in the institution of the guru. This institution developed early in Hinduism as certain spiritually advanced men withdrew to the forest or mountain fastness with their bands of disciples to study and worship in an ashram ("spiritual retreat").

In more recent times, however, the ashram in its earlier form has all but disappeared, and the guru has carried on his work in an urban setting, either in the homes of his disciples or in retreat centers in towns or cities such as Varanasi, Vrindaban, Hardwar, and Rishikesh. Although some gurus have small followings, a few have large numbers of devotees, called chelas. These charismatic gurus have become founders of personality cults. In contrast to the simplicity of life in the earlier ashrams, some of the present cult centers are "big business," with impressive buildings, extensive institutions, and active publishing houses. When the opportunity was given to me to return to India, after an absence of several years, I determined to spend the time in research relating to the history, teachings, and programs of the more prominent of the personality cults in contemporary Hinduism.

Traditionally, religion for the Hindu has been largely an individual matter, except at the time of the occasional melā ("religious festival"). Congregational worship, as practiced in the West, was almost unknown. When the Hindu felt inclined to worship his deity he went alone or with his family to the local temple. Although temples are not entirely deserted today, Hindus in increasing numbers are going to the cult centers for religious instruction and to engage in corporate worship with fellow devotees of the guru. It became apparent to me that certain crises in the life of the Hindu have brought about this change. Among these may be noted the breakup of the feudal system, known as zimindari, permitting greater mobility on the part of the common people, the introduction of Western forms of education by the British and their extension by the present government, the growth of an industrial economy leading to the migration of rural peoples to urban centers, removing them from contact with their ancestral local temples, the development of the various media for public information, the failure of traditional institutionalized religion to keep abreast of the times, and the freedom of worship now permitted in a secular state. Mention should also be made of the influence that the Christian religion and Western philosophy and science have had on Indian life.

Of the seemingly countless number of personality cults to be found in India today I selected nine of the more prominent for my study. Although significant differences in organization and practices exist, certain concepts of traditional Hinduism are apparently accepted by all. Central among these are beliefs concerning the nature of the Absolute Reality, Brahman, and the relation of the Self to this Absolute. The most widely accepted explanation of the nature of the Absolute is that taught by Shankara, who was born about A.D. 788. His is a monistic system based on the Vedanta (the "end" or "goal" of the Veda). In contrast to the later theistic interpretations of Ramanuja and Madhva, his is nontheistic, known as *Advaita* ("nondualism"). *Advaita* is the most popular system of faith and philosophy in India today and has been gaining ground in the West as well. In one form or another I found it to be the basic teaching of all the personality cults with which I became acquainted.

According to Shankara, the Absolute Reality is Brahman, and there is no other reality but Brahman. Brahman is *Sat-Chit-Ananda,* Absolute Existence, Absolute Consciousness, and Absolute Bliss. Brahman is *nir-guna,* without qualities or attributes, without distinctions within it or outside it. It is impersonal. The world was not created by Brahman itself, but by its magical power, *māyā.* "Maya as a power of Brahman is indistinguishable from Brahman, just as the burning power of fire is from fire itself. It is by this that Brahman, the Great Magician, conjures up the world show." [4] Those who are ignorant of the true nature of reality believe the world to be real, but the wise who can see through the illusion realize that Brahman is the only reality.

Shankara further taught that from the purely philosophical or transcendental standpoint, Brahman cannot be described in human terms at all. Even to speak of it as *Sat-Chit-Ananda* is only for the purpose of asserting that it is not nonexistent, unconscious, or subject to the experience of misery. Shankara speaks of the transcendent aspect of Brahman as Parabrahma, the Supreme or the Absolute, the All without distinctions. But from a practical, nonphilosophical point of view the Absolute may be conceived as Brahman *sa-guna* (Brahman "with attributes"). Thus understood, the Absolute may be considered the creator, sustainer, and destroyer, and the world as real. Shankara spoke of this aspect of the Absolute as Ishvara, the God who is worshiped by man. But only those who regard the world as real look upon the Absolute as creator. "For the wise few, however, that know the world is a mere show, there is neither any real world nor any real creator, just as for the man who sees through the magician's trick there is neither any magic nor any magician." [5]

Just as Shankara's philosophy of the Absolute has strongly influenced the founders of the personality cults, so has his teaching concerning the nature of the Self. The *Advaita* ("unqualified monism") of Shankara rejects all distinctions between objects and objects, the subject and the object, the Self and Brahman as unreal and illusory. Man is really identical with Brahman. He is apparently composed of the body, the mind, and the Self. But the body and the mind, like other material objects, are merely appearances. When this is realized, the reality that remains is the Self, which is nothing other than

Brahman. Owing to ignorance, which is beginningless, the Self erroneously associates and identifies itself with the body. This means bondage for the Self. In this state it forgets that it is really divine and it behaves like a finite, limited creature. Liberation from bondage is attained through the realization of the Self's identity with Brahman. The identity is a real fact from the very beginning, only it has been forgotten for the time being and must be recognized. The means to liberation is the study of the Vedanta under a Master, a Guru, who has himself realized Brahman.[6]

The more successful the Guru has been in leading his chelas to Self-realization, to God-realization, the more popular he has become. Thus, cults developed around these charismatic personalities. In earlier days, the most prominent were probably those formed by Shankara, Ramanuja, Chaitanya, and Kabir. Today, the number of cults, large and small, is apparently without number! I was forced, therefore, to confine my investigation to the nine which, according to the best information available to me, had the largest number of adherents. I was fortunate in having the assistance of a Christian young man, a former student of mine, P. D. Shamrao. He himself grew up in a Hindu home and was intimately acquainted with the many Hindu technical terms that we needed to handle. In addition, his fluency in several Indian languages supplemented my somewhat faulty Hindi. The time we spent in each center depended upon the size of the institution and the complexity of its organization. We were cordially received in every center, and the leaders were most cooperative in providing us with the information we sought. Unfortunately, most of the large amount of materials published by the cults visited is not available outside of India. Whenever possible we attended services of worship not only in the headquarters center but in local centers as well. This enabled us to become acquainted with a considerable number of the adherents of the various cults. Our conversations with them after the service, or on other occasions, added to our store of information. Shamrao and I made rather extensive notes of our conversations with leaders and adherents, and these notes, along with our investigations of the publications of the cults, form the basis of the present work.

Some of the concepts and incidents recorded in the following pages will appear strange, if not unbelievable, to persons in the West. I have attempted to report objectively and factually what was told me by adherents of the cults, or what I have read in publications by or about the cult leaders. Whether miracles have occurred or not, it is a fact that the persons who reported them believe that they did. Whether the cult founders were superhuman or not, many of their devotees believed them to be so. As far as I have been able to do so, therefore, I have attempted to reflect the faith experiences of the adherents of the personality cults with whom I have become acquainted without attempting to evaluate those experiences. I trust that all who read these accounts may be convinced of the sincerity of those whom they will meet, whether or not they find it possible to agree with their point of view.

Some years ago the late Carl Michalson, observing that there was very little interest in Eastern religious thought on the part of Western theologians and philosophers, wrote, "There is a language curtain that admits light from West to East, but stubbornly thwarts all theological illumination from East to West." [7] This situation is now gradually changing. The influence of the contemporary personality cults, for example, is not confined to India.

Especially in the form of Vedanta, Hinduism is beginning to make its impact on Western religious thought as well. While it would be untrue to attribute this development entirely to Ramakrishna, Vivekananda, Aurobindo, Radhakrishna, Meher Baba, and other Vedantists, the widespread circulation of books and articles about Vedanta by their followers has certainly made their influence felt. Nels Ferré observes:

> The supernatural, personalistic, classical Christian faith is now being undermined by an ultimately nondualistic, impersonal, or transpersonal faith. The winds are blowing gale-strong out of the Orient. Our seminary students prate, sometimes innocently, about "the transcendence of subject-object relations." Ministers are reading everywhere theologies that call a personal God and real life everlasting preliminary, symbolic doctrines until the fuller meaning of true ontology is understood and accepted.[8]

While Nels Ferré has possibly overstated the influence of Vedanta in the West, it is undoubtedly true that issues which, though not entirely new to Western thinkers, are nonetheless being presented in new forms, and perhaps in strange terms, by contemporary non-Christian religions. The flow of religious philosophies is no longer from West to East only. More and more, philosophical concepts from the East will find a place in our Western culture. The majority of the cults presented in this work have established centers in the West and are carrying on missionary activities, and all of them have Western adherents who are devoted to their Eastern gurus.

My purpose in presenting these cults to the West is not to win converts, but rather to give, in brief form, information concerning their historical development and teachings to any who may have become interested in, or puzzled by, them. I have been encouraged to attempt this work because of the growing interest in the religions of the East as evidenced by the large number of books published recently dealing with various aspects of these religions. The fact that very little attention has been given, however, to the contemporary personality cults in Hinduism may justify the appearance of yet another book. It is my hope that this work may be of value both to the casual reader and to the student of the history of religions. If the former should find some of the material rather too technical, he may pass quickly over Sanskrit words and philosophical terms to matters of greater interest. The scholar, on the other hand, who might consider the treatment not technical enough may find the original sources consulted useful for a more in-depth study of one or more of the cults. Some of these sources are available in Western libraries.

Some explanation should be given concerning my use of terms from Sanskrit and other Indian languages. Words that have already found their way into English usage, such as guru (religious preceptor), swami (monk), ashram (hermitage), yoga (ascetic practice), Brahmin (highest Hindu caste), pundit (an authority), and Vedanta (a monistic philosophy), have not been italicized. Nor have the titles of religious personalities, such as avatara (God-Man, or incarnation), Sat-Guru or Sad-Guru (a Perfect Master), Sat-Purusha (Perfect Man), Sant (Saint), and Sant Sat-Guru (Saintly Perfect Master), been italicized. Italics and capitalizations in quotations have not been altered, for Indian writers capitalize religious and philosophical terms more frequently than do American authors. No attempt has been made to indicate the pronunciation of Hindu terms, for this would involve an extensive discussion and is beyond the scope of the present work.

2

THE FAKIR:
Sri Sai Baba of Shirdi

A festive air greeted us as Shamrao and I alighted from
the station wagon at the decorated gateway and entered
the little town of Shirdi. Crowds milled about in the narrow streets, laughing and talking and occasionally greeting friends with shouts of joy. Merchants in the temporary,
open-front shops called out to passing visitors, inviting
them to stop and purchase fruit and candy, flowers and
garlands, pictures and souvenirs. A public-address system
blared forth music from a record player. To the accompaniment of Indian musical instruments a soloist was singing in the local dialect:

> All the holy places of India are concentrated
>   in Shirdi,
> All of our hopes are laid at the feet of Sai
>   Baba,
> He is great among the saints.
> Shirdi is our place of worship,
> God dwells here in the form of Sai Baba,
> And devotees forget themselves at the sound
>   of His Name.

The scene must have been far different a hundred years or
so ago, when our story begins.

In the year 1854, there appeared in this village of Shirdi, situated in the Ahmadnagar District, in the State of Maharashtra, a boy who appeared to be about sixteen years of age. He wore the garb of a fakir (a "Muslim holy man"), but his language and teachings were largely Hindu. When asked about his parentage and caste, he gave noncommittal answers, speaking largely in parables. He took up his residence at the foot of a sacred neem tree and surprised the villagers by the severity of his austerities. Neither heat nor cold seemed to bother him. He did not go from door to door begging, but ate only what was brought to him by those who were attracted to him. The wonder of the people grew, and so, it is said, one day God assumed the form of a holy man and came by. The people requested him to reveal to them the identity of the young fakir. They were instructed to bring a pickax and to dig in a specified place. To their amazement some bricks were found, and underneath, a stone. When the stone was removed a cave was disclosed. In the cave certain objects used in worship were seen. The stranger told them, "This lad practiced penance here for twelve years." When asked to explain this, the young fakir told them that the cave was his own guru's place, and he asked them to guard it well. The hole was closed and this spot has become holy ground. Later, a shrine was erected here under the neem tree and an image has been installed. After residing under the neem tree for about three years, the young fakir disappeared suddenly from Shirdi.[1]

The scene now shifts to a mango tree near a village in Hyderabad State. In this village there lived a wealthy Muslim named Chand Patil. One day while Chand Patil was on a business trip his horse got away from him, leaving him only his saddle. In vain he searched for the horse. As he trudged along home, with the saddle on his shoulder, he came to the mango tree. There he saw a *ratna* (a "queer fellow") wearing a long robe and having under his arm a short thick stick. He was preparing to smoke his *chillum* ("pipe"). The young man called out to Chand Patil and invited him to rest while joining him in a smoke. When he was told about the lost horse, he instructed Chand Patil to go search in a stream bed nearby. Miraculously, the horse was there, and Chand Patil realized that the stranger was no ordinary man, but an *Avalia* (a great saint or Spiritual Master). When he returned he found that the pipe was ready for smoking, but two things were missing, a coal with which to light the tobacco and water with which to dampen the cloth through which the smoke is drawn. The young fakir took a pair of tongs, and thrusting them forcibly into the ground, brought up a live coal with which the pipe was lighted. He threw the short stick on the ground, and water oozed out. Amazed at what he had observed, Chand Patil invited the young fakir to come to his house with him. Some days later, Chand Patil and his family went to attend a wedding in Shirdi, and the young man accompanied them.

When the party arrived in Shirdi, the carts were stopped in a field near the Khandoba temple. As the young fakir alighted from a cart he was addressed by a priest standing nearby, "*Ya Sai*" ("Welcome, Sai"). Others addressed him as "Sai" and thenceforth he became known as "Sai Baba." He now took up his abode in an abandoned *masjid* ("Muslim mosque") not far from the temple.[2]

Miracles

One of Sai Baba's peculiar habits was to keep an oil lamp burning continuously. He would beg oil from the shopkeepers. One day the merchants plotted to tease him and refused to give him the oil. Unperturbed, Sai Baba returned to the *masjid*, followed by some of the shopkeepers. He put dry wicks in the lamp, took up a tin vessel in which there was a small amount of oil and poured some water into it. He then drank from the vessel, thus "consecrating" its contents, and poured the water into the lamp. He lighted the lamp, and to the amazement of all, it began to burn and kept burning throughout the night. Sai Baba's name soon spread widely, and his fame was further enhanced by the various miracles he performed. He often used them as the basis for a discourse on some spiritual matter.

Such was the case with the grinding of the wheat. Early one morning Sai Baba spread a sack on the floor and placed a hand grinding mill on it. He then took up handfuls of wheat, dropped them into the mill and began to turn the handle. Since it is most unusual for a man to grind grain in India, a crowd soon gathered. Finally, several women pushed him away from the mill and continued the task until a sackful of wheat had been ground. Then, to the surprise of all, instead of distributing the flour to the poor, as was his practice, Sai Baba gave instructions that the flour should be taken out and scattered on the ground in a circle around the village. This was done, and it was explained that a cholera epidemic was spreading through the community, and this was Sai Baba's remedy for checking it. He was not grinding wheat but cholera, which was thus ground to pieces and cast out of the village. The cholera epidemic soon subsided, but there was an even deeper meaning to this incident, it was explained. As he ground the wheat Baba was grinding the sins, the mental and physical afflictions, and the miseries of his numerous devotees. The two stones of his mill consisted of *karma* ("deeds") and *bhakti* ("devotion"). The handle with which Baba turned the mill was *jñāna* ("knowledge" or "wisdom"). Knowledge of Self-realization is not possible until all the evil deeds, sinful impulses, and unholy desires have been ground to pieces.

Among the best-known of Sai Baba's miracles were those of healing. Leprosy was cured, sight was restored to blinded eyes, and the lame were enabled to walk. A fire was kept burning in the *masjid,* and the *udi* ("ash") from the fire is reported to have produced many cures. Even since the death of Sai Baba the fire has been kept burning and the holy ash has been distributed to devotees in many parts of the country to be used when needed. At a Sai Baba center many miles from Shirdi, I witnessed *udi* being distributed to several persons who requested it for members of their families. When I visited Shirdi later, I was given a little packet of the holy ash to be used should I ever need it!

Two instances of vicarious healing are recorded by N. V. Gunaji in *The Wonderful Life of Shri Sai Baba.* On one occasion Sai Baba was sitting by the fire warming himself. Suddenly he stuck his arm into the fire and it was severely burned before his attendants could pull him away. When asked why he had done this thing, he explained that in a distant village the wife of a blacksmith was working the bellows of the furnace. Accidentally her child fell into the furnace. Seeing this, Baba said: "I immediately thrust my hand into the furnace and saved the child. I do not mind my arm being burned, for I am glad that the life of the child is saved." On another occasion a mother whose son was suffering from bubonic plague came in distress to Sai Baba. Baba assured her that her son would soon be well, and opening his robe he showed her large buboes on his own body. He added, "See, how I suffer for my devotees; their difficulties are mine." This extraordinary *līlā* ("deed") convinced Sai Baba's devotees that he in truth suffered vicariously for his disciples.[3]

But Sai Baba could also fly into a rage at the action of a devotee. This happened when some of the disciples decided to put a roof over the area in front of the *masjid*. Thinking it would be a pleasant surprise for Sai Baba, they did not ask his permission. Baba alternated between spending the night in the *masjid* and in the *chavadi* (a small building nearby), so on the night that he was absent from the *masjid* they set up iron posts and trusses for the roof. However, when Baba arrived the next morning he flew into a rage and tore the structure down. He then caught one of the devotees, Tatya Patil, by the throat, snatched off his headgear and threw it into the fire. When several of the others tried to come to the rescue of the unfortunate Tatya, Sai Baba picked up some pieces of brick lying around and threw them at them. After a short while Baba's anger cooled down, and sending to a shopkeeper, he secured a new headpiece which he himself tied around Tatya's head. All who witnessed this strange incident were amazed. But, we are told, such conduct is not unusual on the part of spiritual guides who resort to strange methods for the instruction of their disciples.

The Guru

It is generally believed by Hindus that true progress toward Self-realization is not possible without the guidance and grace of a guru. As a Self-realized Master only he is qualified to grant initiation and to prescribe the *sādhana* ("spiritual discipline") indicated for each seeker. Because of his own spiritual attainments, Sai Baba became the guru for a large number of disciples.

The institution of the guru is almost as old as Hinduism itself. There are scattered references to the preceptor or religious teacher in the Vedas and Upanishads; for example, in the Rig-Veda IV, 5:6, the guru is described as the source and inspirer of the knowledge of the Self, and he is the one who enables the seeker to attain knowledge of the Self. In the Yajur-Veda VII, 27, the guru is described as the one who blesses the disciple and as the one who enhances his spiritual life. The Upanishads are more explicit in insisting that one must have a master, or guru: "Approach a teacher (*gurū*)," says the Mundaka (I:ii:12), "with humility and with a desire to serve." In the Katha Upanishad we read: "To many it is not given to hear of the Self. Many, though they hear of it, do not understand it. Wonderful is he who speaks of it; intelligent is he who learns of it. Blessed is he who, taught by a good teacher, is able to understand it" (I:ii:7). The Katha Upanishad further warns that "the truth of the Self cannot be fully understood when taught by an ignorant man, for opinions regarding it, not founded on knowledge vary one from another. Subtler than the subtlest is this Self, and beyond all logic. Taught by a teacher who knows the Self and Brahman as one, a man leaves vain theory behind him and attains to truth" (I:ii:8). Complete submission to the direction of a competent teacher is essential if one is to attain this knowledge of God. Only he can initiate the disciple into the secrets of spiritual unfoldment. There are said to be two kinds of *diksha* ("initiation"): *sambhavi* and *mantri*. *Sambhavi* occurs when the disciple immediately experiences divine vision, attaining the supreme knowledge by the mere wish or touch of the guru. In the *mantri* form of initiation the guru initiates the disciple by revealing to him a secret *mantra* (a sacred word or formula). It is believed that a person may effect a complete change in his character by meditating upon or by repeating the *mantra*.[4]

It appears that at an early date respect for one's guru evolved into a form of devotion similar to that given to

God. We read in the Taittirya Upanishad, "Let the *Acharya*
("teacher") be your God" (I:ii:2). And the Bhagavata
Purana teaches that the preceptor (*guru*) is to be regarded
as the Deity (XI:iii) and worshiped (X:86).[5] It is only
natural that the concept of the grace (*kripa*) of God
should develop into the grace of the guru (*guru-kripa*)
and to the teaching that enlightenment can come to a
disciple only through the grace of his guru. "Sciences,
contemplation, devotion and various practices are of no
avail without his grace. Trees bear flowers and fruits only
when the spring sets in; devotion bears fruit only when
one is blessed by the grace of the *guru*." [6] As improbable as
worship of a human teacher may appear to one unac-
quainted with the Hindu personality cults, the sincerity of
this worship cannot be doubted as one talks with and lives
among the devotees.

Teachings

Sai Baba's teachings were in harmony with the traditional
Vedanta as reflected in the Bhagavad-Gita. For example,
while interpreting V:15, 16:

> The All-pervading Spirit does not take on the sin or the
> merit of any. Wisdom is enveloped by ignorance; thereby
> creatures are bewildered. But for those in whom ignorance
> is destroyed by wisdom, for them wisdom lights up the
> Supreme Self like the sun[7]

he pointed out:

> Destroying ignorance is Wisdom. Expelling darkness
> means light. Destroying duality (*dwaita*) means non-dual-
> ity (*adwaita*). If one wants to achieve oneness with the
> Absolute he must destroy the sense of duality within him-
> self. . . . The disciple (*shisya*) like the True Master
> (*Sad-guru*) is really the embodiment of Wisdom (*Jnana*).

The difference lies in the attitude, high realization, marvelous super-human Beingness (*Sattva*) and unrivalled capacity and divine powers of the True Master. The True Master (*Sad-guru*) is *Nirguna, Sat-Chit-Ananda* (The Unmanifested Absolute, Absolute Existence, Consciousness, Bliss). He has indeed taken human form to elevate mankind and raise the world. But his real *Nirguna* nature is not destroyed thereby. His beingness (or reality), divine power and wisdom remain undiminished. The disciple is in fact of the same form (*swarupa*). But it is overlaid by the effect of the desires (*samskaras*) of innumerable births. . . . He got the impression, "I am a *Jiva*, a creature, humble and poor." The *guru* has to root out these off-shoots of ignorance and has to give *upadesh*, or instruction. To the disciple . . . the *Guru* imparts the teaching, "You are God, you are mighty and opulent." . . . The perpetual delusion under which the disciple is laboring, that he is the body, that he is a creature (*jiva*) or ego, that God (*Paramatma*) and the world are different from him, is an error inherited from innumerable past births. . . . To remove this delusion, this error, this root ignorance, he must inquire: "How did this ignorance arise? What is it?" The *guru's* instruction (*upadesh*) is to give him the answer.[8]

Sai Baba understood himself to have been the Unmanifest Absolute who took human form in order to destroy ignorance and guide his disciples into that wisdom (*jñāna*) which would free them from the cycle of rebirths that had bound them. Shortly before his death, echoing somewhat the words of Sri Krishna to his disciple, Arjuna, Sai Baba said to his own disciples:

He who loves Me most, always sees Me. The whole world is desolate without Me. He tells no stories but Mine. He ceaselessly meditates upon Me and always chants My name. I feel indebted to him who surrenders himself completely to Me and ever remembers Me. I shall repay this debt by giving him salvation (Self-realization). I am dependent upon him who thinks and hungers after Me and who does not eat anything without first offering it to Me. He who thus comes to Me, becomes one with Me, just as a river goes to the sea and becomes one with it. So, leaving pride and egoism, you should surrender yourself to Me who am seated in your heart.[9]

For sixty years Sai Baba healed the sick, fed the poor, comforted the distressed and taught his disciples. His simple words of instruction and advice were treasured by thousands. He counted among his devotees doctors and lawyers, high court judges and state officials, professors and religious leaders, as well as the "common man." The sacred ash (udi) from his fire was given freely to all who asked. No one, apparently, was ever turned away. Increasing numbers came to Shirdi to have a darshana ("vision") of Sai Baba and, in faith and love, to touch his feet. His disciples, and even strangers, were often surprised to have their hidden thoughts revealed to them by Sai Baba. Many reported having heard his voice or having seen his form in their own homes in faraway towns. Although there were those in the early years who called him "the Mad Fakir," and many others looked upon him as a saint, we are assured that those who really knew him "regarded Him and still regard Him as God Incarnate." [10] In Hindu terms, he would be called an avatāra of the Supreme Being, Brahman.

The Avatara

The average Hindu probably finds the concept of the Absolute as taught by Vedanta unintelligible as well as unsatisfying. One of the most characteristic features of contemporary Hinduism, therefore, is bhakti, the loving devotion paid to one or more of the Hindu gods, conceived as personal. *Bhakti* means adoration of Bhagavan, the Adorable One.

As conceived in its contact with finite man the Absolute is Ishvara, Brahman sa-guna (Brahman "with attributes"), who "descends" to man as an avatara.

The Bhagavad-Gita has Krishna declare to his disciple, Arjuna:

> Many are my lives that are past, and thine also, O Arjuna; . . . Though I am unborn, and My self is imperishable, . . . establishing My self in My own nature, I come into being through My power (*maya*). Whenever there is a decline of righteousness and a rise of unrighteousness, then I send forth My self. For the protection of the good, for the destruction of the wicked, and for the establishment of righteousness, I come into being from age to age.[11]

Although the term *avatāra* is often rendered into English as "incarnation," some Hindu scholars strongly deny that the "descent" of the deity is a true incarnation. For them the term *avatāra* implies that "the Supreme Lord appeared in this world in His own Eternal Form out of His Own Inconceivable Prerogative without accepting any physical body." Although the "birth" of Sri Krishna is mentioned in Hindu scriptures and his birth anniversary (*janmastami*) is celebrated, it is insisted that the deity simply "appears" before the world in "His Own Eternal Transcendental Form." He never accepts an "unholy body" of a human being. Sri Krishna was not born of his "father" and "mother," Vasudeva and Devaki. "Having *appeared* in His Eternal Divine Form, the Lord spoke to Vasudeva and Devaki for some time, and then, before their very eyes, transformed Himself into his Own Krishna Form —a Divine Form, looking like a human child, but not human." [12]

The adherents of the contemporary personality cults, however, do not agree entirely with this point of view. The founders of their cults, whom they adore as divine personages, manifest certain human as well as divine qualities. Their understanding of the nature of the avatara is probably well expressed by Swami Saradananda, a disciple of Sri Ramakrishna, who is believed by his followers to have been an avatara:

> Unlike a *Jiva* ("a mortal being") he (the *avatara*) never gets entangled in or bound by his actions, for, content in the Atman (i.e., Divine Self) from his very birth, no selfish idea of worldly enjoyment arises in his mind, as it does in the case of a *Jiva*. His whole life is dedicated to the good of others. Being always free from the meshes of Maya, he retains the memory of his previous lives. It may be asked: Does he have that unbroken memory from childhood? The Puranas reply: Although latent in him, it is not always manifest during his childhood. But as soon as his body and mind mature, he becomes aware of it with little or no effort. This applies to all his actions. Since he assumes a human body, he has to behave in all respects like a human being. As soon as the body and mind of the incarnation fully develop, the aim of his life is revealed to him.[13]

The "revelation" of which Swami Saradananda speaks came to some of the avataras who have founded the personality cults in a dramatic manner, such as with the bite of a scorpion, a trance in a cave, or the kiss of a Great Master. The revelation has usually been followed by the public announcement of his mission by the divine personage, and he is recognized as a God-realized Being.

It should be noted, however, that although all avataras are God-realized Beings, not all God-realized Persons are avataras. While the Divine may "descend" into the human level, a human being may also "ascend" into the Divine.

The Last Days

Sai Baba "dropped his body" on October 14, 1918. Looking back later to events prior to his passing away, his devotees realized that he had given them several indications of his pending death, even as to its actual date. One of these was in connection with the construction of the building that now contains his tomb, the Samadh-mandir ("tomb-temple"). Shriman Bapusaheb Booty, one of Sai Baba's wealthy devotees, had a dream in which Sai Baba instructed him to build a substantial house for himself at Shirdi. He had been living in temporary quarters. Within the house there should also be a temple in which an image of Lord Krishna should be enshrined. Later, when the matter was presented to Sai Baba, he gave his approval and added: "After the temple is completed I will come there and stay. After the house is completed we shall use it ourselves, we shall live, move, and play there, embrace each other and be very happy." The true meaning of these words did not occur to his devotees then. Various difficulties prevented the placing of the image of Krishna in the temple, but just before he passed away Sai Baba instructed, "Place or keep me in the temple," and in due time his body was placed in the central shrine.

Two years before his death Sai Baba confided to two of his disciples the fact that a third disciple, Tatya, would die during Dasara (Vijayadashami) two years later. He pledged them to keep this information secret. True to Sai's word, Tatya fell sick at the time indicated. Sai Baba also developed fever. Vijayadashami approached and the two devotees were greatly concerned about their friend, Tatya, for he grew steadily worse. Vijayadashami dawned and Tatya's pulse became weak. His end was apparently at hand, as Sai Baba had predicted. But the two devotees were entirely unprepared for that which actually transpired. By noon Tatya began to improve but at 2:30 Sai Baba was dead! In recording this strange event Nagesh Gunaji, Sai Baba's biographer, says: "People said that Baba gave up his life for Tatya. Why did he do so? He alone knows as His ways are inscrutable. It seems, however, that in this incident [that is, foretelling the date of Tatya's death], Baba gave a hint of His passing away, substituting Tatya's name for His own." [14]

The question now arose as to the disposal of Sai Baba's body. Some Muslim devotees suggested that it should be interred in an open field and a tomb be built over it. Hindu devotees believed that it should be cremated in accordance with Hindu practice. It is said that Sai Baba himself gave the answer to that question. That night he appeared to one of his devotees in a dream and indicated that he should be buried in the temple area in the house that Shriman Bapusaheb Booty had constructed. On the following evening Baba's body was brought in procession and buried with due formalities in the temple that had been intended to honor Sri Krishna. For his disciples, this was most fitting. To them he was the incarnation of Sri Krishna himself.

Worship in the Sai Baba Centers

Although Sai Baba attained *mahasamadhi* (final release from the physical body) in 1918, he had promised: "I shall remain active and vigorous even after leaving this earthly Body. I am ever living to help those who come to me and who surrender and seek refuge in me." [15] Believing that he is present with them whenever they meet to remember him, his devotees gather in local centers in many towns and cities on Thursday evenings. The service held in

Jabalpur, Madhya Pradesh, is probably typical. The center is located in a room in the business section of the city. On the occasions when I attended, some twenty-five or thirty devotees sat on the floor facing the shrine at one end of the room. The shrine was a shelflike arrangement on which a large picture of Sai Baba had been placed. Below the shelf was a picture of the god Dadatare, an incarnation of Vishnu. Many consider Sai Baba to be Dadatare returned. Oil lamps and incense sticks burned in front of both pictures. Garlands of flowers had been placed around the pictures. The walls of the room were profusely decorated with pictures of Sai Baba in various poses. Pictures of other saints and of many of the Hindu deities also found a place. In a small glass case on one side of the room there was a figure dressed in red rather than the usual saffron. This figure would hardly be identified as that of Sai Baba were it not for the sign on the case. Although a garland had been placed on the case, no other attention was given to the figure during the service.

The *pūjā* ("worship service") was conducted by Sita Ram Baba, a handsome young man twenty-eight years old. His long black hair fell below his shoulders, but was parted and brought across his shoulders to the front. He had an attractive, sensitive face, and wore a spotlessly white robe. The mother and the sister-in-law of Sita Ram Baba, we learned, had been devotees of Sai Baba. On various occasions they had seen Sai Baba in visions or in dreams. Sita Ram had been nurtured in the faith of Sai Baba. As his faith grew, he too had a vision of Sai Baba in which he was called to be his priest and was told to officiate at Jabalpur. During *pūjā*, Sita Ram Baba refilled the burning lamps with oil, lighted fresh incense sticks, and poured *ghī* ("clarified butter") into the flames. While this was being done, *bhajans* ("hymns of praise") were sung by the devotees. Two soloists, accompanied by two drummers, alternated in singing the *bhajans*. The other devotees joined in the chorus. As from time to time the tempo became faster and the volume greater the sound in the small room became almost deafening, and sometimes both the musicians and the congregation grew almost frenzied in their devotion. One of the *bhajans*, which was sung over and over, was as follows:

> In Shirdi, Sant Sai Nath has become a saint.
>> Krishna's *bhaktas* ("devotees") say that Sai
>> is Krishna Himself,
> Christians say that Sai is Christ,
>> Muslims own him as their own.
> God alone knows who you are.
>> In Shirdi, Sai Nath has become a great
>> saint.[16]

As the singing continued, a woman sitting near the shrine grated fresh coconuts that had been broken and offered as *prasad* ("consecrated food") before the shrine by Sita Ram Baba. The shredded coconut was then passed to a man sitting nearby who mixed it with sugar and added raisins, and placed small amounts in packets. At the conclusion of the *pūjā*, a packet of the *prasad* was given to each person present, and Sita Ram Baba placed a small smudge of *udi* (sacred "ash" from Shirdi) on their foreheads with his thumb. Some ate the *prasad* before leaving, others took it home with them.

The year 1968 marked the fiftieth anniversary of the *mahasamadhi* of Sai Baba. Extensive preparations were made in Shirdi for the celebration of this event. Temporary shops were set up to sell food, flowers, and mementos of the occasion. Tents were erected to provide living quarters for the several hundreds of thousands of devotees and visitors expected to attend the month-long gathering. The most important building in the village was the house built by Bapusaheb Booty in which the *samādh* ("grave") of Sai Baba was located. In it was a long hall, divided by an iron grille. Within the enclosed area was a marble platform, approached by steps covered with silver and surrounded by a low railing of silver. The full-length grave, set into the platform, was covered with a polished marble slab over which a cloth of gold had been placed. At the rear of the platform was a square pedestal on which a larger-than-life statue of Sai Baba in gray marble was seated. The seated figure wore a huge crown of gold and had a shawl of cloth of gold thrown around its shoulders.

On the left side of the main platform was an opening in the railing and the *paduka* ("footprints") of Sai Baba in marble were set into the floor. Devotees filed past this opening and touched or kissed the *paduka,* some prostrating themselves in order to reach and touch the grave also. In the late afternoon the *arati* ("worship") service was held. For this, the grille was opened and ropes were fastened to the two front corner posts of the platform. Men lined up to the left of one of the ropes and the women to the right of the other. A young priest presided. He was seated, facing the image of Sai Baba. From time to time he poured *ghī* into several lamps placed in front of the image, threw flower petals in front of the image, and performed other functions. A number of *bhajans* in praise of Sai Baba were sung by the devotees, led by the priest. After about a half hour of this, the priest arose and placed the smaller of the burning lamps upon a tray. The lamps were then swung in graceful circles in front of the image. By thus "encircling" or "framing" the image, the power of the image—of Sai Baba himself—was drawn into the flames. The tray was then passed through the hall and each devotee passed his hands over the flames and touched his face, eyes, or head. Thus the spiritual power and blessing—the *kripa* ("grace")—of Sai Baba was imparted to each devotee. After some further singing the congregation dispersed quietly.

The next day, Thursday, was a special day, for throughout the day devotees were permitted to perform their individual *pūjās* to Sai Baba. The hall was crowded with people, often entire families, seated on the floor waiting their turn to approach the *samādh*. Sai Baba had promised: "My shrine will bless my devotees and fulfil their needs. My relics will speak from the tomb." [17] Hundreds had gathered that day to experience the fulfillment of his promise. Each had paid a small fee for the opportunity of approaching the tomb, and each had provided himself with materials for offerings. Most had some type of tray on which were placed such items as a coconut, a garland of flowers, a box of sweets (candy made from milk and sugar), or a bag of popcorn. The more wealthy also presented pieces of cloth, which were later auctioned off in a tent erected nearby. As each devotee came forward he handed his gifts to a priest, who touched the image of Sai Baba with them, put the garland around the neck of the image, placed some of the food and cloth on a large tray, and handed what was left back to the donor as *prasad*—a consecrated offering that the devotee would take with him and long cherish. Before moving back to his place in the hall, each spread his hand over a burning lamp and touched his face, eyes, or head. As one watched the faces of these devotees, an expression of adoration, of wonder, of joy, could be observed, for each felt that he had been, if only for a fleeting moment, in the very presence of his Lord.

Sai Baba formed no organization to carry on his work after his death. No imposing buildings were constructed in Shirdi. He wrote no book. But his words are remembered and treasured by thousands of his devotees. His shrine at Shirdi is a place of pilgrimage and devotion. In scores of centers on Thursday evenings his devotees, believing him still available to them, join in his worship, singing:

> Oh, everlasting God, how shall I praise thee?
> How shall I approach thee, or think of thee?
> Oh, Sainath, thou didst live in this world,
> And thou wert a gift to human beings.
> I pray thee, grant my request:
> By joining my hands, with great love,
> Let me serve thee forever, Oh, Sainath.[18]

3

THE SAINT WHO SUFFERED:
Sri Upasani Baba Maharaj

Some distance from the tomb of Sai Baba in Shirdi stands an old, abandoned temple. It was constructed many years ago by a saint called Khandoba. It was not interest in Khandoba, however, that caused me to peer into the dark, dusty interior of the temple through a crack in the closed door. Rather, it was because this old shrine had served for a number of years as the hermitage of one who was tormented and ridiculed by the townspeople, who was called a madman, one who, in his search for Self-realization suffered as few men have been called upon to suffer. In that dark cell he had been held as a virtual prisoner by the command of his guru, Sai Baba.

Kashinath Govind Upasani Sastri, later known as Sri Upasani Baba Maharaj, was born on May 5, 1870, at Satana, in the State of Maharashtra. He came from a Brahmin family which had ministered as priests to the families of the community. Kashinath lived with his grandfather, Gopala Sastri, a scholar who had served in the court of the maharaja of Baroda. Gopala lost his position upon the death of the maharaja, and the family was plunged into poverty. Kashinath's father lived in another city, where he was a clerk in the civil court during most of his son's childhood and youth. The example and teachings of the elder

Sastri had a profound and lasting influence upon the life of the growing youth. But it would appear that Gopala Sastri, as other grandfathers are said often to do, "spoiled" and indulged his grandson in certain of his whims. Because of his dislike for his teacher, Kashinath was permitted to drop out of school and to receive casual instruction at home. Applying the traditional teaching that the body is the prison of the Self, he looked upon his body as an enemy and observed, "It fattens upon our labors and forces us to endure the drudgery and pain of education and the pursuit of a calling for its sake." He began to punish this "enemy" by refusing to eat or to engage in the natural activities of youth that would develop his body.

He was apparently attracted much more to the weird and the supernatural side of his grandfather's teachings than to their practical and vocational aspects. He was impressed with the stories of the power of *mantras* ("sacred invocations") and *tapas* ("austerities") recorded in the Hindu Epics and Puranas. He began to practice breath control (*asan* and *pranayama*) and the repetition of sacred syllables (*mantra japa*) at home or at the cremation ground, "by day and by night." The result of his strange actions was that he was both pitied and scorned by those around him. How was it possible, they asked themselves, that "such a goose had been born in a family of swans"? Kashinath came to think of himself as "good for nothing." [1]

When Kashinath was fourteen, the older members of the joint family of which he was a "nonvoting member" decided that he should be married. He protested that he was unable to support even himself, much less a wife, but to no avail. He was married to a girl of eight. Perhaps his parents thought that if responsibility were put upon him, he would respond, but married life only served to deepen his depression. A few months later he ran away from home and took up his residence with friends of the family in another town. A letter informing him that his mother was seriously ill brought him home again. Shortly after this his wife died, and within a few weeks he was again married, this time to a girl nine years of age. But a year later he again left home, leaving his wife with his relatives. Days passed as he lived with starving or half-starved beggars in a temple on the outskirts of Poona. The food that he begged from house to house he shared with his fellow beggars. His steps now led him westward to Kalyan. Here he met rebuff until an old Maharatha woman took pity upon the starving youth. Along with the offer of food she gave him a Maharathi verse which he was later to repeat many times over:

> Maintain life even on water, if you get nothing else. Love God. Endure your lot. Bear up under misfortunes. Should Fortune smile, reject her. Burst the bonds of desire. Forsake not saintly company.[2]

Four years had now passed since his second marriage. He was nineteen. He decided to return to his home. His journey took him through a thick wood, in the midst of which there was a hill. High up the precipitous cliff he saw a small cave. The idea now came to him that this would be an ideal spot for *prayopavesha* ("fasting unto death"), for in that unfrequented spot he could wait quietly without food and drink for death to come to bring an end to his suffering. Two days passed without food, drink, or sleep. Then the thought came that while waiting for death, he should think of God. He began the silent repetition (*japa*) of holy *mantras*. While he was thus absorbed, he entered into *samādhi* ("loss of all consciousness"). When he awoke from *samādhi* "he found the figure of someone standing by his side pulling off the entire skin which left

his body, like the slough cast off by a serpent." The shock
aroused him to full consciousness and he became aware of
intense thirst. His entire body, with the exception of his
right forearm, was so stiff that he could not move. Suffering intensely, he slipped back into unconsciousness. When
he again awoke he found that a heavy thunderstorm had
arisen and soon torrents of rain began to fall. A small pool
was formed in the cave, and with his free hand he scooped
up water to quench his thirst. He also managed to massage
his body and restore feeling. After three days he had another vision. "A Hindu and a Muslim standing by his side
pulled off his entire skin and thereby disclosed his divinely
glowing body within. Pointing to that body they said, 'We
will not let you die,' and disappeared." Thus assured that
some divine destiny awaited him, he determined to leave
the cave, but he was so weak that with great difficulty he
slid down to the foot of the hill. Half crawling, he made his
way out of the forest and arrived at last at the village of
an aboriginal tribe, where he was given food. He calcu-
lated that he must have spent many months in deep
samādhi in the cave.

Now began a new period in Kashinath's life. Upon his
return to his home he was now received as a tapasvi, one
who had gained great power through his spiritual discipline. Soon after, his father died and his grandfather became ill. Nursing him and preparing his medicines led
Kashinath to decide to take up medicine as a profession.
After the death of his second wife and his marriage a third
time he left home and took up the study of Ayurvedic
medicine. During the next ten years he became extremely
successful and wealthy. To invest his funds he decided to
buy up a large tract of land on which a number of villages
were located. From rents on the land he expected to increase his wealth, but the tenants refused to pay their

rents. Government taxes soon exhausted his resources. Unable to reestablish his medical practice, he and his wife determined to set out on a pilgrimage, visiting certain holy shrines. At one of these, Kashinath decided to revive his old practice of *pranayama* ("breath control"). After a short while his wife noticed him lying unconscious, apparently not even breathing. By throwing water in his face she was able to restore consciousness, but not normal breathing. With difficulty she was able to get him back home, and thinking that his illness might be due to her evil *karma* created in a previous existence, "she walked 125,000 times around a sacred fig tree." All efforts medical and religious, however, proved to be of no help and Kashinath determined to search out a yogi who could cure him.

The first yogi he approached urged him to go to the Avalia (a Muslim term for a Spiritual Master) Sai Baba at Shirdi for further instruction in the religious life. But assuming that Sai Baba was Muslim, Kashinath, a Brahmin, refused this advice. Shortly after this he met an old man who advised him to drink water as hot as his tongue could stand and to stop drinking cold water. Kashinath refused this advice and soon entered into *samādhi*. On the eighth day, seeing a stream, he knelt down to drink. Suddenly the old man stood beside him and addressed him in angry tones: "Did I not warn you to avoid drinking cold water and to drink only hot water? Go to that nearby village, get hot water there and drink it." With these words, the old man disappeared. Kashinath followed this advice, and finding it beneficial, followed this practice the rest of his life. Being again advised by a yogi to visit Sai Baba, he arrived in Shirdi in June, 1911. Thus began a most amazing relationship.

It was morning when Kashinath had his first meeting with Sai Baba. From disciples in Shirdi he learned of the remarkable powers of the saint, but he had no intention of staying. In the evening, when he went to Sai Baba to take permission to leave, he was urged to stay, but declined. "If you must go away," said Sai Baba, "come back in eight days." Kashinath took up his lodging in a temple some distance away, but was irresistibly drawn back to Shirdi. It is not surprising, therefore, that on the eighth day he was again in Sai Baba's presence. Sai Baba then explained that he had been responsible for all of Kashinath's actions during the past eight days and, in fact, for a much longer time. He revealed on a later occasion that it was he who had appeared as the old man who had first instructed Kashinath to drink only hot water and who had reprimanded him when he did not do so. As indicated earlier, it is believed by his devotees that Sai Baba had the power, in fact still has the power, to appear to a disciple in need even at a distance far removed from Shirdi.

Sādhana

It is often said by Hindus that the disciple does not select his guru, but, on the contrary, is chosen by him. When the guru perceives that a future disciple is mature enough to receive instruction, he draws him to himself in some mysterious way not realized at the time by the disciple. Having drawn him, the guru reveals his authority and begins the spiritual discipline (sādhana) of the seeker. This discipline prescribed by the guru, if faithfully followed, leads ultimately to samādhi, the mystic trance in which Self-realization or God-realization is achieved. In classical Hinduism the eight steps leading to samādhi are: yama ("restraint"), niyama ("observances"), āsana ("posture"), pranayama ("regulation of the breath"), pratyahara ("abstraction of the senses"), dhārana ("concen-

tration"), *dhyāna* ("meditation"), and finally, *samādhi*
("trance"). These steps are described in detail in the Yoga
Sutra.[3] Although there were variations in details from
cult to cult, I found that all the personality cults that I
examined prescribed some form of *sādhana* for their members involving most, if not all, of these exercises.

The *sādhana* prescribed for the disciple may be complex. For example, Sri Rupa Gosvami describes in detail
the sixty-four "indispensable Parts or Functions (*Angas*)"
from "(1) Submission to the Feet of the *Guru* (Spiritual
Master)" to "(63) singing the Name of the Lord in the
company of many devotees; and (64) living in Mathura-
mandala" (the Krishna temple in the city of his birth).[4]
It is possible that the stricter members of the Chaitanya
cult still perform all the exercises of this *sādhana*, but
most of the contemporary cults have apparently relaxed
somewhat the requirements. This was certainly true of
the cults that I visited. It was agreed by all, however,
that *mukti* ("release," "salvation") and God-realization are
impossible without *sādhana*, and that only a Sat-Guru
("True Spiritual Master") is able to prescribe an effective
sādhana.

Kashinath soon found that the devotees of Sai Baba
regarded their Master as divine, and yielded unquestion-
ing obedience to his every command as he directed their
sādhana. Though he rebelled at first, Kashinath found
himself doing the same. One such command was that he
should take up his residence in the dilapidated Khandoba
temple and should speak to as few people as possible.
This in itself was a severe hardship, but worse was to
come. A few weeks later when Kashinath asked permission to leave Shirdi and return to his home, Sai Baba
replied, "Kashinath must remain four years at Shirdi."
He then consoled the startled and distressed disciple by

assuring him that at the end of four years the "full grace of God would be showered upon him."

Concerning this incident Sri Narsimha Swami comments:

With these words of Sai—the fate of Pundit Kashinath was sealed. He was doomed to renounce home life (*grihasta-srama*). That old chapter of his life was closed. He was to emerge into a new life as a God-man with myriads of worshippers, with power to grant them salvation and earthly blessings also. In one word, the Sad-Guru Sri Sai had definitely blessed Kashinath with the promise of his grace, to turn him into a Sat-Purusha or Sad-Guru; and the actual manifestation of the traits of Sat-Purusha was a mere question of time—a thing to be brought about in the succeeding four years of his stay there. "Wherever you are," Sai Baba told Kashinath, "you are God—you will realize everything." [5]

Some unusual experiences are said to have come to Kashinath during the next few years. For long he had been accustomed to depend upon others for his food. On a certain occasion his request for food was refused and he came to the conclusion that for food men "fawn, cringe, bow and become dependent." He determined to reject all food, even if it should be offered to him, and we are told that for a full year he ate no food at all. As a result, he not only became emaciated but passed through his *bhramishtavasta* and *unmathavasta,* that is, states resembling insanity, in which he saw visions, and external objects took on unusual and fantastic forms. All of this was, it is said, a part of his training carried on under the power of Sai Baba.

And so it came to pass that on Gurupoornima (the sacred day on which the devotee worships his guru) Sai Baba sent Chandrabai, one of his female devotees, to the Khandoba temple with the instructions that Kashinath be formally and devoutly worshiped in the same way that he himself was worshiped. Kashinath was taken by surprise and was considerably annoyed by the attention shown him, but Chandrabai insisted that this *pūjā* was at Sai Baba's command. In traditional Hinduism, when a new image is installed in the temple a ceremony known as Pratishta Kumbhabhisheka is performed, after which the image may become the object of worship. Sai Baba intimated by commanding Chandrabai to perform *arati* (the waving of the lighted oil lamp) before Kashinath and offering *pūjā* to him that he was now worthy of the worship of men. From that time on he was known as Upasani Maharaj or Upasani Baba.

The Sat-Purusha

But Upasani Baba's *sādhana* ("spiritual discipline") was not yet complete. No one can ever become a Sat-Purusha (a true saint or Perfect Man) until he has conquered completely the three "urges," *aham* ("egotism"), *kanchan* ("love of possessions"), and *kamini* ("the sex urge"). Sai Baba aided him in the conquest of these urges by creating a number of tempting visions before Upasani Baba or by demanding that he undergo certain severe tests. And finally the time came when Sai Baba said to Upasani, "There is no difference between you and me."

For three years Upasani Baba endured the trials of the rigorous spiritual discipline imposed upon him by Sai Baba. But in July, 1914, he accepted the invitation of a certain Dr. Pillai and secretly left Shirdi late one night. Although food would have been provided for him in Dr. Pillai's home, he preferred to beg his food from Brahmin families. A portion of this food was given to Dr. Pillai and his family as *prasad*, that is, food sanctified by his touch.

Although efforts were made to keep his identity secret, word soon spread in the community that a Sat-Purusha (a true or God-realized saint) was living among them. Devotees began to come to him in increasing numbers to worship at his feet. He then took up his residence in a coolie's hut next to the quarters of the outcaste sweepers and scavengers. Yet Brahmins and other high-caste people came to him and even took *prasad* from his hands. Many were attracted to him also by the spiritual discourses that he gave and by the miracles that he is said to have performed. Not all those who came to him, however, were friendly, and one of his miracles is said to have been performed at a time when a hostile group of Brahmins arrived to do him harm. It was evening and Upasani Baba was seated on the porch of the house speaking to a group of high-caste ladies. Some outcastes were seated a short distance away also listening to the discourse. The Brahmins arrived with lanterns and inquired of a bhangi ("scavenger") where Upasani Baba was. The bhangi replied that he was on the porch. They went up to the porch but could see no one. The bhangi informed them that because their hearts were not pure they could not see Upasani Baba. In anger the Brahmins departed. Upasani Baba had made himself and those around him invisible to his tormentors! Another miracle of a different kind is reported. One day a woman devotee presented Upasani Baba with an orange. He opened it and proceeded to give a slice to each of those around him as *prasad*. Though some thirty devotees were present, Upasani Baba kept on giving each a slice until all had received one.

It is believed by his followers that Sai Baba was aware of all that had been happening to Upasani Baba. Toward the end of the year of his disciple's absence from Shirdi he drew him back to his side, and Upasani Baba took up his abode again in the deserted temple. Sometime later, it was in 1917, a group of farmers from the village of Sakuri, a few miles distant, invited Upasani Baba to come to their village. They constructed a hut at the edge of the village, near the cremation ground. Sakuri now became the permanent center for Upasani Baba's work. His spiritual discourses attracted devotees from increasing distances. The story of his life produced by a well-known writer, Madhav Nath, spread his fame. In 1923, Baba's lectures began to appear in a Marathi monthly called *Sai Vak Sudha,* and were later published in book form under the title *Upasani Vak Sudha.* Others of his discourses were published under the title *The Unpublished Talks of Upasani Baba.* A third book dealing with the duties and role of women in society bears the title *Sati Charitra* ("The Character of a Wife").

Miracles are reported to have occurred during this period also. An official who was discharged from a government position was reinstated after Upasani Baba took an interest in his case. Various diseases were healed, evil spirits were cast out, and financial troubles were solved. All these occurrences are attributed to the faith of his devotees. In fact, he demanded "blind faith" in all who came to him. To his devotees, their guru was divine. Everything he demanded of them was for the best. There was nothing unknown to him in the past or future, and there was nothing beyond his power.

As the number of devotees grew, their gifts made it possible for Upasani Baba to develop the physical features of his ashram. A temple to the god Sri Dattatreya, whom Upasani Baba held in high esteem, was first constructed. Later, smaller shrines to other deities—Siva, Khandoba, Shanti, and Ganapati—were erected. The *zopadi* ("main hall") in which the *samādh* ("tomb") of Upasani Baba now lies, the Yajna Mandir ("House of Sacrifice"), the temple in honor of Upasani's mother, a temple to the Virgin Goddess, Kanya Kumari, an office building, and hostels for visitors and permanent residents were gradually added.

As early as 1920, Upasani Baba began to travel extensively throughout Western and Central India. Groups of his devotees were formed in numerous centers as his fame and influence spread. As a result, ashrams were established in Satana, Nagpur, Surat, Dharampur, and Hyderabad. Temples and hostels are associated with several of these. Smaller meeting places in which the worship of Upasani Baba takes place regularly are to be found in many other places. Although Upasani Baba was himself a Hindu, he has won followers from other religious groups in India as well. One of my first contacts with the movement was with a Parsi gentleman, the retired owner of a large cement factory, while we were traveling in a railway carriage. I was going to witness the Fiftieth Anniversary Celebration of the Mahasamadhi of Sai Baba at Shirdi. This gentleman had been an ardent devotee of Upasani Baba, and then of Godavari Mata, his successor, for many years and was on his way to spend a month in his own cottage at Sakuri in the presence of Godavari Mata. Baba counted in the ranks of his followers persons from all stations of life, maharajas, government officials, businessmen, scholars—and outcastes.

Perhaps one explanation for the wide appeal of Upasani Baba was his own confident self-awareness. A number of his statements about himself in his *Upasani Vak Sudha* are illuminating. "You will not be able to grasp it if I tell you about my divine state. Such a state of Perfection such as mine is noticed after several centuries." He probably meant that such a nature as his is generally manifested only after the lapse of several centuries. He continues: "I am the Ancient One. I am in the Beyond-State, beyond Duality and Non-duality. I am in the world, but not of it. Because I have to behave like a man of the world, do not misunderstand me. I experience simultaneously the World-state and the God-state. I live eternally in the state of divine-consciousness. I am everything." [6]

Possibly another source of his appeal was his understanding of the nature and purpose of suffering. In a land of widespread and intense suffering such as India his own deep experience of suffering must have struck a responsive chord in the lives of many. Upasani Baba sought to find spiritual meaning in suffering. He likened it to *tapas,* the severe austerities that saints of old had practiced to attain spiritual boons or to experience God-realization. He sought to make those who suffer feel that in the involuntary suffering which had befallen them, they had the same opportunity for spiritual benefits which the ancient tapasvis had in their forest life. People should rejoice at having to suffer, when suffering comes. The ascetics of old sought suffering. Suffering is needed for spiritual growth and is divinely ordained. Suffering is that which raises man from the brute to Godhood. The more one suffers, the more godly he becomes. When Baba spoke thus of suffering, his own life seemed to authenticate his words.

The misfortunes of this world can be overcome and the reward of a better life in future births can be assured by absolute faith in and dependence upon one's guru and by *sat-karma* ("true or good works"). For Upasani Baba, good works consisted largely, it would seem, in performing the various ceremonies and offering the numerous sacrifices (*yajña*) enjoined by the Hindu faith. "If one simply goes on observing all the fasts, feasts, ceremonies and observances shown in each year's calendar," he declared, "his or her salvation is assured." [7] Under the guidance of Upasani Baba all the major Hindu festivals were observed in traditional form, and a schedule of worship and devotion was designed for those living in the ashram for twenty-four hours of the day. Most of these are being observed to the present time.

Two incidents in the later years of Upasani Baba deserve special mention, his imprisonment in his *pinjrā* ("cage"), and the establishment of the Kanya Kumari Sthan ("Ashram for Virgin Maidens"). When the devotees came on the evening of December 25, 1921, to have their *darshana* ("vision") of Upasani Baba, they were amazed to find him enclosed in a small cage made of bamboo canes. When they remonstrated with him, he replied that just as one man may go to jail for the crimes of another, so he was imprisoned to bear the sins of his devotees. With him in the cage were the gods and saints of all religions. Sai Baba and Upasani Baba would forever be present in their subtle form, whether physically existent or not. Whoever would worship the cage would have all his sins forgiven. For three full years Upasani Baba never left the cage even for a moment. Soon the women devotees organized a *saptah* ("worship service") in the Datta temple to secure his release. They were later joined by the men, the women carrying the responsibility for continuous worship from noon until midnight, and the men from midnight to noon. *Pūjā* ("worship") and *arati* ("waving of lighted lamps") in front of the cage were also started, and have been continued until the present. In 1928 the devotees replaced the bamboos of the *pinjrā* with silver bars, but upon Baba's insistence a few of the bamboos, which still can be seen, were returned to their former positions.

Before describing the foundation of the Sri Upasani Kanya Kumari Sthan, it is well to look for a moment at Upasani Baba's teaching concerning women, and especially unmarried women. He starts by insisting that a married woman should follow the Code of Manu, the great Hindu lawgiver, which teaches that the wife should look upon her husband as God and should serve him wholeheartedly. But woman, as such, taught Baba, is *satvik* ("bright," "pure") and innocent by nature. She is without ego and has no *prarabdha* ("inherent sinfulness"). She is worthy to attain God-realization. Thus, if a woman does meritorious acts, beneficial results will follow not only for herself but for her whole family, and even for her ancestors also. According to Upasani Baba, the word *kanya,* generally translated "virgin," is composed of two syllables, *ka* and *nya. Ka* means "Supreme Godhead" and *nya* "to lead." *Kanya* means, therefore, "one who leads others to the Supreme Godhead." *Kumari,* generally "a young woman," is composed of *ku,* which means *a-sat* ("nontruth"), and *mari,* "to kill or destroy." A kumari is thus one who destroys untruth. The tradition of dedicating a young woman or girl in "marriage" to a deity is very ancient in India. Similarly, she may be offered in spiritual marriage to a Sat-Purusha, a God-realized saint. The Sat-Purusha serves as a medium to bring about her union with the Absolute. This is known as *Brahma Vivaha.* It is therefore necessary that a kanya be permanently associated with a Sat-Purusha, either by her own choice or by that of her parents. By virtue of her union with the Supreme, her human attributes are replaced by those of the divine. A *Brahma Vivaha,* in association with the saint, saves the souls not only of her own relatives but the souls of all others who bow before her.[8]

In 1928 a young man came to Upasani Baba in great distress. He felt called to a life of renunciation and wished to dedicate his wife to God. His wife, Godavari, who was fifteen years old, also wished to renounce worldly life.

Upasani Baba agreed to take her under his protection.
Shortly after, another girl, eleven-year-old Prema, was
given as *kanyadan*, the gift of a kanya, to Upasani Baba by
her father, a devotee of Baba. On Gurupoornima, the day
of worshiping the guru, Upasani Baba took a garland,
which had belonged to Sai Baba, from around his own
neck and placed it around Godavari's neck, and spoke
briefly of her future greatness. Shortly after this, the devotees began to worship her as they did Upasani Baba.
Three other girls were brought to Baba as *kanyadan*, and
in 1932 the five were united to Sri Krishna through the
medium of their guru, Upasani Baba. To guide these
young kanyas, and those who were dedicated later, the
Kanya Kumari Sthan, or ashram, was established. At the
death of Upasani Baba, Sati Godavari succeeded him as
Sat-Guru, or head, of the ashram. He had given her his
kripa ("grace"), and his divine powers had passed to her.
But the story of Godavari Mata will be recounted later.

Traditional Hinduism held that only the three higher
castes might read and recite the Holy Scriptures, the
Vedas. Shudras ("outcastes")—and women—were denied
this privilege. Because of his conviction that a kanya who
has performed *Brahma Vivaha*, that is, "spiritual marriage," to a God-man, might be used to save the souls of
many, Upasani Baba decided to defy tradition and not
only permit the kanyas to read the Vedas but also actually
to recite them. Thus, the kanyas in the ashram were taught
Sanskrit and the proper methods of reciting the Vedas. I
witnessed an occasion in which the kanyas recited the
Vedas and was impressed with the precision and ease with
which they performed this extremely difficult task. From
time to time they have been invited to recite the Vedas
in religious festivals in various parts of the country. As far

as I could learn, the kanyas of the Kanya Kumari Sthan
are the only women who are so trained.

Last Years

Upasani Baba's last years were filled with extensive travel,
meeting and blessing his devotees scattered about the
country, teaching the kanyas in the ashram, and supervising the construction and dedication of shrines and temples
made possible through the gifts of his followers. The last
of these was in Satana, the place of his birth. Early in
December, 1941, he made his last visit to Hyderabad and
was entertained as the guest of his devotee, Raja Narsing
Raj. On his return he stopped to speak to devotees in
several cities along the way and arrived in Satana on the
twenty-second. Here he installed with his own hands
twelve *jyotilingas* ("images") in the temple that had been
constructed over the spot formerly occupied by his own
home. He returned exhausted to Sakuri on the twenty-
third and "dropped his body" and entered *mahasamadhi*
on December 24. His body was buried on the twenty-fifth
in front of his cage. Later, the *samādh* ("tomb") which
one sees today was erected, and his image was placed in
the cage. A pair of *padukas*, symbols of Baba's footprints,
have been placed in front of the *samādh*. Here a constant
stream of devotees bow to offer their worship to their departed leader. But for them he is not really gone, for he
had promised them, "I am never absent from Sakuri."
B. V. Narsimha Swami writes in *The Sage of Sakuri:* "The
absence of Baba's physical existence has intensified his
spiritual presence everywhere and in everything. Devotees
have felt him now nearer and dearer than before. Instead
of seeing him behind the bars of the cage, they can now

take his *darshana* ("vision") in the sanctuary of their own hearts." [9]

The character and teachings of Upasani Baba are both paradoxical. Though he talked about spiritual matters, his language was often coarse, sometimes vulgar. Apparently, on the slightest provocation he could fly into a "temper tantrum" in which he would beat or throw stones at his devotees, and the next moment he would shower them with love and affection. His numerous discourses covered a wide range of metaphysical subjects—the nature of the Absolute, *Purusha* and *Prakriti* ("Spirit" and "Matter"), *namasmarana* (salvation through repeating the name of God), *sanyas* ("renunciation"), to mention but a few, yet his language was always that of the common people. He often used simple illustrations to explain a profound spiritual truth: "Rain showers equally on all places, but water gathers in a hollow place, and not on a hillock. Likewise, a saint looks upon all with an equal eye. But, those who are proud are like a hillock, are not granted the experience of his grace, while an humble soul reaps spiritual benefit from him." [10] "Various vessels are used for various purposes. One cannot keep *ghī* ("clarified butter") in a vessel spoilt by rock-oil. One has to clean it before its use. Likewise, one has to purify one's mind before receiving the Grace of God." [11] Upasani Baba was a traditionalist, yet in some respects his outlook was modern. He taught that women should "worship their husbands as God" and that their place is at home, and not in the office or in the professions. They should not get entangled in worldly activities. Yet he worked to raise the status of women in society. He believed that they should be educated, though he stressed religious rather than secular education. He held traditional ideas of the home, yet he advocated "family planning" long before it became a real issue in India.

Although he took no part in the struggle for political independence from Great Britain, he gave his approval to the struggle and advised his followers to become engaged in the independence movement. He emphasized the fact, however, that political freedom without the spiritual regeneration of the nation could never lead to true freedom for the Indian people.[12] Upasani supported the need for social reforms, but revealed his traditionalism by discouraging the removal of the ban on widow remarriage and by supporting the practice of "untouchability."[13] He believed in education, but was not impressed with secular education whose primary aim seemed to fit one merely for material success in life. True education must develop character and responsible citizenship.[14] Thus, there were many paradoxical elements in the life and teachings of Upasani Baba, but perhaps it is the very nature of a "God-Man" to be paradoxical!

4

THE HIGHEST OF THE HIGH:
Meher Baba

"*Jai Meher Baba, Jai Meher Baba*"—"Victory to Meher Baba." This chant can be heard on dozens of American campuses today where students bow before the picture of their newly discovered "Savior." The face that smiles at them from the picture has few of the features of the traditional Hindu swami or sadhu. There is no long hair or hair coiled on the top of the head. There is no beard, but a somewhat heavy moustache. The eyes do not have the faraway gaze of the mystic nor the half-closed eyelids of the yogi. Rather, they have the mischievous twinkle of one who very much enjoys life. The face beams with compassion and love. Perhaps this is why his followers speak of themselves as "Baba Lovers," why they speak often of "Love," why they believe that love is the greatest force in the world, and why they greet each other with an embrace. Who is this saint from the East who has won the devotion of so many youths in the West in recent years?

While many of the adherents of the personality cults claim that their founders were, or are, avataras, and the founders themselves apparently accept this designation, Meher Baba explicitly declared himself to be "the Avatar for this age." He further claimed, "I am the very same

Ancient One, in flesh and blood, who is eternally worshipped and neglected, always remembered and forgotten;
I am that Eternal One, whose Past is worshipped and remembered; whose Present is neglected and forgotten;
whose Future is always much desired and longed for." [1]
Purdom, who has written a biography of Meher Baba under the title *The God-Man*, asserts, "That Baba does declare himself God-Man in the fullest sense there is no
question." [2] This statement occurs in the chapter that discusses Meher Baba's own distinction between the God-
Man, the avatara of God who has descended and assumed
human form, and the Man-God, the "God-realized" human who has ascended into divinity through his own
sādhana.

The designation that Meher Baba often applied to himself was "the Highest of the High." "I am neither a *Mahatma* nor a *Mahapurush,* neither a *Sadhu* nor a Saint,
neither a *Yogi* or a *Wali.* . . . I am the Highest of the
High. . . . If I am the Highest of the High my Will is
Law, my Wish governs the Law, and my Love Sustains
the Universe." [3]

Merwan Sheriarji Irani was born in Poona, India, in
1894. His parents were Persian. His childhood was happy
and he received the education of a middle-class boy. In
1911 he entered the Deccan College, where his favorite
study was poetry. He wrote poems in Persian, in several
Indian languages, and in English, which were published in
local papers. One day, in 1913, as he was riding home from
college on his bicycle he saw an old woman sitting under
a neem tree. His eyes met hers, and she beckoned to him.
He left his bicycle and went over to her. She arose and
embraced him. No word was said, and after a short time
he left her. This was his first meeting with Hazrat Baba-

jan, a Muslim saint said to be well over a hundred years old. From time to time he would stop and sit beside her. Their meetings were in silence. Early in 1914, when he made his usual visit, she kissed him on the forehead. Shortly after he reached home he fell into a deep trance. His eyes were wide open but he saw nothing. This continued for three days, and he began to move about in a daze, unconscious of his surroundings. For nine months he was given medical treatment, but to no avail. He was then taken to certain Perfect Masters to seek their help. First there was Sadgura Narayan Maharaj, and then Tajuddin Baba. Then he was taken to Sai Baba at Shirdi, before whom he prostrated himself. When Merwan arose, Sai Baba looked at him and said, "Parvardigar," which means "God-Almighty-Sustainer." He was then sent to the temple of Khandoba, in Shirdi, where Upasani Maharaj was living under Sai Baba's guidance, naked and fasting.[4] When Upasani Maharaj saw Merwan for the first time, he flung a stone at him, hitting him on the forehead. This was to help awaken him to gross consciousness again. Sometime after this, Upasani Baba began an ashram of his own at Sakuri. Merwan accompanied him to Sakuri and lived under his guidance for several years.

Later, Meher Baba ("Compassionate Father," the title later given to him by his disciples) was to explain that to bring about the incarnation of God the psychic power of five Perfect Masters must be exerted.

What I am, what I was and what I will be as the Ancient One, is always due to the five Perfect Masters of the Age. During the Avataric periods the five Perfect Masters make God incarnate as man. Sai Baba, Upasani Maharaj, Babajan, Tajuddin and Narayan Maharaj are the five Perfect Masters of this age for me. Of these five, Upasani Maharaj and Babajan directly played the main roles. Babajan in less than a millionth of a second made me realize (My Ancient State) that I am God and in the period of seven years, Upasani Maharaj gave me the knowledge that I am the *Avatar,* the Ancient One (established me in that State). Sai Baba made me assert this time what I am. Babajan made me feel what I am. Upasani Maharaj made me know what I am. Babajan gave me Divine Bliss. Sai Baba gave me Divine Power. Upasani Maharaj gave me Divine Knowledge. I am Infinite Power, Knowledge and Bliss. I am the Ancient One, come to redeem the modern world.[5]

Disciples of Meher Baba believe that these experiences explain how it was possible for him to move in two levels of consciousness, the Universal Consciousness and the Cosmic Consciousness. While engaged in his "universal work," carried on in seclusion, such as directing the affairs of men and nations and acting on behalf of his "Lovers" scattered around the world, he moved on the level of his Universal, or God, Consciousness. When communicating with his *mandali* (the intimate band of disciples), meeting visitors, dictating messages to or answering letters from his disciples, he moved on the level of his Cosmic, or Man, Consciousness.

Toward the end of 1921, "Upasani Baba . . . returned Meher Baba completely to normal consciousness of the world with full retention of his Godhead and said to him: 'You are the Avatar, and I salute you.' " [6] Meher Baba left Sakuri and returned to Poona, where a small hut was constructed for him. Disciples were drawn to him and were trained in their *sādhanas.* After a period of intensive training of his disciples Meher Baba established a colony near Ahmadnagar, which is called Meherabad. Here a school for boys, a hospital, and a dispensary were opened. In 1925, telling his disciples that too many words had already been spoken and now was the time for action, Meher Baba began to observe silence. It is believed by his disciples that this silence continued until his death in 1969. His many spiritual discourses and messages were first dictated by means of an alphabet board, but this was discarded in 1954, and he used only unique hand gestures which were interpreted by his disciples. He traveled extensively throughout India. In 1938 he made a tour with a group of Eastern and Western women disciples in a bus driven by Elizabeth Patterson, an American disciple who had driven a Red Cross ambulance during the war. This tour brought him to Jabalpur, where I was living, and there I saw him for the first and only time. When I visited Meherabad thirty years later, he was in strictest "seclusion," doing his "universal work." He visited America on several occasions and stayed at the Meher Baba Center at Myrtle Beach, South Carolina, which had been established for him by Elizabeth Patterson. Centers have also been established in California, New York, Florida, Virginia, and Washington, D.C. Groups of "Baba Lovers" also gather in other parts of the country to sing his praises and discuss his teachings.

Purdom divides the life of Meher Baba into ten periods: The Preparation (1894–1922), The First Ten Years (1922–1931), The Period of World Travel (1931–1939), The *Masts* of India (1939–1949), The New Life (1949–1952), The Free Life (1952–1953), The Highest of the High (1953–1954), The Final Declaration (1954–1957), The *Sahawas* (1958), The Universal Message (1958–1962).[7] Brief reference has already been made to the principal events of the first three of these periods. The fourth period was certainly the most unusual in the life of this unusual man. A foreigner who travels widely throughout India will be impressed with the large number of appar-

THE HIGHEST OF THE HIGH

ently mentally deranged persons he will see. Some of these are actually insane, others suffer from varying degrees of mental illness, and still others are "holy men" who, having renounced the world, have adopted various abnormal activities to indicate their detachment from ordinary life. It is extremely difficult to distinguish one class from another. During the period from 1939 to 1949, Meher Baba gave his special attention to a class that he called *masts*. Concerning this work, Purdom writes:

> Baba began to concentrate upon certain selected men who, though mentally unbalanced or disordered, were not simply insane, though often behaving as the worst examples of feeblemindedness; they were regarded by him as being in a particular spiritual condition. "Such persons," says Baba, "are not mad in the ordinary sense; they are desperately in love with God, and are known as *masts*." The word *mast*, pronounced "must," seems to be Baba's own; it it is probably derived from *masti*, a Persian or Urdu word meaning "overpowered." [8]

These "God-intoxicated souls," as Meher Baba called them, have had their minds so disarranged by "spiritual energies" that they have been led to renounce the world and the normal conditions of living. They are often found living in latrines, graveyards, or garbage dumps, half naked or completely without clothing, and with their bodies covered with filth. They are in this world but not of this world. "They are overcome by an agonizing love of God," says Baba, "and are drowned in their ecstasy. Only love can reach them." [9] Meher Baba spent ten years of his life, from 1939 to 1949, trying to "reach" *masts* in all parts of India. Extensive tours were made to cities, towns, and even villages where *masts* were reported to be living. Four or five members of the *mandali* who accompanied him would be sent out into the "byways and hedges" to discover the *masts*. Then Meher Baba would go in person to visit each one. Baba would bathe them with his own hands, despite occasionally vigorous opposition from the *mast* who preferred his "natural" state, feed them, and sit beside them in silence for a period. Then Baba would move on to the next *mast*. Though he never fully explained the significance of his actions to his followers, Purdom remarks:

> We are intended to understand that *masts* are important to Baba, not only because only he can help them, but, because of their spiritual state, by helping them in their own development he is helping mankind in general through them. They are channels of spiritual impulse of the greatest value.[10]

For several years a special ashram for *masts* was maintained at Meherabad, the center which Meher Baba had established in Maharashtra State. A number of *masts* were gathered from different places by disciples, devious methods sometimes being necessary, and were brought to the ashram. Here Baba attended to them personally. After some days they were taken back to their places.

This period in Meher Baba's life was brought to a close by his "Great Seclusion." For forty days he remained absolutely alone in a small hut that had been prepared for the purpose. For food he had only honey, water, and milkless tea. When he emerged from the hut at the end of his period of seclusion, he appeared none the worse for his long fast.

The New Life

The disciples of Meher Baba found his actions at times exceedingly strange and unpredictable. This must have been especially true at the time he launched his New Life

Movement.[11] In January, 1949, he announced that a complete change would soon take place in the life of his followers. Then, on February 15, he went to Mt. Abu, where he remained in seclusion until August 15. Upon his return to Meherabad he announced that all properties must be disposed of and the *mandali* disbanded. On October 16 he would enter upon the New Life. Accordingly, the properties of the ashram were sold and the proceeds given to the poor, especially to *masts*. The number of the disciples, then about 120, would be drastically reduced. Each disciple was required to submit in writing his decision as to whether he would accompany Meher Baba on his New Life Movement. By October 16 the number who said yes had been reduced to twenty—four women and sixteen men. Early that morning the caravan set out on foot on the trek that was to carry them to the holy city of Varanasi. The monsoons were not yet over, and it soon became necessary to engage a bus for the party. Varanasi is northeast of Meherabad, but the party now turned southwest to Belgaum. Here a month was spent in intensive training and manual labor, in which Meher Baba took part.

From Belgaum the journey was now made to Varanasi by train. In Varanasi all the disciples were required to go out two by two to beg for their food from house to house. They were not permitted to approach storekeepers, as most religious beggars do. This must have been a new and trying experience to some of the disciples who were doctors and other professional men. From Varanasi the party traveled to Hardwar, another holy city, much of the journey being made on foot. Many weeks were now spent, with Hardwar as a center, in visiting the hundreds of sadhus ("holy men") and mahatmas ("great spirits") to be found in the ashrams in surrounding villages. Appeals were sent to disciples who had been with Meher Baba in the Old Life to send funds that might be used to feed those in the ashrams which were now being visited.

Absolute discipline was demanded of the "companions" who had stayed with Meher Baba. Punishment for disobedience was often unusual. For example, a doctor and a companion, who failed to appear at a certain designated time, were required to rub their noses in the mud! This may account, in part, for the fact that the number of "companions" had now dwindled to only ten. On the first anniversary of the New Life, Meher Baba invited his companions to reconsider their decision to join him in the New Life—to rejoin as his servants or to go away and become again his Old Life disciples. He then declared:

> My old life places me on the altar of Absolute Godhead and Divine Perfection. My New Life makes me take the stand of a humble Servant of God and his people. In my New Life, Perfect Divinity is replaced by Perfect Humanity. In my New Life I am the Seeker, the Lover, the Friend. Both these aspects—Perfect Divinity and Perfect Humanity—have been by God's will and both are everlastingly linked with God's eternal life. Anyone may believe me to be whatever he likes, but none may ask for my blessings, miracles, or any rewards of any kind. My New Life is eternal. Those other than my servants in the New Life, whoever and wherever they may be, who desire to live the life, are free to do so in the spirit of it independently.[12]

The next stage in the New Life was taken on October 16, 1951. Meher Baba described this as his determination "to take the step of Annihilation." In Hindi, this is *manonash* ("destruction of the mind"). From mid-October until mid-February, 1952, he went into strict seclusion, permitting only four disciples, "servants" he called them, to remain with him. For the followers of Meher Baba, this "step of Annihilation" was of supreme importance. During the period of the New Life he had voluntarily suspended the state of Perfect Master to become common man and a Perfect Seeker. The *manonash* had effected the dissolution of the natural mind of Meher Baba in its normal workings, and it had been transformed into the Divine and Infinite Mind. He was now prepared for the "Free Life."

The Highest of the High

The years 1952 and 1953 were spent in extensive travel both in India and abroad. While in the United States, he spent some time at Myrtle Beach, South Carolina, where a Center in his honor had been established. It was also while he was in America that Meher Baba was involved in an automobile accident that crippled him for life.[13] On September 7, 1953, the reputed birth date of Zoroaster, Meher Baba made one of the most important of his "declarations." It was a very long statement, but some of the more significant sentences may be extracted:

> When man consciously experiences that he is Infinite, Eternal and Indivisible, he is fully conscious of his individuality as God, and experiences Infinite Knowledge, Infinite Power and Infinite Bliss. Thus man becomes God, and is recognized as a Perfect Master, *Sad-guru*. When God manifests on earth in the form of man and reveals his Divinity, he is recognized as the *Avatar*—thus God become man. The *Avatar* is always one and the same, because God is always One and the Same, the Eternal, Indivisible, Infinite One, who manifests himself in the form of man as the *Avatar*, as the Messiah, as the Prophet, as the Ancient One—the Highest of the High. . . . In the world there are countless *sadhus, mahatmas, mahapurushas* ("Great Men"), saints, yogis and *walis* (Muslim "holy men"). . . . I am neither a *mahatma* nor a *mahapurusha*, neither a *sadhu* nor a *saint*, neither a *yogi* nor a *wali*. . . . The

question therefore arises . . . then what am I? The natural assumption would be that I am either just an ordinary human being, or I am the Highest of the High. . . . If I am the Highest of the High my Will is Law, my Wish governs the Law, my Love sustains the Universe. . . . If you truly and in all faith accept your Baba as the Highest of the High, it behooves you to lay down your life at his feet . . . for Baba's unbounded love is the only sure and unfailing guide to lead you safely through the innumerable blind alleys of your transient life.[14]

In the same vein, in March of the following year, he said to his devotees: "If people were to ask . . . 'Are you God?' I would reply 'Who else could I be?' If they ask me 'Are you *Avatar*?' I would reply 'Why else have I taken this human frame?'"[15] In spite of these exalted claims for himself, Meher Baba insisted that he came neither to teach nor to found a new religion, but to awaken man to the consciousness of his Real Self, which is none other than God. "I belong to no religion," he said. "Every religion belongs to me. My personal religion is my being the Ancient Infinite One, and the religion I impart to all is Love for God, which is the truth of all religion."

The Sahawas

Meher Baba never referred to his followers as "disciples" or "devotees," but as "Baba Lovers." In June, 1954, Meher Baba issued an invitation to all his "Lovers," whether they had ever seen him or not, to attend *sahawas*—"the intimacy of the give-and-take of love"—at Meherabad in September. Although the invitation was intended especially for devotees in India and Pakistan, it was extended to male devotees in the West who also might want to come. Normally, only the members of the *mandali*—the intimate band of disciples—and a few privileged visitors were permitted to spend any length of time with Meher Baba, but on this occasion thousands, some reports say one hundred thousand, were permitted not only to see Baba but to hear him give a number of his most treasured "Discourses." In addition to the more public *darshanas*, a selected group of his followers were permitted to spend a week in close fellowship with Meher Baba as he "discoursed, joked and played" with them. They came in groups of two hundred each, four such groups in all. The day-by-day events of this unusual occasion are described in detail by Don E. Stevens in *Listen, Humanity*,[16] and by C. B. Purdom in *The God-Man*.[17]

It was during this *sahawas* that Meher Baba issued two of his most famous pronouncements, "Baba's Call" and "The Final Declaration." In his Call, Meher Baba said that the time had come for him to repeat the Call that Avataras from age to age had given, inviting men to come to them for spiritual illumination. Because Avataras come in great humility, they are rejected and persecuted. But truth must be proclaimed. God is All. There is nothing but God. This being so, the disciple as well as the Avatara is God. Man must awaken from his ignorance and try to comprehend the fact that not only is the Avatara God, but man, the ant, and the sparrow are nothing but God. The difference is that the Avatara is conscious of his Godhood, while the others are not. The Call closed with the challenge that his followers, even in the midst of their normal activities, should realize their true identity with himself, their Beloved God.

Meher Baba began his Final Declaration with an expression of appreciation to his disciples who had come from all over the world to be with him. He then informed them that the time was fast approaching when the things that he had been teaching them would come to pass. The world is now filled with misery, hatred, jealousy, frustration, and fear. This is all because men live in ignorance of the true nature of reality. The illusion of "manyness" blinds them from realizing the true "oneness" of reality. This illusion had developed with the evolution of consciousness. But the time has come for the "preordained destruction of the multiple separateness" which prevents men from realizing their unity and brotherhood. This destruction, soon to take place, will destroy three fourths of the world. Those who survive will be brought together in a brotherhood of lasting happiness. This catastrophic event, predicted Meher Baba, would coincide with the breaking of his silence. Then he will speak only one Word and thus lay the foundation for the evolution of consciousness that will continue for the next seven hundred years. Prosperity and happiness will then be at their height. Men will have overcome their feeling of separateness, and thus of hostility toward one another, for his Word will have touched the hearts of all mankind. Meher Baba will then return again to begin a new cycle of existence. In closing his Final Declaration, Baba announced that a series of events would soon take place: a strange disease would attack his body, he would suffer humiliation, he would break his silence and say the Word of Words, his glorification would usher in the destruction of three fourths of the world, and then he would "drop his body." [18]

The *sahawas* came to an end with this Final Declaration, and his followers dispersed. During July, 1956, Meher Baba made a whirlwind tour of Europe, America, and Australia, where he was greeted by numerous "Lovers." In December of that year he was involved in a second automobile accident. The injuries that he received were serious, especially those to his right hip and side. Although he was in considerable pain, the year 1957 was spent in extensive travel and in developing plans for *sahawas* at Meherabad in February, 1958, for Eastern devotees, at Myrtle Beach in May for European and American devotees, and in Australia in June. Although *sahawas* had been held in Meherabad in 1957, it was apparently nothing as compared with that in 1958, when special trains brought devotees from all over India to Ahmadnagar, the railway station nearest to Meherabad. The accommodations for nine hundred men were filled to overflowing as each of four batches of "Lovers" spent five days with Meher Baba. To each group he gave discourses on such topics as Love, Obedience, God, and his own avataric mission.

To attend the *sahawas* at Myrtle Beach his devotees, 225 in all, came from England, France, Switzerland, Israel, Mexico, and the United States. The two weeks spent there were filled with informal talks given by Meher Baba and his "Discourses," which were read to the devotees by one or another of the *mandali*. They covered such subjects as the meaning of *sahawas*—the intimate companionship that the Master shares with his disciples; the nature of Love— the mystical relation between the Lover and the Beloved; the "Split Ego"—the real "I" which mistakenly identifies itself with the false "I"; Obedience; Real Birth and Real Death; and a number of others. One of the more unusual discourses was entitled "I am the Son of God the Father and God the Mother in One." In the Beyond state, explained Meher Baba, God is both God the Father and God the Mother simultaneously. In past periods the avataras of God have all been male, Beloved Sons who represent the strength and wisdom of God. In the Beyond state God did not have occasion to play the part of God the Mother. But there is in God a tender side of his nature that suffers. Meher Baba has undergone for the sake of his devotees intense suffering as a result of his two accidents. Thus, he is also the well-beloved Son of God the Mother. In this incarnation of the avatara, God has had the occasion to play the part both of Father and of Mother.[19]

Meher Baba and his traveling companions reached Australia in early June and proceeded to a center about seventy miles from Brisbane that had been arranged by devotees under the direction of Francis Brabazon, poet and longtime disciple. More than fifty devotees from Victoria, New South Wales, and Queensland attended this *sahawas*. As in the earlier gatherings, many of Meher Baba's discourses were read aloud, interspersed with comments by Baba himself. Here, as elsewhere, Baba requested that all who would give him absolute obedience should raise their hands. All but three present did so, a boy and two men. It was explained by the boy's mother that he was too young to understand, and the two men said they were not sure whether or not they would be able to obey.

Another impressive *sahawas* was held in 1962 when Meher Baba invited his "Lovers" to attend an "East-West Gathering" in Bombay. Extensive preparations were made for this assembly, which was attended by a large number of devotees from all around the world. Along with the usual discourses, primarily for his own followers, there were a number of public meetings in which all who were interested were permitted to see and hear "the Avatar of this age." This unusual gathering is described by Francis Brabazon in his *The East-West Gathering*.[20]

The closing years of Meher Baba's life were spent in deepening seclusion. When I visited the center in Ahmadnagar just three months before his death, I was told by Adi Irani, Baba's personal secretary, that even he was

permitted to visit Baba only rarely. Naturally I did not
see him. I was told that he was so deeply involved in his
"universal work" that his own personal servant entered
his room only once a day to bring the meager food that
he allowed himself. Yet word went out in 1968 to call the
"Baba Lovers" of the world to another East-West Gathering of momentous importance to be held in Meherabad in
the spring of 1969. National groups were to come at specified times to meet with Baba. Some felt that this would
be the time when he would "break his silence." This meeting never took place as originally planned, for on January
31, Meher Baba "dropped his body." Nevertheless, many
"Lovers" made the pilgrimage on the scheduled dates. A
planeload went from the United States. Some of those in
this party reported that it was the most deeply moving
experience of their lives, for they felt "Baba's presence
more surely with them than even on those occasions when
they had met him physically." Perhaps the "breaking of
his Silence" actually coincided with his "dropping of his
body," they say, for in their meetings together and in
their day-by-day "work" for him they are keenly aware of
his presence and of his guidance.

To summarize in brief the teachings of Meher Baba is
impossible. Although after 1925 he never spoke and presumably never wrote, nevertheless, five full-length books
and five volumes of "Discourses" are attributed to him.[21]
In addition, his teachings are set forth in detail in several
works by his devotees.[22] It is not the mass of material,
however, which makes summation difficult. Even in his
"Discourses" Meher Baba was no "systematic theologian."
Apparently, he "spoke" spontaneously, using gestures or the
alphabet board, of course, as the occasion suggested. Even
in rearranging the "Discourses" in three "volumes," the
editors, Ivy Oneita Duce and Don E. Stevens, have not

made the task much easier.[23] Yet, in spite of these difficulties, because of the impact of Meher Baba upon the lives of a growing number of "Lovers" some effort must be made to indicate a few of his leading ideas.

The Man-God and the God-Man

There is a Sanskrit word, *Sad-Gurū*, generally translated "Perfect Master," which is roughly equivalent to the English term "Man-God." It is applied to one who has "attained self-knowledge, who has gained mastery over his nature and achieved union with Reality." [24] The Perfect Master realizes his eternal being, his "I-am-ness." He experiences freedom from all limitations. While some God-realized souls leave the body at once, and forever, remaining eternally merged in the unmanifest aspect of God, there are others who retain the body for a time, but their consciousness is merged completely in the unmanifest aspect of God, and they are not conscious therefore of their bodies. They experience continually the bliss, power, and knowledge that God possesses, but they cannot consciously use them to help others attain liberation. A few God-realized souls, however, retain their bodies, yet are conscious of themselves as God both in his unmanifest and his manifest aspects. They know themselves both as the unchanging divine essence and as the constantly changing infinitely varied manifestation of the Divine. They know themselves as the Divine in everything, and are thus able to make other souls realize God. There are fifty-six God-realized souls in the world at all times. For the most part they live and work apart from and unknown to the general public, but five, who act in a sense as a directing body, always work in public. These are known as Sad-Gurus, or Perfect Masters. Each is a "Man-God."

The foremost Sad-Guru who first emerged through evolution, and helped and helps other souls to gain God-realization, is known as the Avatara. But there is a difference between the Sad-Guru and the Avatara. When man becomes God and has infinite consciousness, he is called Sad-Guru—Man-God or Perfect Master. When God becomes man, he is called Avatara—God-Man or Messiah. Neither the Avatara nor the Sad-Guru has a finite and limited mind, because his mind, merged in the infinite, has become the universal mind.[25] A Perfect Master is one who has gone through the process of cosmic evolution and involution and become a Man-God. An Avatara, or God-Man, is one who does not pass through those processes but is born as a man who knows himself to be God. An Avatara, therefore, is not simply a manifestation of God, but God manifested, God become incarnate.[26] Meher Baba points out that both Perfect Master and Avatara are equal in having God's life and are on every level in the world:

Both are simultaneously on the level of the lowest to the highest . . . the only difference is that the Perfect Master *acts* on that level and the Avatar *becomes* on that level. . . . For instance a Perfect Master cannot or will not *fall ill,* but when he appears to have fallen ill, it is just his "acting" of illness . . . when people see the *Avatar* ill, he has *actually fallen ill* and has literally become ill. . . . A Perfect Master *behaves* as the creature of that level . . . whereas the *Avatar* becomes the creature of that level.[27]

Creation

Though Meher Baba was not born a Hindu, his teaching is largely in the Vedantic tradition. However, he often employs Western terminology, and even examples from Christian theology, to express his ideas. For example, in explaining the concept of the unreality of the phenomenal universe, he says: "God is all. There is nothing but God." How shall we, then, explain the origin of man's illusion that the world about him is real? Like Sri Aurobindo, Meher Baba employs the concepts of evolution and involution. Elaborate charts explaining the "stages" of evolution from stone to man and the "planes" of involution of consciousness from "gross consciousness" to "God-consciousness" hang on the walls of Meher Baba centers. These charts are fully explained in *God Speaks*, a work attributed to Meher Baba, though edited by Duce and Stevens. In his "Discourses," Meher Baba describes in detail the "Beginning and the End of Creation" and the "Formation and Function of *Sanskaras*," those impressions on the mind which produce illusion.[28] In the beginning there was only Reality, unconscious of itself. But the evolutionary process was ultimately set in motion by the "will-to-be-conscious" which is inherent in the Infinite. In order to make any sense out of the idea of creation, it is necessary to posit this will-to-be-conscious in the Absolute in an involved state prior to the act of manifestation.[29] "Just as a wave going across the surface of a still ocean calls forth into being a wild stir of innumerable bubbles, the *lahar* (will-to-be-conscious) creates myriads of individual souls out of the indivisible infinity of the Oversoul. But the all-abounding Absolute remains the sub-stratum of all the individual souls." [30] One must not suppose, however, that any real change takes place in the Absolute when the involved will-to-be-conscious makes itself effective by bringing into existence the phenomenal world. Only an apparent change takes place. "The manifoldness of creation and the separateness of the individual souls exist only in imagination." [31]

In the beginning the individual soul had no impressions

(*sanskaras*) and no consciousness. But the infinite, impressionless, unconscious, tranquil state of the soul then reverberated with the impulse that may be called the "first urge" (the first urge to know itself). The first urge was latent in the Oversoul. Simultaneously with the reverberation of the first urge, the infinite Soul *experienced* for the first time. The first experience of the infinite Soul was that it (the Soul) experienced a contrariety in its identity with its infinite, impressionless, unconscious state. This experience of contrariety effected changeableness in the eternal, indivisible poise of the infinite Soul with a recoil or tremendous shock which impregnated the unconsciousness of the unconscious Soul with the First Consciousness of its apparent separateness from the indivisible state of the Oversoul.[32]

Thus, with the evolution of consciousness in the Absolute arose the first impression. It therefore marks the beginning of the formation of *sanskaras*. In the gross sphere the first focus of manifestation—the first center of consciousness—is in the inert stone. But the possibility of self-expression is severely limited in the stone. Therefore the will-to-be-conscious, which is inherent in the vastness of the Oversoul, seeks by divine determination a progressive evolution of vehicles of expression. This process leads progressively to evolution of consciousness and forms through the metal, vegetable, animal, and human planes of existence. When the Oversoul finally takes the human form, consciousness attains its fullest development with complete awareness of the self and the environment.[33] The One *in* the many thus comes to experience itself as one *of* the many, and there is where illusion begins.

We see, then, that illusory thinking results from the interference of impressions (*sanskaras*) accumulated during the process of the evolution of consciousness. The function of consciousness is perverted by the operation of impressions that manifest themselves as desires. Through many lives, consciousness is continually burdened by the aftereffects of the many experiences that the soul undergoes. The thinking soul cannot break through the barrier created by *sanskaras,* and consciousness becomes a helpless captive of illusions created by its own false thinking.[34] The Ultimate Reality, which is symbolically represented by such concepts as "God," can be fully known only by bringing the unconscious into consciousness. The progressive conquest of the unconscious by the conscious culminates in "consummate consciousness." This consciousness is unlimited in scope and unhindered in function. This state is reached through the *involution,* the turning inward, of the soul through the "Seven Planes of Liberating Consciousness." [35]

Even though I were capable of doing so adequately, space does not permit me to deal with further aspects of Meher Baba's thought, such as "The Characteristics of the Seven Different Kingdoms," "The States of Divine Consciousness," "The Beyond the Beyond State of God," "The Ten States of God," and "The New Humanity." [36]

Divine Love

Most of Meher Baba's disciples, however, apparently do not attempt to understand his metaphysical discourses. They turn, rather, to his numerous discourses on Love. One of these is "World Peace Through Love" in which Meher Baba says:

> Everywhere today man is rightfully occupied with the problem of world peace. If there is war, it means nothing short of racial suicide and total destruction. But world peace cannot be assured through dogmas, however

learned, or organizations, however efficient. It can be en-
sured only by a release of unarguing and unconquerable
love which knows no fear or separateness. Humanity is not
going to be saved by any material power—nuclear or
otherwise. It can be saved only through divine intervention. . . . Today the urgent need of mankind is not sects
or organized religions, but LOVE. Divine love will con-
quer hate and fear. . . . I have come to awaken in man
this divine love. It will restore to him the unfathomable
richness of his own eternal being and will solve all of his
problems.[37]

Man himself is not able to generate divine love. Human
love is so limited by human desires and emotions that

the spontaneous appearance of pure love from within becomes impossible. So, when such pure love arises in the
aspirant it is always a *gift*. Pure love arises in the heart of
the aspirant in response to the descent of grace from the
Master. As soon as the disciple is ready the grace of the
Master descends, for the Master, who is the ocean of divine love, is always on the look-out for the soul in whom
his grace will fructify. When pure love is first received as
a gift of the Master it becomes lodged in the consciousness
of the aspirant like a seed in a favorable soil, and in the
course of time the seed develops into a plant and then into
a full-grown tree.[38]

Meher Baba departed somewhat from traditional Hinduism in his attitude toward the world. Although it
is not ultimately real, it is not to be renounced and
avoided. To live the spiritual life one need not retreat
from life, but must involve himself in the life of the world.
Work undertaken with honest intent and love for God is
"Baba's Work," and those who do this are always his.

But the greatest work one can do for Baba is to live the life
of love, humility, sincerity and selfless service in which

there is no trace of hypocrisy. Baba's love is for all: and for each of his lovers to help others know this, his or her own life must be a radiating example of love so that it may become the instrument of Baba's love and the truth of Reality. . . . Baba's love is with his lovers always, helping and guiding them. And they? They should keep their love for him alive and aglow, by making him their constant companion in all their thoughts, words and actions, while carrying on their responsibilities, commitments and all other apparently necessary things of this world, though these have no foundation of their own in the domain of Reality.[39]

Worship

Meher Baba was apparently quite ecumenical in outlook. He often had passages from the Bible, the Koran, the Avesta, and the Gita read in gatherings with his devotees. Prayers, using the various titles for the Divine, were often read by members of the *mandali*. Baba himself prepared a "Universal Prayer," and a "Prayer of Repentance" which were and are often repeated in gatherings of "Baba Lovers." Meher Baba loved music, and religious songs were often sung in his presence. One of his favorites was "He's Got the Whole World in His Hand." Today, gatherings of devotees of Meher Baba follow much the same pattern. A large picture of Meher Baba rests on a table. Garlands of flowers are hung around the picture, and sometimes lamps are burned in front of it. As they gather, "Baba Lovers" greet each other with an embrace, and usually with some quotation from Baba's works. No lamps are swung in front of the picture, as in the *arati* in Hindu shrines, but hymns of praise are sung. Two verses from one of the *aratis* are:

The cause of creation Thou art.
The Saviour of the world Thou art.
Matchless Thou art. There is none but Thee,
O Truth-incarnate Avatar!
  I offer my mind to Thee.
  Accept it, O Meher, as my Arti.[40]

Quotations from the words of Meher Baba are then read, and these are followed with further hymns of praise and the "Universal Prayer" or other prayers approved by Meher Baba. The gathering breaks up with all present saying, *"Meher Baba ki jai!"*—"Victory to Meher Baba."

5

THE DIVINE MAGICIAN:

The Miraculous Life
of Sathya Sai Baba

It is not uncommon for trains to run late in India, and when they do they can often cause considerable inconvenience to their passengers. Such was the case when the Bombay–Madras Mail ran late and I missed the connection that would have brought me into Dharmavaram early one morning. I arrived about six o'clock in the evening instead. Dharmavaram is the station from which one takes the country bus for the thirty-mile trip to Prasanthi Nilayam, the ashram of Sathya Sai Baba. The last scheduled public bus had already departed. About a hundred passengers, headed for Prasanthi Nilayam, had alighted from the train. A few were picked up by friends in private cars; the rest of us were dependent upon commercial transportation. After some two hours of waiting, ninety of us crowded into a "chartered" bus, intended for forty-five, and started the long journey through the night over rough country roads. At one spot where the mud was deep all male passengers had to get out and push the bus through. It was well after midnight when we arrived at our destination, a small village community "in the middle of nowhere."

Although I had written and telegraphed ahead, no one was on hand to meet me or the rest of my companions on the crowded bus, for all were asleep. I soon discovered that we were not the only visitors, however. Since this was the holiday season, hundreds of others had come to have a *darshana* ("vision") of the God-Man of Prasanthi Nilayam. Since there were no quarters for so many, the visitors had stretched out in characteristic Indian style on the ground and had covered themselves with their sheets from head to toe to ward off the buzzing mosquitoes. The camp, in the dim light, had the appearance of a massive morgue with corpses laid out in the open as well as under the trees. In our party there had been a singing group of ten women and their male director. At last a tent was found for them, and Shamrao and I were invited to share their privilege of being under cover.

This was short-lived, however, for we had hardly spread our bedding rolls on the ground before it began to rain— rather, to pour—and a stream of water soon flowed through the tent, weakened the tent pegs, and the whole tent collapsed on us. We managed to disentangle ourselves, but by this time our bedding, our suitcases, and we were thoroughly drenched, with no shelter in sight. We sat down and waited for morning to come. At 4:30 A.M. Shamrao and I went for a bath in the community bath-house, dressed, got breakfast at a tea shop, and took our places with a large crowd for our first *darshana* of Sathya Sai Baba.

All eyes were fixed on a door on the second floor, open-ing on the long veranda that ran across the front of the building in which Baba lived. He would pass from the room on the right in which he slept to his dining room on the left. We watched from about 6:15 to 7:00 A.M. Then Baba came out and stood a moment looking down on the crowd. He smiled and gave a gesture with his left hand, which I was to see a number of times later, and passed on. His devotees greeted him with the palms of their hands placed together in the attitude of prayer and worship. On their faces were rapt expressions of devotion and joy. This was my first contact with one of the most unusual persons it has been my privilege to meet.

There is hardly a shop and there are very few homes in South India in which a picture of Sathya Sai Baba is not to be seen. Even in commercial Bombay a shrine has been erected in which he is worshiped. In numerous places on Thursday evenings prayers are said to him. In 1968 a World Conference of the Bhagavan Sri Sathya Sai Seva Organizations was held in Bombay. A large number of devotees from overseas as well as from India gathered "at the Lotus Feet" of Sathya Sai Baba. For the gathering, a souvenir volume, *At the Lotus Feet of Bhagavan Sri Sathya Sai Baba*,[1] was published. This volume contains articles of appreciation from all over the world. Six are by American devotees.

Sathya Sai was born on November 23, 1926, in the hamlet of Puttaparthi to devout Hindu parents. His devotees believe that he is Sai Baba of Shirdi come again, "exactly as that Avatar of the Lord had promised."[2] Their faith is based on the statement of an ancient disciple of Sai Baba who reports that shortly before his death the saint announced that he would be reincarnated eight years later. That Sai Baba ever made such a statement is denied by his disciples, for it is their belief that he is still alive and that many have had visions of him. It is not clear why Sathya Sai Baba should wish to claim to be the reincarnation of the earlier Sai Baba, but he has continued to insist upon this relationship, although his own fame has surpassed even that of his predecessor. Further, he says of himself, "I am Shiva-Shakti (i.e., the god Siva and his spouse), born in the *gothra* ("family") of Bharadwaja, according to a boon won by that sage from Shiva and Shakti. Shakti Herself was born as Sai Baba of Shirdi; Shiva and Shakti have incarnated as Myself; Shiva alone will incarnate as the third Sai in Mysore State." [3]

The baby born eight years after the death of Sai Baba of Shirdi was given the name Sathyanarayana Raju. It is said that various musical instruments in the house sounded without the touch of human hands, announcing his divine birth. A mysterious cobra was found under the bed of the newborn baby, as if to proclaim that Sheshiasai, Lord of the Serpents, had come to earth. As a lad, Sathyanarayana was very precocious, often giving instructions to his own teacher. His miraculous powers were early manifested. "To his schoolmates he would give sweets and pencils from empty schoolbags." On one occasion, when his teacher annoyed him, by his magic power Sathanarayana prevented the teacher from rising from his chair until he released him. On the banks of the nearby river he would make images of the gods from the sands and turn them into gold by his touch. He organized his schoolmates into a prayer group and instructed them in the teachings of the Hindu scriptures, which he had no need to memorize, for he already knew them by heart. Some of the neighbor boys were formed into a dramatic group and performed religious dramas that Sathya had written.

Early in 1940 he fell into a mysterious trance or coma. Some say that he suffered the sting of a scorpion, but his devotees believe that this was the method he employed to manifest himself to his followers. He had left his body, it is said, to go to the help of a devotee in dire distress. Doctors, exorcists, and others were called to cure him, but to no avail. After remaining in this state for about two months, Sathya "suddenly rose from his bed, called all the members of the house, and distributed sugar candy and flowers produced by the wave of the hand. When the neighbors came, He gave them in addition handfuls of *payasam* ("milk with rice") again produced from thin air. Then He announced Himself, 'I am Sai Baba of Shirdi.'" From this time onward, it is said, people "flocked around him, offering flowers, camphor, and incense. He taught them . . . the prayer 'Worship the feet of the Guru in your mind, and they (the feet of the Guru) will be the means of crossing the vast ocean of *Samsāra* ("Transmigration").'" [4]

On October 20 of that same year, Sathya Sai determined that the time had come for him to undertake his mission. Coming home from school, he threw aside his books and declared to his family: "I do not belong to you. I am leaving; I have full work ahead. Those devoted to Me are calling Me. The task for which I came is yet unfinished; I am starting now." He left home for good. When a neighbor attempted to stop the youth, Sathyanarayana told him: "The illusion has gone. I am no more yours. I am Sai Baba, remember." [5] Sathya Sai Baba took up his abode in a nearby temple, people flocked to see and hear him, and many accepted this teen-age youth as their guru, their spiritual guide. In 1944 a building, now called the Old Shrine, was built by his devotees. The impressive new building, Prasanthi Nilayam ("The Abode of Eternal Peace"), was dedicated in 1950 on his twenty-fourth birthday. From his fourteenth year to the present Sathya Sai Baba has continually moved about India, and even abroad, giving a *darshana* ("vision") of himself to his devotees, instructing them, and initiating them as his disciples. [6]

Miracles

Before I met him in person in Prasanthi Nilayam the one thing that I heard most frequently about Sathya Sai Baba was his ability to perform astonishing miracles. The claims made for him are well summarized in the statement of an American devotee who spent some time with him:

> In the tradition of history's Avatars and greatest Saints and Prophets, Baba heals the sick, the blind, the insane, and casts out evil spirits. He converts one type of matter to another and multiplies small quantities of material things, such as food, to produce large quantities. He travels in his subtle body to far places and there takes any appropriate *mayavic*, or illusory physical form—vanishing at will. Or he takes no form, but is there unseen, bringing protection, blessings, help in problems, and often leaving a sign of his visit. He pierces the barriers of physical space and time, seeing what his devotees are doing at a distance, what they have done in the past, and what will happen to them in the future. He not only reads minds, but moves and moulds them in the right direction, bringing as much influence to bear on a person as individual freedom and considerations of *Karma* warrant.[7]

One of the miracles attributed to Sathya Sai Baba occurred during the construction of the Prasanthi Nilayam. Heavy girders had been brought by train to the railway station some thirty miles from the site. When the engineer in charge of the construction considered the problems involved in conveying the girders by ox cart along the narrow country dirt roads, passing through several villages and across a number of streams, he decided that the task was hopeless and so informed Sathya Sai Baba. He suggested that the plan to use girders be abandoned and the construction plans changed. It was at this time that word was brought to Baba that a traveling crane had been abandoned in another town along the railway because it was out of order and beyond repair. Baba produced *vibhuti* ("sacred ash") and gave it to a devotee, who went and scattered it over the crane. Miraculously, the crane was now found to be in working order, and not only lifted the girders from the railway car but even transported them across the fields to the building site.[8]

During the Dasara ("Ten Day") holidays in October and his birthday celebrations in November, many thousands of devotees (sometimes as many as fifty thousand) go to Prasanthi Nilayam to have a *darshana* of Sathya Sai Baba and to witness his miracles. One disciple, a former chief scientist in the Government's Ministry of Defense, insists that Baba is "beyond the laws of physics and chemistry, a divine phenomenon, an incarnation."[9] A particular Thursday during Dasara is especially auspicious, for on that day Sathya Sai Baba draws from his mouth two gold *linga* (the phallic symbol associated with the god Siva) which, it is said, he has formed magically within himself. It is also during this time of pilgrimage to Prasanthi Nilayam that accounts of his numerous other miracles are given. A leading lawyer swears that Baba cured him of Parkinson's disease with the wave of his hand. Another devotee reports that when he was traveling with Baba the car ran out of gas, but, unperturbed, Baba simply turned a bucket of water into gasoline.[10] Charles Penn, a captain in the Civil Air Patrol in California, was caught in a severe hailstorm while crossing a mountain in search of a lost plane. In the midst of the storm he saw Baba sitting beside him, and knew that he was being directed by Baba. "Penn! You need not look out," he heard the voice of Sathya Sai say. "I shall look for you." Thus assured, Penn completed his mission in safety.[11]

Although I did not personally witness any of these miracles, I talked with many people who had. I saw a golden coin (incidentally, bearing the image of Sathya Sai Baba!) that had been produced out of thin air. I talked with a father whose infant son had been healed of a disease, declared "incurable" by doctors, by the application of *vibhuti* ("sacred ash") which Sathya Sai Baba had produced by the wave of his hand, and saw the lad himself, now about twelve years old. Others had had "visions of Baba" in places far removed from Prasanthi Nilayam.[12]

Sathya Sai Baba's most spectacular miracle occurred in July, 1963. The incident is described in detail by his biographer and personal secretary, N. Kasturi. On June 28, Baba announced that he would not grant any interviews during the next week. Early the next morning, as he crossed the veranda from which he usually gave *darshana* to his devotees, he fell to the floor with a massive stroke. It was soon discovered that his entire left side was paralyzed. This stroke was followed by four heart attacks. Several doctors were called, but apparently could give no relief to the intense suffering through which Baba was going. The situation was made more difficult by the fact that, although he was unconscious, Baba resisted all efforts at administering medication. This situation continued for five days. On several occasions death seemed imminent. On the sixth day Baba returned to consciousness, and in a weak voice demanded that all the devotees be called together to receive his *darshana*. Two days later, supported by two of his disciples, with his left foot dragging and his left arm hanging useless by his side, he made his way to the Prayer Hall. After he had been seated he gestured that he wanted a glass of water. He sipped a few drops and then, dipping the fingers of his right hand into the water, he sprinkled a few drops on his left hand and arm. Next, with both hands he stroked his left leg. Then, to the amazement of all present, he stood up, healed. For the next hour and a half he spoke to his devotees with the force and eloquence with which they were familiar! During the course of his address he informed them that one of his devotees, who had no other helper, had appealed to him when overtaken with a stroke and later with four heart attacks.

> My *Dharma* ("duty") is *Bhaktarakshana* ("protection of devotees"). I had to rescue him. I am the only one who could have survived the heart attacks. This is not the first time that I have taken on the illness of those whom I want to save. You may call these miracles; they are part of my essential miraculousness. This is my nature. It is part of the task for which I have come.

It was then that Sathya Sai Baba revealed that Siva and Shakti had incarnated themselves in him, that he himself is the Lord in human form.[13]

Prasanthi Nilayam

The little village of Prasanthi Nilayam, in Andhra Pradesh, takes its name from Prasanthi Nilayam ("Home of Supreme Peace"), the building in which Sathya Sai Baba resides. It is situated on a fairly large plot of land in Puttaparthi, a hamlet girded by rugged hills. The river Chitravati runs through the village, which has its own post office, bank, police station, hospital, school, and bookstore. A number of Baba's devotees have built their private cottages in the village in order that they may spend time in his presence. Some motel-like buildings and a number of small restaurants and tea shops provide for the needs of the multitudes of devotees and visitors who come to see Sathya

Sai Baba. The two most imposing buildings are the auditorium, which will seat from four to five thousand people,
and Prasanthi Nilayam itself.

As one approaches this "Home of Supreme Peace" one
sees first a round enclosure which, through its flower arrangement, symbolizes the teaching of Sathya Sai Baba:
"After crossing the six internal enemies of man—Lust, Anger, Greed, Attachment, Pride, and Jealousy—the *sādhaka*
("seeker") comes to the green meadow of *Prema*—Love.
Beyond that we have the expanse of *Shanti*—Quiet—
where all agitations cease and the mind is at ease in its own
silence. Now is the chance to establish oneself in Yoga, the
discipline of spiritual union with the Universal Power, the
Absolute Wisdom, the Eternal Verity. The consciousness
ascends through the six centers, marked on the *Yoga
Danda* ("pole") in the center of the circle. The Lotus of
the Heart blooms, the petals unfold, the fragrance per-
meates the universe." [14] This last symbolism is represented
by a pole, cut by six ascending circles, and crowned with a
spreading lotus flower. Each time I approached this enclosed garden I saw a number of people bowed in prayer,
possibly meditating upon these words of Baba.

Prasanthi Nilayam is an impressive two-storied building. Across the front of the building, on both levels, run
wide verandas. It is on the upper veranda that Sathya Sai
Baba appears several times a day to give *darshana* to his
devotees. The large room on the ground floor is the Prayer
Hall, at the western end of which is the shrine on a raised
platform. On either side of the shrine is a life-size picture,
one of Sai Baba of Shirdi and the other of Sathya Sai Baba.
Between them, on a pedestal, stands a silver image of Sai
Baba, and underneath, a small portrait of Sathya Sai Baba.
It is said that these are not objects for worship, but are in-
tended to assist one's meditation. On the walls of the

Prayer Hall are portraits of the various "manifestations of the Godhead," including one of Christ among those of the many noted saints of India. On the ground floor are two other rooms in which Sathya Sai gives interviews to devotees and visitors. The second floor is occupied with the living quarters of Sathya Sai. In the center of the second-floor veranda is a marble image of the Hindu deity Sri Krishna in his traditional pose, playing his flute. On the flat roof of this veranda is a marble bust of Sathya Sai Baba, and his flag, of saffron color with the *cakra* ("symbolic wheel") in the center.

Discourses by Sathya Sai Baba and by learned pundits (Vedic teachers) are given in the auditorium, and between times verses from the Hindu scriptures are chanted by teams of readers and broadcast throughout the village over a public-address system. Meditation and worship take place at stated times in the Prayer Hall. At 4:45 A.M. the mystic *mantra* "*Om*," the symbol of the cosmic Word, is chanted for some time. About 6:00 A.M. Sathya Sai Baba appears on the upper veranda to give *darshana* to his devotees. This is followed by two *bhajan* sessions, in which songs of praise are sung by selected groups of singers. It is considered a great honor to be invited by Baba to present a *bhajana* at Prasanthi Nilayam. The *arati* (service of worship), with the waving of lamps and the burning of incense before Baba's picture, is conducted at 11:00 A.M. The afternoon may be given to interviews and other activities. An interesting feature of the interviews is that, while individuals may indicate to the secretary their desire to talk with Sathya Sai, it is Baba himself who generally selects, it appears almost at random, those from the audience to whom he will give interviews. It is explained that he knows intuitively those who are in most need of his help. At 7:00 in the evening all gather in the auditorium to hear a discourse by

Sathya Sai or by someone who has been invited by him to speak.

Teachings

Sathya Sai Baba's message to his disciples and to the world is given through his writings and his many discourses. In 1958 he began the publication, in English and the principal Indian languages, of a monthly magazine, *Sanathana Sarathi* ("The Timeless Charioteer"), in which a number of his own articles appeared. These, along with his numerous discourses, have been published in his five-volume *Sathya Sai Speaks*[15] and some half dozen other books in the major languages of India. His message centers largely around the exposition of the meaning of the four aspects of the "task" to which he set himself: *Dharmasthapana* (Establishing the Faith on Firm Foundations), *Vidwathposhana* (Fostering of Scholarship), *Vedasamrakshana* (Preservation of the Vedas), and *Bhaktarakshana* (Protection of the Devotees).[16] For him, the "Faith" is the *Sanatana Dharma,* the Eternal Religion of the Hindus revealed to the rishis ("sages") of long ago; "Scholarship" is the studying, learning, and teaching of the Vedas, the sacred and eternal canonical scriptures; and "Protection of the Devotees" means protecting them from the destructive influence of secularism and materialism. But the devotees also have their "tasks." These are expressed by the five words that occur again and again in his writings and discourses: *Dharma* (performing the duties laid upon them by their religion and by his command), *Sathya* (discovering and living by the truth revealed to them), *Shanti* (living the life of peace and of quietness), *Prema* (exhibiting love in all relationships), and *Dhyāna* (living the life of discipline and obedience). Each of these ideas is developed by

Sathya Sai in a separate book, the *Dharma Vahini,* the *Sathya Vahini,* and so on.[17] The list of books by, or about, Sathya Sai Baba is indeed impressive.

Without any apparent sense either of embarrassment or of boasting, Sathya Sai says and writes much about himself:

> When someone asks you, in great earnestness, where the Lord is to be found, do not try to dodge the question. Give him the answer that rises up to your tongue from your heart. Direct them to come to Puttaparthi and share your joy! Tell them He is here in the Prasanthi Nilayam.[18]

Baba's style is conversational, simple, spiced with humor and with references to familiar folk tales or with quotations from the scriptures of Hinduism, Buddhism, and Christianity. Although his topics deal with immediate needs and situations, his thought is based squarely on the traditional *Sanatana Dharma,* the Eternal Religion, as expounded by the Vedanta philosophers. Because of his awareness of being an *avatara* he speaks with a disarming lack of embarrassment about himself and his deeds as a supernatural person. He speaks with authority and demands obedience of his devotees. A brief summary of one of the discourses that I heard him give will illustrate these points.

Some three or four thousand of us gathered in the large auditorium for the afternoon discourse, which lasted for an hour and a half! But because Sathya Sai Baba is a most impressive speaker, he held his audience from beginning to end. As he often does, he started with a song of his own composition, sung with a fine baritone voice. Then, with marvelous inflection of tone, sweeping gestures, humor, parables, and stories he gave a commentary on the song that he had just sung:

A boy once went to a learned man and, showing him his ring, asked him what it was made of. He was told that it was made of gold. The lad insisted that it was made of silver, but the learned man would not agree. Another learned guru gave the same reply, but when the boy insisted that it was made of silver the guru answered, "Yes, maybe it is so." Then the boy said, "No, it is made of brass." The guru agreed and said, "Yes, it may be so." The young man was surprised and asked, "Guruji, how is it that you agree to whatever statement I make?" The guru replied: "My dear boy, to me there is no gold or silver or brass. All are the same to me." Applying this lesson, Sathya Sai pointed out that only Brahman exists. Neither "you" nor "I" exist in the ultimate sense. When one realizes that he is Brahman, he ceases to exist as a being apart from Brahman. To realize this is salvation. We love our bodies as though they were our permanent abode, but at death we must leave them. Nothing in this world belongs to us; neither do we belong to anyone.

Self-realization, God-realization, is possible only to one who accepts the authority of his spiritual teacher and practices what he has learned. Once Jesus entered the Temple at Jerusalem, pointed out Sathya Sai, and drove out those who were misusing that place of worship. Then some scribes and Pharisees appeared on the scene and demanded, "By what authority do you do these things?" Jesus told them this story: Once a father had two sons. To the elder he said, "Son, go into the field and take care of it." The son said, "Yes, father, I will do so." But he never went. Then the father called the younger son and said, "Son, go into the field and take care of it." The younger son said, "Father, I will not be able to go." But later, he did go and fulfilled his father's desire. After narrating this story Jesus asked who was true and loyal to his father. All re-

plied saying that the younger son was. Thus, pointed out
Sathya Sai, only those who obeyed his teaching were
worthy of receiving *moksha* ("salvation"). Just to listen
without obeying would be like taking the doctor's prescrip-
tion and putting it under one's pillow, expecting then to
be healed. Only after buying the medicine and taking it as
the doctor has prescribed can one save one's life.

People today, insisted Sathya Sai, are not interested in
the spiritual life. Day and night they think only of accumu-
lating wealth. To emphasize this point he told the story of
Lakshmi, the goddess of wealth, and Vasudeva, the god of
knowledge. One day Lakshmi said to Vasudeva, "I have
more disciples in the world than you do, Vasudeva." Vasudeva, taken aback, challenged Lakshmi to prove it by their
both becoming avataras. Lakshmi became a famous pundita
who promised people: "If you will give one rupee to the
poor, you will gain two. For silver you will get gold." Thus,
wherever she went she blessed people with wealth and
gained many followers. On the other hand, Vasudeva became a famous pundit, teaching the way of salvation by
renunciation and meditation. He, too, gained many disciples. But one day the devotees of Vasudeva heard of the
pundita and her blessings and invited her to come to their
village. But she replied, "Unless you drive the pundit out
I will not enter your village." Sorrowfully, the devotees of
Vasudeva returned, for they did not want to hurt the famous pundit. But in the end they requested him to leave.
Thus, pointed out Sathya Sai, people care nothing for
spiritual knowledge; they want gold, silver, and jewels.

Secular learning today, continued Sathya Sai, is making
people proud and scornful of religious knowledge. There
was in a certain village a father who had an "educated"
son. One day this educated son observed his father doing
his *pūjā* ("worship"). He noticed that his father would

take small quantities of water from a vessel and, after repeating each *mantra*, would take a small sip. The educated son said to himself: "It appears that my father is thirsty. But I do not understand why he should drink water in such a miserable way. Why does he not take a tumblerful and drink it all at once?" So he brought a glass of water and placed it before his father, saying, "Here, father, drink this if you are so thirsty." The father looked up and said: "Dear son, I am not thirsty. I am performing *pūjā*. This way of drinking holy water is part of the ritual." The son laughed and went away. Later, the father observed his son writing a letter. He was using a pen and a bottle of ink. From time to time he would dip the pen into the ink and write. After a while the father said: "Dear son, if you want to pour ink on that paper, why do you do it in that miserable way? Why don't you just turn the ink bottle onto the paper?" Picking up the ink bottle, he held it over the paper. "Shall I do it for you?" The "educated" young man quickly caught on to his father's meaning!

Institutions

This story, and the point that it was intended to emphasize, underscores Sathya Sai Baba's attitude toward contemporary developments in Indian life. The spiritual life of the nation is being undermined. To counteract the trends toward secularism and materialism and to save men from their influence he has become incarnate.[19] To carry out his purpose he has established institutions through which to enlist the aid of those who share his ideals. His program and philosophy are probably well expressed in the words of one of his devoted disciples, Sri Ratan Lal:

> In our country, we are passing through a disintegrating phase on account of giving up the ancient way of life. . . .

We are today facing many problems of an unprecedented character. If we are to solve them, we must have men and women who have the true spirit of religion. . . . The basis of our civilization is to be found in the philosophy of the Upanishads. . . . We must go to the Upanishads for our inspiration. . . . When we have failed, our defeat is due to our infidelity to the teachings of the Upanishads. It is therefore essential for our generation to grasp their significance and understand their relevance to our problems.[20]

Thus, while Sathya Sai Baba uses modern methods of communication and travel, his way of life, the program at Prasanthi Nilayam, and his message are essentially traditional.

The two significant institutions established by Sathya Sai, other than Prasanthi Nilayam itself, have as their purpose the propagation of the wisdom of the Vedas.

In order to encourage the younger generations to benefit from the teachings of the Upanishads (the Vedas), and thereby spread the message of the real *Bharati Sanskruti,* a Trust known as "Sri Satya Sai Education Foundation" has been registered and has been charged with the responsibility of establishing new institutions or assisting present institutions to spread the light of Vedantic knowledge.[21]

The first institution established under this Trust was the Veda-Sastra Patasala, the Academy for Vedic and Sanskrit Study, a school at Prasanthi Nilayam in which young boys are taught to chant the Vedas by heart. The second institution is the Akhila Bharathai Vidwanmahasabha, the All India Academy of Vedic Scholars, established in 1965 when two hundred pundits responded to Sathya Sai's invitation and assembled in a great convocation. Since then, branches of the Academy have been formed by Vedic scholars in a number of cities in South India.

It was somewhat unfortunate for me that I could visit

Prasanthi Nilayam only during the holiday season when thousands of devotees had come to have a *darshana* of this one whom they consider divine. Although Sathya Sai Baba, spotting me in the crowd, stopped long enough for me to take his picture, there was no opportunity for me to talk with him. Because of the additional features that had been added to the daily program, no interviews were being given. Seen close up, he is an impressive figure, with a handsome face, and crowned with a massive head of hair. He wears a long red or golden robe. At his every appearance his devotees bowed before him in adoration. Although some of his followers were somewhat more restrained, the majority with whom I talked agreed, it appears, with the assertion, "Satya Sai Baba is indeed God with the three qualities of omnipotence, omniscience, and omnipresence. . . . He is the *Guru* of *Gurus*, the *Vid* ("Wisdom") of the Veda, goal of man, the Supreme Power, and God in all His manifestations." [22]

6

THE SOUND THAT LIBERATES:
The Radhasoami Satsang

Agra is well known to tourists as the city of the magnificent
Taj Mahal, the "Dream in Marble." Not known to them is
another institution of considerable interest. On the outskirts of the city is a large colony known as Dayalbagh
("Garden of Compassion"). This is the center of one division of the Radhasoami Satsang.[1] As one approaches he
sees on the left-hand side of the road a hospital, followed
by a long, rather low building which houses a number of
offices. Next, there is an impressive gateway through
which can be seen a new building being constructed in
marble. On the other side of the gate is a row of shops. On
the right side of the road, and extending for nearly a mile,
can be seen a number of brick buildings. Behind these are
small private residencies. Continuing down the road, on
the left are open fields: a grape orchard and farmland. On
a low hill is a modern dairy. Beyond the buildings on the
right are further fields, planted in a variety of crops. The
colony gives the appearance of an active community.

But to one familiar with the history and teachings of the
cult, these signs of modernity seem strangely paradoxical,
for fundamental to the Faith of the Radhasoami Satsang is
the belief that the *Surat Shabda Mauj* ("Spiritual Sound

Current") emanating from the Feet of the Supreme Being, who is enthroned in the Region of Pure Spirit and Light, descends through other Regions, penetrating spiritual-material, material-spiritual elements until it finally vibrates in this world of materiality and evil far removed from the Region of Spirit and Light. Then, through the practice of *Surat Shabda Yoga,* the individual *surat* ("spirit" or "soul"), which is trapped in this material world, is lifted through Region after Region until it is finally absorbed into the Supreme Being.

Since the Radhasoami Satsang gives such importance to the concept of the *Shabda,* and since it finds a place in the teachings of the other cults also, it may be well at this point to look more closely at the concept. The effective power of correctly articulated sounds is an accepted belief in Hindu thought. It is said that sounds can create and destroy. The world was created, it is believed, by the utterance of the proper sounds, and it is maintained by the repetition of the proper sounds, just as the sun is kept in its proper position only because people worship it regularly with the proper sounds, called *mantras.* A *mantra* is a mystic word or religious text which has been revealed to men by a seer. It is said to have the property of saving the soul of one who cherishes it. A *mantra* may be of one syllable, as in the case of the sound *Om,*[2] or it may be a verse from the Vedas. For the Hindu a *mantra* is not a mere formula or a prayer. It is an embodiment in sound of a particular deity. It is the deity itself. Because the *mantra* is the embodiment of a deity in sound, it must be repeated in that form alone in which it first revealed itself to the mind of a seer. It is not to be learned from books, but from the voice of a living guru. It is generally given, and its mystic meaning is explained at the time of initiation.[3] The purpose of *japa,* the frequent repetition of the *mantra*, is to produce the gradual transformation of the personality of the worshiper into that of the worshiped. The more a worshiper advances in his *japa* the more does he partake of the nature of the deity whom he worships, and the less is he himself.[4]

Sahabji Maharaj, the Fifth Sat-Guru of the Radhasoami Faith, in his *Yathartha Prakasa*, quotes extensively from the Vedas, Brahmanas, and Upanishads "creation stories" in which Brahma or Prajapati, through the creative act with his female counterpart, *Vani* ("word" or "sound"), brought forth all creation.[5] The contemporary literature of the cults teaches that this "creative Word" is still active, some say "vibrating," and that it is mediated through the *Sat-Guru* ("True Master") and the *mantra* given at the time of initiation.[6]

The Divine Founder

The teachings of the Radhasoami Satsang, it is claimed, are similar to those of other Faiths, collectively and separately known as the "Religion of Saints," as taught by Kabir, Nanak, Jagjivan Sahab, and others. Param Guru Shri Shiv Dayal Singh Sahab, founder of the Radhasoami Satsang, known to his followers as Soamiji Maharaj, was born in Agra in 1818. He was of the Kshatriya caste. From the early age of six, it is said, he began performing spiritual practices and would often sit for hours in a closed room deep in meditation. He soon also began to expound profound spiritual teachings to his family and companions. Many gathered to hear his words of wisdom. He was married, but we know little of his wife. Apparently, he would occasionally dress as Krishna and she as Radha, and they would instruct their disciples through enacting scenes from the Puranas. In 1858, Rai Salig Ram, who subsequently succeeded Soamiji Maharaj as the Second Revered Leader of the Faith, became a disciple and it was at his request and the requests of other devotees that Soamiji Maharaj founded the Radhasoami Satsang in 1861.

The founding of the Satsang was announced publicly through the following proclamation: "It is hereby proclaimed for the benefit of *Adhikaris* that the Supreme Being Almighty Lord Radhasoami, on observing the Jivas undergoing extreme suffering and being subjected to delusion, has Himself assumed the Form of the Sant Satguru and manifested on this earth for their redemption and through His Supreme Grace, explains the secret of His Original Abode by means of the *Surat Shabda Marga*. It behooves the Jivas that they should engender within themselves love and faith in His Holy Feet." [7] By the members of the Satsang, Soamiji Maharaj is believed to be this "Incarnation of the Supreme Merciful Radhasoami," the Supreme Being. The name "Radhasoami" is apparently a form of "Radha" and "swami," representing "Lord" Krishna and his devoted *gopi* companion, Radha. The teachings of the First Leader of the Faith are embodied in two volumes, one in prose and the other in poetry, each with the title *Sar Bachan* ("Essential Utterances"). At the time of his death in 1878, Soamiji Maharaj said to his devotees: "Let no Satsangi, whether a householder or a Sadhu, feel distracted. I shall be with one and all and they shall be looked after with more and more Grace." [8]

As the number of followers of Soamiji Maharaj increased, the house in which he was living in Agra became inadequate. A spot about three miles outside the city was selected for a new center, and the foundation of Radhasoami Bagh, now known as Soamibagh ("The Lord's Garden"), was laid. After some living quarters and a place for worship had been constructed, Soamiji Maharaj made this his permanent residence. Near the rooms in which he lived there was a mound. On this mound his ashes were deposited in a building constructed as a mausoleum. The colony, to which reference has already been made, grew up around this spot. A later Leader of the Faith conceived the plan of constructing a magnificent building, enclosing the earlier one. When completed, this may well rival the Taj Mahal in beauty.

As a rule, it appears, the element of miracle is not emphasized in the Radhasoami Faith. Yet, in *A Brief Account of the Progress of the Radhasoami Satsang*, published in 1961, a number of miracles attributed to Soamiji Maharaj are recorded. During the construction of a building at Soamibagh, the builders discovered that a sacred neem tree stood in the way. The laborers refused to uproot the tree. "The matter was brought to the notice of Soamiji Maharaj. He went to inspect the site, garlanded the tree and returned home and to the surprise of all, the tree began to dry up from that time and soon died out. The impediment was thus easily removed." [9] In 1877, because of the failure of the monsoon a serious drought occurred. Villagers came to Soamiji Maharaj for help. "Soamiji Maharaj ordered that all should repeat the Holy Name 'Radhasoami' in chorus during Satsang and all Satsangis and Sadhus repeated the Holy Name in chorus. A shower of rain soon followed." [10] A certain sadhu, by name Hans Das, was commanded to develop a colony, to be called Radhabagh, in the vicinity of a dried-up, deserted well. "Hans Das, in obedience to orders, took up his residence there and in a few days he repaired the well and water collected in it to a depth of six feet. During the famine that soon followed this event, water rose so high in the well that Hans Das provided water daily to hundreds of cattle of the neighboring villages." [11] The land around the well was sandy and apparently unfit for cultivation. But Soamiji Maharaj insisted that it must be cultivated. A garden was laid out and then "farms and fields have developed there . . . in an area of four square miles around Radhabagh and good crops and vegetables are now grown there year after year." [12]

The Second Revered Leader of the Radhasoami Faith was Rai Bahadur Salig Ram, who was known as Param Guru Huzur Maharaj. He was born in Agra in the year 1829. After graduation from Agra College he entered the service of the Postal Department and rose to the position of Postmaster General in the North-Western Provinces. Even shortly after his birth, it is said, it was known that Salig Ram would have a remarkable future. "On studying his horoscope astrologers had predicted that He would be free from all evils and passions and would be mercy and piety personified. A Sadhu had also predicted that this child would be famous and would benefit mankind by bestowing both religious merit and material prosperity." [13] According to family custom, Salig Ram was asked to accept a certain teacher, Gosainji by name, as his personal guru. But the questions about religion which Salig Ram put to him were so difficult that Gosainji was unable to answer them. Salig Ram refused to accept him and determined to find a Sat-Guru, a True Master. His search carried him to many pandits and maulvis (Hindu and Muslim learned men) to the study of many scriptures, but to no avail until the year 1858. Then, by accident, it appeared, he met Seth Pratap Singh, the youngest brother of Soamiji Maharaj. Guided by him, he presented himself before Soamiji Maharaj, who answered his many questions on various religious topics satisfactorily. After attending his discourses for two years, Salig Ram became a devoted disciple of Soamiji Maharaj. From that time, until the death of his Lord, Salig Ram served Soamiji Maharaj "with his (a) body (*Tan*), (b) mind (*Mana*), (c) wealth (*Dhan*) and (d) spirit (*Surat*)." This type of service has become the pattern in the Radhasoami Faith. Service with the body (*tan*) consists in providing any and all types of menial service which may be required for the care of the guru. Service with the mind (*mana*) involves the complete surrender of one's will to the guru. Service with money (*dhan*) consists in placing one's entire wealth and income at the disposal of the guru. All one's personal needs are then met by the guru. Service with the spirit (*surat*) implies employing every possible minute absorbed in repeating the name "Radhasoami" and in concentrating on his form, that is, the "mind is busy in the contemplation of the Beloved, while the hands are busy performing worldly duties." [14]

Upon the death of Soamiji Maharaj in 1878, Salig Ram became the Second Revered Leader of the Radhasoami Satsang, with the title "Huzur Maharaj." Under his leadership a large number of satsangis were initiated, and the Satsang became more widely known. Max Müller, in his book *Rama Krishna, His Life and Teachings,* speaks of the widespread influence that Huzur Maharaj had. It appears that it was he who was largely responsible for giving permanent form to the Satsang and systematizing its teachings. He began the publication of a journal called *Prem Patra* (literally, "The Love Journal"). His articles on the Faith, first published in the journal, were later published in a six-volume work under the title *Prem Patra.* His teachings are also set forth in his *Prem Bani,* in four volumes, and his *Radhasoami Mat Prakash.*

Miracles are also attributed to Huzur Maharaj. For example, it is recorded that a "Satsangi was suffering from leprosy. His wife prayed to Huzur Maharaj to grant him relief from the disease. Huzur Maharaj gave instructions that water used by Himself for his bath on next Sunday be collected and given to the lady for her husband to bathe with. This was done and the patient bathed with the said water and was cured of his leprosy." [15]

Pandit Brahma Shankar Misra, known as Param Guru Maharaj Sahab, became the Third Revered Leader of the Satsang upon the death of Huzur Maharaj in 1898. By this time the activities at the center in Agra had become so extensive and the management of the branch Satsangs so much a burden for the Revered Leader that Maharaj Sahab established the Central Administrative Council, in 1902, to look after the affairs of the Satsang. Two years later the Radhasoami Trust was formed to look specifically after the properties of the Satsang. Maharaj Sahab had also planned to organize a number of secular institutions such as schools and workshops when his death, in 1907, prevented. Sri Kamta Prasad Sinha, a lawyer, became the Fourth Revered Leader of the Radhasoami Satsang, with the title "Param Guru Sarkar Sahab."

His succession was disputed, however, by a majority of the members of the Central Council, although 111 of the 116 branch Satsangs accepted him as the Sat-Guru. A division occurred, therefore, in the movement. The Central Council, being in charge of the *samādhs* ("tombs") of the first three Leaders, refused to permit the followers of Sarkar Sahab to hold worship services at the *samādhs*. Ghazipur, which had been the ancestral home of Kamta Prasad Sinha, became the center of the Satsang which recognized Sarkar Sahab as Sat-Guru. In 1910, when all efforts at reconciliation had failed, the Ghazipur satsangis adopted the constitution of a new body, known as the Radhasoami Satsang Sabha. This section of the Satsang became known, later, as the Radhasoami Satsang, Dayalbagh,

while the other section was known as the Radhasoami
Satsang, Soamibagh. For clarity, we will deal with each of
these sections separately, continuing first with the Dayalbagh Satsang.

Upon the death of Sarkar Sahab in 1913, he was succeeded by Anand Sarup, who became known as Param
Guru Sahabji Maharaj. His selection was confirmed, it is
said, by a strange incident. Although many of the satsangis
had been looking for the manifestation of the *Nij Dhar* of
the Supreme Being Radhasoami in one of their number, it
was not until Anand Sarup entered the room where a number were gathered that they were amazed to see his form
change first to that of Soamiji Maharaj and then to that of
Huzur Maharaj.[16] "Thereafter, Sahabji Maharaj observed,
'The Spiritual Current is flowing with all its majesty and
force. It behoves all of you to offer obeisance.' He then
allowed Satsangis to offer obeisance. Satsangis, one after
the other, bowed to Him and offered obeisance in turn."[17]
Sahabji Maharaj brought dynamic leadership to the Faith.
In 1914 plans were made to transfer the headquarters of
the Satsang back to Agra. A large tract of land was secured
which surrounded the earlier colony, known as Soamibagh,
on three sides, and in January, 1915, the colony of Dayalbagh ("Garden of Compassion") was founded. The Radhasoami Educational Institute was established in 1917. In
time this became an arts college. In the same year the
Model Industries was established. This has expanded into
a number of branches, manufacturing a variety of con-
sumer goods. A dairy, considered one of the best in the
country, came into existence in 1930. The Saran Ashram
Hospital, now a well-equipped modern institution, was established in 1921. In the meantime a flood of books poured
forth from Sahabji Maharaj's pen. Among the more prominent of these was the *Yathartha Prakasha,* in three vol-

umes, a scholarly survey of the major religions. His *Discourses,* in three volumes, and his *Prem Sandesha* expound in detail the teachings of the Radhasoami Faith. The versatile nature of his activities attracted wide attention, and he was knighted by the British Government in 1936.

As early as 1921, it is said, Sahabji Maharaj had given indication that his successor would be Mehtaji Sahab, a civil engineer who rose to a high position in the Punjab Government. Not without some opposition, Mehtaji Sahab became the Sixth Sat-Guru in 1937. Under his able leadership impressive progress has been made by the Radhasoami Satsang Sabha, Dayalbagh, in the areas of education, industrial manufacturing, medical and other social services, the dairy, publications, and so forth. An extensive agricultural program has also been introduced in which all members of the colony take part. The organization of the Satsang has also been widely extended. There are now seven registered Regional Radhasoami Satsang Associations, supervising the activities of District Satsang Associations and some 600 branch Satsangs. A number of these worship in their own Satsang halls. A Satsang colony has been established in Delhi and plans are under way for colonies in other parts of India. The educational institutions at Dayalbagh deserve special mention. The institute for boys, established in 1917, has developed into a degree-granting college with departments in arts, science, commerce, law, and agriculture. A high school for girls is now a woman's college granting the B.A. degree. A woman's teacher training college offers courses through the master's degree. A technical school has departments in mechanical, electrical, and automobile engineering, and the engineering college offers degrees in mechanical and electrical engineering. The equipment in both these latter institutions is up-to-date, as I myself observed when I visited Dayalbagh.

In addition to the primary and secondary schools at Dayalbagh colony itself, similar institutions have been opened
in several of the Indian States. The extensive activities of
the colony are described in the booklet *Dayalbagh: A Brief
Description of the Origin, Early History and Development
of the Colony and Its Institutions.*[18]

The Radha Soami Satsang, Beas

Before we turn to a consideration of the teachings of the
Radhasoami Satsang, the story of a further division that
took place in the Satsang must be given. This came about
through the activities of Baba Jaimal Singh, who was born
in the Punjab in 1839. As a youth, while studying the
Granth Sahib, the scriptures of the Sikhs, he discovered
reference to "the Five Melodies in man which are said to
be constantly reverberating in him and might be heard, by
proper training." Since no one in his community could explain to him the meaning of the "Five Melodies" he set
out in search of a Master who could. After many months of
searching he met a sadhu who told him that in Agra there
lived a perfect mahatma who could instruct him in the
"Five Melodies." In Agra he was finally directed to Soamiji
Maharaj, who welcomed him and gave him instruction in
the "Five Melodies," which form a part of the teaching of
the Radhasoami Satsang also. These are said to be *Niran-
jana, Om, Rarang, Sohang,* and *Sat.* In time, Soamiji
Maharaj initiated Jaimal Singh and instructed him in the
spiritual practice of the Faith. Urged by Soamiji Maharaj
to earn his own living, he joined the army and remained
in the service for thirty-four years. His spiritual practice
continued unabated, and he began to initiate some of those
who attended his discourses. After his discharge he went
to Beas, near Amritsar, and began to hold *satsang.*[19] This

led to a break with the Satsang under Maharaj Sahab, and the Radha Soami Satsang, Beas, now became a separate movement. While Radhasoami Maharaj was believed to be the incarnation of the Supreme Being, Merciful Radhasoami, and his *Sar Bachan* was the basic scripture of the Satsang at Beas, certain innovations were introduced that were unacceptable to the Satsang at Agra. The breach that developed has never been healed.

Before his death in 1903, Baba Jaimal Singh nominated Sardar Sawan Singh as his successor. Sawan Singh had had a distinguished career in the army, but was searching for a Master to serve as his guru. One day Baba Jaimal Singh visited the town where Sawan Singh was stationed. As the young officer passed them Baba Jaimal Singh remarked to a disciple, "That is the man we have come to initiate." The disciple replied, "How can that be when he does not even notice you?" The saint replied, "On the fourth day he will come to us." And so it happened that on the fourth day Sawan Singh, having heard that a holy man was holding *satsang* nearby, came to see and hear him. He was greatly impressed by the character and teachings of Baba Jaimal Singh, and after a short time sought initiation by him. From that date until the death of his Master he visited Baba Jaimal Singh on every occasion possible and sat at his feet.

Under the leadership of Sawan Singh, who was known to his followers as the Great Master, the Radha Soami Satsang at Beas made considerable progress. It was not long after the death of Baba Jaimal Singh, we are told, that his disciples "became aware of the divine nature of His successor." [20] Following his retirement from military service in 1911, Baba Sawan Singh Ji settled at the colony in Beas, to which he gave the name "Dera Baba Jaimal Singh" in memory of its founder. During the years of his leadership the colony grew from a small collection of huts by the riverbank into a large and flourishing spiritual community. He was not content to confine his labors to the colony, however, but also traveled extensively throughout North India establishing branch Satsang centers. Visitors from overseas were also attracted to Beas and before his death those calling themselves disciples were to be found in Europe and America.[21] The spiritual autobiography and teachings of Baba Sawan Singh are recorded in his *Spiritual Gems.*[22]

Although, as I have mentioned before, the Sat-Gurus of the Radhasoami Faith minimize the importance of miracles, a number of miracles are nonetheless attributed to the Beas Sat-Gurus also. One of the best known of the Great Master's miracles is recorded in Katherine Wason's *The Living Master.*[23] An Indian professor of the Vedanta philosophy decided to make the pilgrimage to the sacred Armanath Cave in the high Himalayas. To reach the eighteen-thousand-foot height, he rode horseback.

"Our journey was without incident," said the professor when relating his story, "until we reached a height of sixteen thousand feet where the ground and the surrounding mountains were completely covered with snow. We were moving slowly, single file, and deep chasms yawned their depths at our side. Suddenly I felt a peculiar faintness creeping over me and found myself helplessly falling from the horse. The gorge swam mistily before my eyes, thousands of feet below, and I knew I was going to plunge downwards. But then I felt a strong arm, and in those few minutes of semi-consciousness, I saw the face of the one who saved me. I had never seen Him before, nor ever dreamed such a one existed, for there was a strange light, a radiance all around His figure.

"After that I do not know how long I remained senseless.

It might have been ten or fifteen minutes or more. When I regained consciousness I found my head in the lap of that figure. He was lightly touching my head with his right hand. 'Well, goodbye, my friend. We will meet again,' said He, and vanished." Although the professor inquired of his traveling companions who had seen him fall from his horse, no one had seen the strange figure.

This was not the end of the professor's miraculous experience. On the way back to his university he was mysteriously drawn to Beas. There, to his amazement, he saw seated on a dais in the midst of the satsangis the radiant figure who had so opportunely come to his aid. The Great Master called him to his side. Continued the professor: " 'Well, well,' He said, smiling in a way I had never seen before. It was not a smile, it was the Presence of God. 'You have come. We will have ample time to talk, but now you may take some rest.'

"At the Colony I remained for weeks afterward—until the opening of college. For I found my God there. All Vedanta and Yoga were forgotten in the delight of meeting my Lord."

As his successor, the Great Master appointed Sardar Bahadur Jagat Singh Ji, an elderly disciple who had been initiated as early as 1909. Until he retired in 1943 and moved permanently to Beas he served as a professor of chemistry at an agricultural college in the Punjab. Many of his former students, who had been impressed by his deep spirituality, joined him at the colony. In the five intervening years before he himself became the Sat-Guru of the Faith he spent nearly all his time in deep meditation. His thoughts are set forth in his *The Science of the Soul*.[24] During the three and one half years that he served as Master he is estimated to have initiated approximately twenty-six thousand into the Radhasoami Faith.[25]

It is said that the present Sat-Guru of the Satsang was identified as a future Master when he was still a youth. As the Great Master was approaching the end of his life two of his disciples asked him: "Will you tell us in whose hands you will leave us? Who will be the Master after you?" For some time Sawan Singh Maharaj attempted to turn the conversation in other directions. Just then the Great Master's grandson, Charan Singh, appeared at the corner of the house and approached him. "There he comes," said the Master in a whisper. This conversation was not revealed to others until many years later, but thus informed, the two satsangis began increasingly to notice signs of the unusual spirituality of the young man. One day, for example, when the sky was clear and the sun was shining brightly, arrangements were being made to hold the *satsang* out-of-doors. Young Charan instructed those in charge to hold the *satsang* indoors. They paid no heed, and the Great Master had hardly begun his discourse when a fierce storm accompanied by rain burst with such severity that it was impossible to remove the carpets on which the satsangis sat before they became thoroughly soaked.

Just before his death Sardar Jagat Singh did announce Charan Singh to be his successor. Between the time of the incident just recounted and his assumption of the leadership of the Satsang in October, 1951, Charan Singh had secured his law degree and was engaged in the successful practice of law. As the present Master he has given vigorous leadership to the Radha Soami Satsang, Beas. A number of new buildings have been constructed in the colony, including a magnificent Satsang Ghar ("House of Worship"). The building is in the shape of a giant T, with a series of wide marble steps, stately rows of pillars, marble terraces, and tall arched windows on all eight facades. Covering the interior is a great plateaued roof around

which seven gold-tipped towers rise, a tower at each corner of the T, and a central tower crowning all with a lofty
dome.[26] A thriving community spreads out from the center, extending to the river Beas in one direction and to
wide cultivated fields in the others. What was once a desert
waste of sand, rocks, and gullies has now been made to
"blossom like a rose."

Maharaj Charan Singh Ji has traveled extensively, in
India and abroad, speaking to large audiences, and instructing and initiating satsangis. Among those who have
lived at the colony and who have received initiation are a
number of disciples from overseas. These are now to be
found in North and South America, Europe, Africa, and
the Middle East. A number have written and published
books describing their spiritual pilgrimages in the Satsang.
Maharaj Charan Singh Ji has also written a number of
books, both in English and in the languages of Northern
India.[27]

The Radhasoami Satsang, Soamibagh, Agra

Reference has been made earlier to the division that took
place between the Central Administrative Council, with
headquarters at Soamibagh, Agra, and the followers of Sri
Kamta Prasad Sinha after the death, in 1907, of the Third
Revered Leader, Maharaj Sahab. Refusing to accept the
claim of the followers of Sri Kamta Prasad Sinha, known as
Sarkar Sahab, that the Spiritual Current from the Merciful Radhasoami had passed to him as the Fourth Revered
Leader, the Administrative Council recognized the sister
of Maharaj Sahab as the true Sant Sat-Guru. She became
known as Buaji Maharaj. Her brief period of leadership
was cut short by her death and the Soamibagh Satsang
recognized Rai Saheb Madhav Prasad Sinha, the grandson

of Soamiji Maharaj's elder sister, as the Fifth Sant Sat-Guru. Known as Babuji Maharaj, he continued in government service until 1919, when he retired and gave his full time to the Satsang. Under his leadership the Soamibagh Satsang made considerable progress. His discourses on the Radhasoami Faith, which led to the initiation of a large number of followers, are recorded in S. D. Maheshwari's *Teachings of the Radhasoami Faith Based on Babuji's Discourses* and in *Notes on Discourses by Babuji Maharaj*, by Myron H. Phelps, an American satsangi who spent some years as a seeker in the colony at Soamibagh.[28]

Babuji Maharaj named no successor before his death in 1949. The Soamibagh Satsang holds to the belief, however, that there must be a living guru to guide the Faith. They explain the present situation as an "interregnum" between "manifestations." The present Guru is alive somewhere in the universe but has not chosen to manifest himself as yet. Upon the death of Babuji Maharaj the Spiritual Sound Current which had been brought to earth by Soamiji Maharaj, and which has been passed on to his successors, has also entered the present Guru, and from his hidden state he is directing the affairs of the Faith. The authority to administer initiation into the Faith has been granted to certain spiritual persons by the Administrative Council. Initiation is not a ritual or ceremony, but consists in imparting the mysteries of the Faith and the Spiritual Practices (*Surat Shabda Marga*) to the initiates. In this way the Satsang continues.

Although no social-welfare institutions have been developed by the Soamibagh Satsang, a most ambitious building program has been undertaken. Its center is the *samādh,* or mausoleum, which will preserve the ashes of Soamiji Maharaj, the founder and the First Sant Sat-Guru of the Radhasoami Faith. The foundation for the building was laid by Maharaj Sahab in 1904. After his death in 1907, there was a temporary suspension of the construction until 1923, when Babuji Maharaj ordered its resumption. Since then the work has been carried on uninterruptedly, and when I visited Soamibagh the ground floor, or crypt, and the first floor of the main structure had been largely completed. The main structure will consist of a hall 68 x 68 feet, surrounded by verandas 15 feet wide on all sides. These will rise from a wide marble platform extending 55 feet in each direction. The central structure will be capped by a golden dome, and the whole *samādh* will be 193 feet high. It is difficult to find words to describe the portion of the building already completed. Delicately arched doorways give access to the main hall. Intricately carved panels of marble carry the messages of the several Sant Sat-Gurus and *shabds* ("hymns") from the scriptures of the Faith. These have been placed on the walls both inside and outside the main hall. The letters at places have been filled with mother-of-pearl and other semiprecious stones. Almost all the distinctive Indian fruit trees and flowers find a place in the panels that are being carved or have already been placed in position. The marble used is of different colors. Graceful minarets will rise from the four corners of the platform. The main building, above the platform, will be composed of a series of galleries that will appear ingeniously as verandas on the outside and balconies on the inside.[29]

I was told that it may take as long as two hundred years to complete the *samādh,* for such work cannot be hurried and the construction will be carried on only as resources are available. Contributions will be received only from members of the Soamibagh Satsang. Because of the division between this Satsang and the other two, funds will not be accepted from members of the others, and, in fact, members of the Dayalbagh and Beas Satsangs are not even permitted to enter the *samādh* area to visit the tomb of the founder of the Faith. When completed, if ever, the *samādh* of Soamiji Maharaj may well rival the famous Taj Mahal in beauty and magnificence.

The Radhasoami Faith

While the teachings of the three sections of the Radhasoami Satsang differ in minor details, they all go back to the orginal "revelation" given by Soamiji Maharaj in the *Sar Bachan* ("Essential Teachings" or "Essential Utterances").[30] It would be impossible, in a short work such as this, to give a full account of the Radhasoami Faith, or even one that would be reasonably intelligible to the average reader. It is certainly the most esoteric Faith I have encountered. It is literally "out of this world," for it deals with regions of existence unknown until revealed by Soamiji Maharaj.

According to the Radhasoami Faith, there are three main divisions, or Regions (*Desha*), in creation and each main division has six subdivisions (*Loka*). The highest of the main divisions is *Nirmal Chetan,* the Pure Spiritual Region. In this Region there is no materiality at all. Next is *Nirmal Maya,* or *Brahmananda,* the Spiritual-Material Region. Into this Region matter has entered, but it is said to be "pure matter." The lowest of the Regions is *Malin Maya,* or *Pind,* the Material-Spiritual Region. This is the Region in which we live, and it is the Region of "impure" or "gross" matter. The subdivisions of *Nirmal Chetan,* beginning with the highest *Loka,* are said to be *Radhasoami Dham,* the abode of the Merciful Radhasoami, *Agam, Alakh, Anami, Satloka,* and *Bhanwargupha.* It is said that these *Loka* ("Lands") were unknown and had never been described before the coming of Soamiji Maharaj, for they are *Anami* ("nameless") and *Akeh* ("indescribable").

The six subdivisions in *Brahmananda* ("abode of Brahman") are said to be *Sunn Loka,* or *Daswan Dwar, Trikuti Loka, Sahasdal Kamal Loka, Vishnuloka, Brahmaloka,* and *Shivaloka.* Each of the *Loka* in *Brahmananda,* as also those in *Nirmal Chetan,* is presided over by a spiritual ruler created by Dayal Radhasoami (Merciful Radhasoami) and directly responsible to him. The various *Loka* in *Brahmananda* have been described partially in other religions under such titles as Heaven, Nirvana, Paradise, and so forth. The avataras, gods, saints, and gurus who have promised salvation to their followers can take their devotees no higher than the *Loka* from which they have themselves descended. Thus, only the Radhasoami Faith can carry the soul to the highest abode of all.

Pind exists both externally in the universe and internally in the *jīva* ("living" person). Externally it exists in six centers in the universe. These correspond to the six spirit centers in the human body, our world corresponding to the heart. The six spirit centers in the human body are the six ganglia, or nerve centers. The first is the point between and back of the two eyes (the *til*) and is the abode of the *surat* ("soul," "spirit"). From this center it spreads by degrees into the body, through the five lower centers. The second ganglion is at the throat. It is the region of the *prāna,* or vital force of the body. The third ganglion is at the heart, the center of emotions and desires. The fourth is at the navel, the fifth at the organ of reproduction, and the sixth at the rectum.

In the beginning only Dayal Radhasoami, the Supreme Spiritual Being, existed. Then, from the Holy Feet of the Merciful Radhasoami emanated the *Mauj.* The *Mauj* (literally, "flow" or "overflow") is said to be the Overflow of

Love or Will from the Supreme Being. It is the "Current" of the *Surat Shabda*, the Spirit Sound or Melody. From the *Mauj* came the creation of the *Desha* and *Loka* ("Regions" and "Lands") below the *Dham* of Dayal Radhasoami. As it descended it came into contact with *māyā* ("materiality" or "matter") and the Pure Spirit became diluted, so to speak, and the second Region is *Nirmal Maya*, or the Spiritual-Material Region. In the third Region, *Malin Maya*, the Material-Spiritual Region, gross matter predominates.

The *surat* ("spirit" or "soul") of the *jīva* ("individual") has also come from the Supreme Being. It is a ray from the Eternal Sun, a drop from the Boundless Ocean. But as it descended from the Abode of Radhasoami it became imprisoned and encased in layers of materiality. And now, in this present world of human existence, it is totally incapable of freeing itself. It was for this reason that the Supreme Being, Dayal Radhasoami, took incarnation in the human form of Soamiji Maharaj, in order to instruct seekers in the *Surat Shabda Yoga*, the Spiritual Practices through which alone the soul can find its way home. Although these practices are secret, and are revealed to the seeker only at the time of his initiation, they are said to consist of two main parts: first, *Sumiran* (repetition of the holy name "Radhasoami") and *Dhyan* (contemplation of the holy form), and second, the "Sound Practice," which is revealed to the initiate by the Sat-Guru when he is deemed ready. Just as a single light shining in the darkness may guide the wanderer home, the Spiritual Sound Current, it is said, guides the spirit entity back to its original home. Perhaps a more accurate analogy for the present day would be the radio wave that guides the plane safely to the airport! Only a Sant Sat-Guru can impart this saving knowl-

edge to the seeker. By means of the *Surat Shabda Yoga*
the soul is drawn stage by stage, through Region after Region, until it is absorbed in the Supreme Being, aided in
each by the Ruling Spirit of that Region.[31]

Reference should be made to one other important teaching of the Radhasoami Faith, that concerning the *Nij
Dhar*. The *Nij Dhar* is "that Supreme Tide which issues
forth from the Supreme Spiritual Ocean and expands into
the lower creation for the gracious object of redeeming
spirit-entities (*jīvas*)." The followers of the Radhasoami
Faith look upon Soamiji Maharaj, the founder of the Faith,
as the incarnation of the Supreme Being, Merciful Radhasoami. This implies that the *Nij Dhar* of the Supreme
Being manifested itself in human form for the emancipa-
tion of *jīvas* imprisoned in materiality and ignorance. The
Nij Dhar, it is contended, cannot exist in more than one
human body at a time. After the departure of Soamiji Maharaj, the *Nij Dhar* began its redemptive work through another human form, that of Param Guru Huzur Maharaj,
and thus through the succeeding Sat-Gurus.

The allegation that the satsangis worship a mere human
being, which has been brought against the Faith, is denied. Worship and homage is done only to the *Nij Dhar* of
the Supreme Being manifested in the Sant Sat-Guru. There
is no special ceremony when, after the departure of the
Sant Sat-Guru, his successor manifests himself. "Manifestation means the dawn of knowledge to the Satsangis that
the *Nij Dhar* has entered some particular Personality.
When the *Nij Dhar* begins to function in a new body, the
new Form grants internal and external experiences to the
devotees and gradually draws them to His Feet. By and by
the glory and greatness of the new Human Form fills the
hearts of all the followers." [32]

The worship services that I attended in the Satsang at Dayalbagh, Agra, and in a local branch Satsang, in Jabalpur, were simple but impressive. In Dayalbagh the Satsang was held in a large hall, divided by a partition some six or seven feet high. Men sat on one side of the partition and women on the other. There was no such partition in the branch hall in Jabalpur. In Dayalbagh the Sant Sat-Guru, Mehtaji Sahab Maharaj, sat in a chair so arranged that he could be seen by both men and women satsangis. In Jabalpur, a picture of Mehtaji Sahab Maharaj, placed on a table, indicated the presence of the Sant Sat-Guru in the Satsang. The service opened with the singing of several *bhajans* ("hymns of praise") by a smaller group of singers, followed by *bhajans* sung by all the satsangis. A discourse was then given by the Sant Sat-Guru, if present, or by the reading of a discourse by one of the members. Previous to the opening of the Satsang one or more members had brought food offerings and placed them before the Sat-Guru or his picture. The satsangis now sang a *bhajan* in which they asked Merciful Radhasoami to accept and sanctify the offering. This was then distributed to the worshipers as *prasad,* an offering which has been touched or looked upon and blessed by the Supreme Being. Some of the satsangis ate the *prasad* then and there, others took it home with them to be eaten later. The service closed with the members addressing one another with the greeting, "Radhasoami!" In the branch Satsang at Jabalpur the worship service was followed by a fellowship hour in which light refreshments were served by a member and a discussion of the Radhasoami Faith was held with the visitors present.

Nothing can be learned by one who is not a satsangi about the nature of the Spiritual Discipline (*Surat Shabda*

Yoga) revealed to the satsangis, for they are sworn to secrecy, but one gathers that all strive to so discipline themselves that they may one day hear the *Surat Shabda*, the Divine Five Melodies, which will guide their own souls back to their original abode.

7

THE PRIEST OF KALI:
Sri Ramakrishna

It may appear strange that the act of repairing a broken image could have started a youth on the path which was to lead to the recognition by thousands across the world that he was an avatara of the Supreme Being, but such was the case. His birth took place in the village of Kamarpukur, in Bengal, in the home of a devout Brahmin named Khudiram and his wife Chandra Devi. In 1835, Khudiram made a pilgrimage to Gaya, a shrine that had been erected near the footprint of Lord Vishnu. It was while on this pilgrimage, it is said, that he had a vision in which Lord Vishnu promised to be born as his son. At the same time Chandra Devi, in front of the Siva temple in Kamarpukur, had a vision foretelling that she would give birth to a divine child. On February 18, 1836, the child, "to be known afterwards as Ramakrishna and honored as the God-man of modern India was born. He was given the name of Gadadhar, 'the Bearer of the Mace,' an epithet of Vishnu." [1]

As a boy Gadadhar showed great interest in religion, and his delight was to listen to recitals of stories from Hindu mythology and the Epics. These he would afterward recount from memory, to the great joy of the villagers. At the age of six or seven Gadadhar had his first ex-

perience of spiritual ecstasy. While out walking he saw a
dark thundercloud. A flight of snow-white cranes passed in
front of it. The beauty of the contrast overwhelmed him
and he fell to the ground, unconscious. A neighbor, passing
by, picked him up and carried him home. Gadadhar was
never sent to school, and he remained illiterate to the end
of his life. At the age of sixteen he joined his older brother,
Ramkumar, who taught in a small local school in Calcutta
and served as priest to a number of Brahmin families.
Gadadhar assisted his brother in his priestly duties.

The Black Goddess

There lived in Calcutta a rich widow named Rani Rasmani.
She was not a "queen," as her name might imply, for she
belonged to the Shudra, that is, the lowest, caste. The
name Rani, given her as a pet name by her mother, was
not altogether inappropriate, however, for she was a
"regal" figure, accustomed to having her own way. She was
known also as a woman of great piety. On the banks of the
Ganges River at Dakshineswar, about four miles from Calcutta, she had constructed a temple to her favorite deity,
the "Black Goddess," Kali. Several other shrines were also
constructed in the temple garden, twelve to Lord Siva and
one to Lord Krishna. When the time came for the installa-
tion of the image of Kali and the dedication of the temple
area, Rani Rasmani ran into difficulty. No Brahmin priest
was willing to officiate at a shrine owned by a Shudra. In
great distress, Rani Rasmani appealed to Ramkumar, who
was known as an authority in such matters, for advice. He
suggested that the legal ownership of the temple area be
deeded to a Brahmin, while she would retain the management of the shrine. This was done, but still to no avail.

Rani Rasmani now urged Ramkumar to officiate. With great reluctance he agreed to do so, and became the priest in charge of the Kali temple. Another Brahmin was persuaded to preside at the Krishna temple. Gadadhar strongly disapproved of his brother's action, and for many days refused to visit the shrine. But after certain adjustments were made to meet his scruples, he took up his residence at Dakshineswar.

One day, while dressing the image of Lord Krishna, the priest in charge dropped the image and broke one of its legs. Rani Rasmani was greatly distressed, for she loved the little image. According to Hindu custom, a broken image should not be used as an object of worship. She was advised to throw it into the river. Gadadhar disagreed. "If your son-in-law should break his leg," he asked her, "would you throw him away?" "Of course not!" she replied. "I would have a doctor heal him." Gadadhar then offered to repair the broken leg, and did it so skillfully that the break could not be seen. The priest who had been responsible for the mishap was discharged and Gadadhar was put in charge. Mathur Mohan, Rani Rasmani's son-in-law, suggested that the young priest should be called Ramakrishna, and this became his name from that time onward.

For Ramakrishna, the image of Krishna was the Lord himself, to be fed and clothed, waked up, bathed, put to bed. The zeal with which he performed his duties as priest soon attracted the attention of all who came to the temple area, and Rani Rasmani and Mathur were greatly pleased. They were especially impressed with the deep spirituality of the youthful priest. It was only natural, therefore, that when in 1856, Ramkumar died, Ramakrishna should have been appointed to assume his duties as priest of the Kali temple.

He soon came to realize what a strange goddess she was. To the ignorant she is the terrible destroyer. She stands upon the prostrate body of her consort, Shiva. Her neck is encircled with a garland of human skulls, her waist with a girdle of human arms. She has four arms. One holds the bloody head of a human victim, another a bloody sword. But to her true worshippers she is the benign, all-loving "Mother." One hand is lifted in blessing and another calms the fears of her children. She is the Shakti, the Creative Power, inseparable from the Absolute. She now became to Ramakrishna the only Reality.[2]

There is another image of the Black Goddess, in Calcutta. In fact, the city gets its name from this image, "Kali Ghata," Kali on the bank of the river. This image, which I had seen on previous visits to Calcutta, had greatly impressed me by its size. I had not visited Dakshineswar, however, but had supposed the image there might be similar. I was surprised, therefore, to discover that it was hardly larger than a big doll! I decided that Ramakrishna must have had a vivid imagination to be able to picture this Kali as his "Mother." Nevertheless, he often sought her presence and spoke to her in most personal terms. And as he conducted the worship services morning and evening he began to ask himself:

Is there anything behind this image? Is it true that there is a Mother of Bliss in the universe? Is it true that She lives and guides this universe, or is all a dream? Is there any reality in religion? [3]

Seeking an answer to these questions, he began to spend hours night and day meditating before the image of the Divine Mother. So intense was his concentration that he often passed into *samādhi* ("unconsciousness"). He became possessed with the passionate desire that Mother

Kali would reveal herself to him in her cosmic form. Because the vision was denied him, he wept bitter tears and cried aloud. His strange conduct caused many to think him insane. But through it all Rani Rasmani and her son-in-law, Mathur Mohan, stood by him, believing his conduct the sign of his deep spirituality. Later, he described to a devotee this agony of soul and its outcome:

> There was an unbearable pain in my heart because I couldn't get a vision of Mother. Just as a man wrings out a towel with all his strength to get the water out of it, so I felt as if my heart and mind were being wrung out. I began to think I should never see Mother. I was dying of despair. In my agony, I said to myself: "What's the use of living this life?" Suddenly my eyes fell on the sword that hangs in the temple. I decided to end my life with it, then and there. Like a madman, I ran and seized it. And then—I had a marvelous vision of Mother, and fell down unconscious. It was as if houses, doors, temples and everything else vanished altogether; as if there was nothing anywhere. And what I saw was an infinite shoreless sea of light; a sea that was consciousness. However far and in whatever direction I looked, I saw nothing but waves, one after another, coming toward me. They were raging and storming upon me with great speed. Very soon they were upon me; they made me sink down into unknown depths. I panted and struggled and lost consciousness.[4]

Marriage

Previous to this experience his cousin, Hriday Ram, had come to Dakshineswar to join Ramakrishna. Hriday's concern for his cousin's condition was only deepened by the situation that followed the vision of the Mother. States of unconsciousness became more frequent and more prolonged. The bulk of the responsibility for the temple worship fell upon Hriday, who began to question Ramakrishna's very sanity. Word reached Ramakrishna's mother in Kamarpukur that he was indeed demented, and to prevent further embarrassment to the family he was sent back to his village. Plans were now made for his marriage, with the thought that responsibility for a wife might prevent him from entering into the frequent trances that had occurred while in the presence of the Kali image. Though he soon discovered what the family was plotting on his behalf, he accepted the idea without objection. To everyone's surprise, in fact, he showed a childlike pleasure as he talked of his marriage. Because of the poverty of his family, difficulty was experienced in finding a suitable bride, a young woman beautiful enough to distract his attention from his obsession for "the Mother." At last, Ramakrishna himself indicated where the bride whom he had himself chosen would be found. "You must go to the family of Ram Mukhopadhyaya in the village of Jayrambati. Fate has marked my bride with a straw." The expression "marked with a straw" referred to a Bengali custom of tying a straw around a fruit or vegetable that one wished to offer to the Lord.

Though Saradamani, the bride thus identified by Ramakrishna, was discovered to be only five years old, there seemed to be no alternative but to arrange the marriage. In May, 1859, the twenty-three-year-old Ramakrishna, accompanied by his brother Rameswar, journeyed to Jayrambati, where the ceremony was performed. Saradamani accompanied Ramakrishna back to Kamarpukur for a brief visit, and then returned to her own home. Some time later, in spite of his mother's protests, Ramakrishna returned to Dakshineswar.

Religions and Religion

Ramakrishna now adopted in sequence several *sādhanas*—
Tantric, Vaishnava, Vedanta, and others. His purpose was
to experience continuous *samādhi*, the state of God-realization, the awareness of identity with the Absolute. On one
occasion, after a period of intense concentration, he fell
into a deep trance, in which he remained for three days.
As he gradually returned to consciousness, he believed that
Kali "asked him not to be lost in the featureless Brahman,
but to remain in *Bhavamukha,* on the threshold of Absolute Consciousness, the border-line between the Absolute
and the Relative." To the end of his days, he "oscillated
back and forth across the dividing line. Ecstatic devotion
to the Divine Mother alternated with serene absorption in
the Ocean of Absolute Unity." [5]

The knowledge of Brahman in the *virvikalpasamadhi*
(the highest state of *samādhi*, in which the aspirant realizes his total oneness with Brahman) now convinced
Ramakrishna that the gods of the different religions are
but so many manifestations of the Absolute on the Relative Plane. He believed that all religions lead their devotees
by differing paths to one and the same God. He began to
explore some of the other religions. Under the guidance of
a Muslim teacher he dressed as a Muslim and repeated the
name of Allah. After three days he saw a radiant figure
whom he took to be Muhammad. "This figure gently approached him and finally lost himself in Ramakrishna.
Thus he realized unity with the Muslim God. Thence he
passed into communion with Brahman. The mighty river
of Islam led him back to the Ocean of the Absolute." [6]
Eight years later he desired to learn the truth of the
Christian religion. He began to listen to readings from the

Bible and became fascinated with the life and teachings of Jesus. One day while he gazed intently at a painting of the Madonna and Child, the figures of the picture, he believed, took life, and rays of light emanating from them filled his soul. Christ had possessed his soul. Three days later as he walked in the garden "he saw coming toward him a person with beautiful large eyes, serene countenance, and fair skin. As the two approached each other, a voice rang out in the depths of Ramakrishna's soul, 'Behold the Christ, who shed his heart's blood for the redemption of the world, who suffered a sea of anguish for love of men. It is he, the Master Yogi, who is in eternal union with God. It is Jesus, love Incarnate.' The Son of Man embraced the son of the Divine Mother and merged in him. Sri Ramakrishna realized his identity with Christ, as he had already realized his identity with Kali." [7]

As a result of these various experiences Ramakrishna declared:

> I have practiced all religions—Hinduism, Islam, Christianity—and I have also followed the paths of the different Hindu sects. I have found that it is the same god toward whom all are directing their steps, though along different paths. You must try all beliefs and traverse all the different ways once. Wherever I look, I see men quarrelling in the name of religion—Hindus, Mohammedans, Brahmos, Vaishnavas, and the rest. But they never reflect that He who is called Krishna is also called Shiva, and bears the name of the Primal Energy, Jesus and Allah as well—the same Rama with a thousand names. A lake has several *ghats* ("banks"). At one the Hindus take water in pitchers and call it *"jal";* at another the Mussalmans take water in leather bags and call it *"pani."* At a third the Christians call it "water." Can we imagine that it is not *"jal,"* but only *"pani"* or "water"? How ridiculous! The substance is one under different names, and everyone is seeking for the

same substance; only climate, temperament, and name create differences. Let each man follow his own path. If he sincerely and ardently wishes to know God, peace be unto him! He will surely realize Him.[8]

Sarada Devi

In 1872, Saradamani, who had been married to Ramakrishna as a child bride, came to Dakshineswar. She had received word that Ramakrishna was indeed insane. It was reported that on one occasion he had dressed as a woman and had lived in the women's quarters in the temple area, calling himself Yashoda, the foster-mother of Krishna. On another occasion, declaring himself to be Hanuman, the servant of Rama, he had jumped around like a monkey. He had dressed as a Muslim and had insisted on having his food prepared in Muslim style, thus breaking the Hindu rule against eating meat. Thinking that her place should be at the side of her husband, Saradamani hurried to Dakshineswar. Ramakrishna greeted his young wife and encouraged her to stay with him, for he was eager to undertake her spiritual training. A bed was arranged for her in the room where he had been living, but Ramakrishna said to Saradamani:

> As for me, the Mother has shown me that she resides in every woman, and so I have learned to look upon every woman as Mother. That is the one idea that I can have about you; but if you wish to drag me into the world, as I have been married to you, I am at your service.[9]

Saradamani had no such wish, and their marriage was never consummated in physical union.

Some months later, when Sarada asked Ramakrishna, "How do you think of me?" he replied, "I always see you as a form of the blissful Divine Mother." In the spring of

1872, Ramakrishna confirmed these words in a symbolic act. On the day set for the worship of the goddess Kali, he seated Sarada on the seat reserved for the goddess. He sprinkled over her water that had been made sacred by the recitation of the proper *mantras,* and made to her the sixteen ritual offerings appropriate for the worship of a deity. He treated Sarada now as the goddess in person. Then both he and Sarada Devi, as she was to be known henceforth, fell into *samādhi.*

Ramakrishna and His Disciples

Possibly Ramakrishna would have remained unknown outside Bengal were it not for a group of young intellectuals whom he attracted to himself. His blunt words and often tactless manner tended to alienate older persons who came to him seeking either spiritual guidance or to satisfy their curiosity about this strange man. Perhaps he did not encourage them to become disciples, for he said of them that "they could no more be taught spirituality than a parrot can be taught to speak after the ring of colored feathers has appeared around its neck." [10] Christopher Isherwood quotes Ramakrishna as expressing deep yearning for young disciples:

> "In those days there was no limit to my yearning," he would recall. "During the daytime, I could just manage to keep it under control, though the talk of worldly-minded people tormented me. I would yearn for the time when my beloved companions would come to me; I kept thinking what a relief it would be to talk freely and openly to them about my experiences. . . . I kept planning what I would say to this one and what I should give to that one, and so forth. I was tortured by the thought that another day had passed and they hadn't arrived! . . . I would cry out at

the top of my voice in the anguish of my heart, 'Come to me, my boys! Where are you? I can't bear to live without you!' " [11]

His "cry" must have been heard, for from about the year 1880, there gathered about him a group of young men from high-caste homes in Calcutta. Most of them had had an English education and were searching for a deeper spiritual experience than they had found in their family religion. One of these was Narendranath Datta, the son of a wealthy lawyer of the Calcutta High Court. With his astonishing memory he imbibed a large amount of Hindu lore in a traditional Indian school. In high school he was always first in his class, and this record was maintained in the University of Calcutta. He enrolled in the Scottish Church's College, where he developed a keen interest in philosophy. In the company of a group of Hindu young men he visited Ramakrishna. From time to time, out of curiosity aroused by the strange priest, he visited Ramakrishna, but was unimpressed by his *Advaita* ("nondualism"), a teaching that he considered atheistic. But one day a miracle occurred. As Ramakrishna was deep in a trance, his foot touched Narendra, and he too fell into a trance, seeing nothing but "God." Even after he returned home he was unable to shake off this strange experience. Shortly after this his father died, practically bankrupt because of certain extravagances. Greatly shaken, Narendra went to Ramakrishna for advice. "Go to the temple and pray to the Mother," he was advised. "She will grant you whatever you ask." The youth obeyed. When he returned, his face was "transfigured." He had decided to become a swami. Just before his death Ramakrishna initiated the young disciples as monks, making Narendra their leader and giving him the name Vivekananda, i.e., "Bliss of Discrimination—between the Real and the Unreal."

Early in 1885, a sore developed in Ramakrishna's throat, which did not respond to treatment but gradually grew worse. Later in the year, his throat began to bleed. Several well-known physicians who were called in diagnosed the case as cancer. To get him into a quieter place and nearer the doctors a house was found in Calcutta, and Ramakrishna was moved. The young disciples moved in with him so as to tend to him night and day. Ramakrishna continued to grow weaker. Thinking the air of Calcutta was further aggravating the sore in his throat, he was then moved to a house in Cossipore, located in a large garden. Ramakrishna began to prepare his little band of disciples for the end. "Before I go," he said, "I'll cast my whole secret to the winds. When many people have discovered who I really am, and start to whisper about it, then this body will cease to exist, by the Mother's will." January 1, 1886, was a memorable day for the young disciples. As they were gathered in the garden, Ramakrishna came among them. He began to touch them, one after another. Some went into *samādhi*. Others felt themselves endowed with a supernatural power. "All said later that they felt that Ramakrishna had that afternoon for the first time revealed himself as a divine incarnation." [12]

One day in August, Naren was in Ramakrishna's room. Looking down at the frail figure on the bed, he asked himself whether this suffering creature could indeed be an incarnation of God. "If he would declare his divinity now, in the presence of death, I'd accept it." Slowly Ramakrishna spoke in a weak voice. "O Naren, aren't you convinced *yet?* He who once was born as Rama, and again as Krishna, is now living as Ramakrishna within this body—and not in your Vedantic sense." [13] By this he implied that he was not merely the *Ātman* present in every being, but that he was an avatara and the reincarnation of former avataras.

Early on August 16, 1886, Ramakrishna smiled at those standing around him, and went into *samādhi*. He never returned to consciousness. He had entered into *mahasamadhi*, "the final state in which he who has realized his identity with Brahman leaves the physical body, never to return." His body was cremated late that afternoon. His ashes were collected in a copper urn by one of the disciples.

Shortly after the death of their Master the little band gathered in the garden at the home of one of their number. It was Christmas Eve. As they were meditating on the life and teachings of Ramakrishna, Vivekananda broke the silence and told them the story of Jesus Christ as he had heard it in his college days. He then charged his brothers "to become themselves Christs, to aid in the redemption of the world." Standing in the light of the fire around which they had gathered, the youth took the vow of *sannyasa* (i.e., poverty, chastity, and obedience) and the Ramakrishna Order was definitely formed. The Order became an entirely new movement in Hinduism, for it sought to combine the traditional ideas of the life of meditation and world-renouncing monasticism with the ideals of service and works of mercy. Although some of the swamis remained in the monastery, others, Vivekananda among them, scattered throughout India to proclaim the teachings of Ramakrishna. Word came to Vivekananda of a World's Parliament of Religions to be held in Chicago. Longing to preach to the West, he sailed for America in May, 1893. In Chicago he met a wealthy American woman who introduced him to the chairman of the Parliament. He was invited to address the assembly. Speaking fluently in English, he captivated his audience. His Chicago appearance created speaking invitations which carried Vivekananda from coast to coast. Finally, he established himself in New York and founded the Vedanta Society, in 1894. Swamis were called from India to assist, and other centers were established. Vivekananda returned to India in 1897 and established the Ramakrishna Mission. A large tract of land, to become the headquarters of the Mission, was secured at Belur, near Calcutta, on the banks of the Ganges. Back in America in 1899, Vivekananda undertook a whirlwind lecture tour. In churches he lectured on the subject "Christ, the Messenger," and in public auditoriums on "The Way to the Realization of a Universal Religion." In 1900, he returned to India again and spent his last two years establishing new centers of the Ramakrishna Mission.[14]

Worship at the Ramakrishna Math

The worship service (*arati*) conducted in the temple at the Ramakrishna Math ("monastery") in Belur is impressive, especially that held on Sunday afternoons. Many devotees from Calcutta and elsewhere join the inmates of the monastery, filling the large shrine. Fortunately for Shamrao and me, the swami who acted as our guide during our visit conducted us to the very front of the congregation so that we might have an unobstructed view of the service. The service took place in front of the more than life-size seated marble image of Ramakrishna. A single swami, a rather young one, performed the *arati*, but a number of others sitting together in front served as a kind of choir which led in the chanting, or singing, of the *bhajans*. A small organ, drums, and cymbals maintained the rhythm. The young swami rang a long-handled bell continuously by a graceful twist of his left wrist and hand.

The *arati* consisted in offering to the Supreme Being, of whom Ramakrishna was an avatara, symbols of the five elements that composed the "body" of the Supreme: fire, water, ether, earth, and air. First, an Indian oil lamp, held in the right hand, was swung in wide circles for some minutes before the image, symbolizing the offering of fire. The lamp was replaced by a conch shell, filled with water. From time to time water was deliberately spilled out in front of the image. A folded piece of saffron-colored cloth symbolized ether; a rose, earth; and a whisk, air. There seemed to be a regular pattern in the swinging of the votive objects: a single upward movement, but a number of loops in the downward stroke. The upward stroke was to the right, facing the altar, while the downward stroke, with the loops, was on the left. But with the whisk a new pattern was followed: while the whisk was twirled by the fingers, it was swung vertically to the image alternating with the circles parallel to the altar. For the members of the Rama-krishna Order the *arati* is understood as worship offered to Sri Ramakrishna as one who is still present, blessing the devotees and guiding the affairs of the Order. To them, he is Ishvara, the manifest form (*sa-guna*) of the Un-Manifest Brahman (*nir-guna*), as were Rama and Krishna. Follow-ing the service of the offering of the five elements, there was a series of short prayers sung by the swamis and con-gregation, to the accompaniment of the organ. The whole service was dignified, restrained, and impressive.

Later Developments

After Vivekananda's death, centers continued to be de-veloped not only throughout India but overseas as well. In the United States, for example, centers were opened in New York, Chicago, Boston, St. Louis, Seattle, Providence, Washington, Portland (Oregon), Hollywood, and a retreat was established on Lake Tahoe. Today there are eleven such centers, and the Vedanta philosophy introduced by the Ramakrishna swamis has had a significant influence in our country.

The religious, educational, medical, and other philanthropic activities of the Ramakrishna Math and Mission are impressive. The movement started with only sixteen monks—the direct disciples of Ramakrishna. Today there are hundreds of monks, and many more dedicated laymen, serving in institutions around the world. There are 150 centers, about fifty outside India. The Mission operates in India a dozen modern hospitals and sixty clinics, eight colleges, and thirty-five high schools, and more than a hundred lower schools, and ninety student homes and hostels. Sixty-five thousand students are enrolled in these educational institutions. An impressive Cultural Center in Calcutta provides research facilities for international scholars as well as numerous cultural activities for Indians. The Ramakrishna Mission has rendered significant relief to victims of famine, flood, cyclone, earthquake, communal riots (i.e., between Hindus and Muslims), and other calamities that India has experienced during the past seven decades. Orphans have been given homes and the destitute have been given relief. The Ramakrishna Mission is, therefore, a pioneer and almost unique as a religious institution engaged in social welfare.[15]

But perhaps more important than the contributions that the institutions of the Mission have made to man in his physical needs has been the impact that the life and teachings of Ramakrishna had upon his immediate disciples, and through them and the Ramakrishna Math upon a large number of persons in India and around the world. Presented as Vedanta, the teachings of Ramakrishna and his interpreters are influencing philosophical and theological thought in the West.

As summarized by Christopher Isherwood, an American disciple of Ramakrishna, Vedanta teaches four fundamental truths:

(1) That man's real nature is divine. If, in this universe, there is an underlying Reality, a Godhead, then that Godhead must be omnipresent. If the Godhead is omnipresent, it must be within each one of us and within every creature and object. Therefore man, in his true nature, is God. (2) That it is the aim of man's life on earth to unfold and manifest this Godhead, which is eternally existent within him, but hidden. The differences between man and man are only differences in the degree to which the Godhead is manifest. . . . "Right" action is action which assists the unfoldment of the Godhead within us: "wrong" action is action which hinders that unfoldment. "Good" and "evil" are, therefore, only relative values. Because the Godhead is within each one of us, Vedanta teaches not merely the brotherhood, but identity of man with man. Every soul is your own soul. Every creature is yourself. If you harm anyone, you harm yourself. (3) That truth is universal. Vedanta accepts all the religions of the world, because it recognizes the same divine inspiration in all. Different religions suit different races, cultures, temperaments. (4) Vedanta is impersonal, but it accepts all the great prophets, teachers, and sons of God, and all those personal aspects of the Godhead who are worshipped by different religions. . . . It believes that all are manifestations of the one Godhead. Accepting all, it does not attempt to make converts. It only seeks to clarify our thought, and thus help us to a truer appreciation of our own religion and its ultimate aim.[16]

8

THE LIFE DIVINE:
The Vision of Sri Aurobindo

Anyone who goes to Pondicherry, in South India, expecting to find the Sri Aurobindo Ashram in some secluded spot, away from the activity of modern life, is likely to be surprised, for the town of Pondicherry with its scores of brick or concrete buildings housing numerous commercial enterprises and thousands of inhabitants *is* the ashram. It was not that way when Aurobindo Ghose arrived in that little village in French Territory, in 1910, as a political refugee. The change has been brought about by this Indian man with a Western education and a Frenchwoman, known as "the Mother," who has imbibed the best of Indian culture. "Sri Aurobindo," writes Herbert Jai Singh, is "among the great architects of the Indian Renaissance. His phenomenal contributions to the fields of politics, philosophy, religion, education, and art make him one of the most creative thinkers of our century. The central aim of all his endeavors, however, was to 'bring down God into the lives of men.' " [1] It was to sit at his feet that thousands of seekers were led to make Pondicherry their spiritual Mecca.

Aurobindo Ghose was born in Calcutta on August 15, 1872. His father, Dr. Krishnadhan Ghose, while completing his medical training in England, became thoroughly enamored of Western ways and determined that his son should have an English rather than a traditional Indian education. Thus, at the age of seven Aurobindo was sent to England and placed under a tutor. In 1884, he entered St. Paul's School in London, where he distinguished himself as a student of languages, learning Latin, Greek, Italian, German, French, and Spanish. His excellent record at St. Paul's won him a scholarship to King's College, Cambridge. There he won a number of prizes for his Greek and Latin poems, and secured a first-class in the classical tripos. After staying for fourteen years in England, Aurobindo returned to India, where he became a lecturer in French, the professor of English, and finally vice-principal of Baroda College.[2]

The Baroda period was a time of further literary activity. Soon after his return to India, Aurobindo began writing poetry inspired by Indian themes. One of these was a long narrative poem, in Bengali, entitled *Urvasie,* based on Kalidasa's Sanskrit *Vikramurvasie.* This was followed by another narrative poem, *Love and Death,* and a drama in blank verse, *Perseus the Deliverer.* Then came a number of shorter poems which appeared in the pages of *The Bandemataram,* the weekly news magazine of which Aurobindo became coeditor. Aurobindo's literary fame outside India rests also on his English translations, generally free rather than literal translations, of the gemlike verses of Bhartrihari and the plays and poems of Kalidasa and other great masterpieces of Sanskrit literature. Perhaps his best-known poetical work is his massive philosophical poem, *Savitra.* Further consideration of Aurobindo as a literary figure lies outside the scope of this study, but a useful treatment of the subject will be found in *Sri Aurobindo,* by K. R. Srinivasa Iyengar, professor of English at the Andhra University, Waltair.[3]

The Patriot

Brief reference must also be made to the political movement in which Aurobindo became an active leader. Bengal, his native state, was the center of the independence movement. In 1905, Aurobindo returned to his native Bengal and threw himself into the effort to rid his country of British rule. For him, political freedom for India became a religious as well as political passion. On one occasion he wrote to his wife that he was in the grip of three mighty convictions. "Mad ideas, the world would call them—three supreme frenzies." First, he firmly believed that all his possessions were his only in trust—they really were God's. As such, they must be spent on *dharmakarya* ("spiritual work") on behalf of his needy countrymen. Secondly, he desired with all his heart to see God face to face, and, thirdly, to carry on a campaign (*mahavrata*) to free his Mother, India, from the demon that was sucking her lifeblood, using not the weapons of the warrior (*kshatratej*) but the power of God (*brahmatej*).[4] His pen was active, and article after article appeared in the pages of *Bandemataram*, which soon became a Nationalist paper. He also began to accept invitations to make patriotic speeches. In 1908 he was arrested on the charge of sedition and was thrown into jail. While in prison he turned to the study of the Hindu scriptures, especially the Bhagavad-Gita and the Upanishads. Impressed by the instructions given to Arjuna by Sri Krishna, he began the practice of the Yoga of the Gita. In the seclusion of his prison cell Aurobindo experienced the call to a new life. He had a vision of Sri Krishna of the Gita enveloping all existence: "I looked at the jail that secluded me from men and it was no longer by

its high walls that I was imprisoned; no, it was Vasudeva
(Krishna) who surrounded me. . . . I looked at the pris-
oners in the hall, the thieves, the murderers, the swindlers,
and as I looked at them I saw Vasudeva; it was Narayana
whom I found in these darkened souls and misused bodies." [5] This vision was soon to transform Aurobindo from a
political agitator to a mystic searching for the deeper
meanings of life.

Even the circumstances of his prison life did not prevent
him from composing poems that gave expression to his
newfound faith. In fact, his present hardships made him
realize that the path which God calls his devotees to follow is no easy one. Courage and faith are demanded. To
one who would ascend the windswept uplands toward true
freedom he says:

> Stark must he be and a kinsman to danger
> Who shares my kingdom and walks at my side.[6]

During the year of Aurobindo's imprisonment the British Government attempted to meet the increasing unrest in
the country with mass deportation of Nationalist leaders.
Upon his release, he found the Nationalist Party in Bengal
almost nonexistent, so he started publishing two weekly
papers, the *Karmayogin* in English and the *Dharma* in
Bengali, with the purpose of reviving the party and edu-
cating the public. So successful was he that he again came
to the attention of the British officials, and in January,
1910, he received word secretly that he was soon to be de-
ported. He now took the final decision to retire from Calcutta to the neighboring French Territory of Chander-
nagor. But even this was too near the storm center of the
Nationalist movement, so, after a short stay, he took up his

abode in Pondicherry, where he might pursue the *sādhana* of Yoga. Here he remained from 1910 until his death in 1950.

The Life Divine

The next four years were spent in comparative seclusion. A few disciples joined him, and the foundations for an ashram were laid. In 1914, among those who visited his ashram were a French couple by the name of Richard. They were in search of a "Master in whom they could recognize a World Teacher." With their assistance Aurobindo started an English journal, *Arya,* and a French journal, *Revue de grande synthèse.* The pages of *Arya* were to carry, in serial form, most of the philosophical writings, poetry, art criticism, and essays on Indian culture that were to bring Sri Aurobindo recognition and fame. The French edition was discontinued after the first seven issues, but *Arya* was published for nearly seven years, until 1921. During these years there appeared in serial form some of Aurobindo's best-known works: *The Life Divine, The Secret of the Veda, Essays on the Gita, The Psychology of Social Development, The Ideal of Human Unity, The Future Poetry, A Defence of Indian Culture,* and *The Synthesis of Yoga.*[7]

The First World War caused the Richards to return to France. In 1920, Mira Richard, having separated from her husband, returned to Pondicherry and has remained there to the present time. She gradually took over the responsibility of running the ashram, which had grown considerably during the intervening years, thus enabling Sri Aurobindo to devote himself entirely to meditation and writing. She has acquired the symbolic title of "the

Mother," and it is under her leadership that the ashram has continued to grow after the death of Sri Aurobindo. November 24, 1926, is celebrated as the day of victory by the followers of Sri Aurobindo, for on that date his long years of *sādhana* were ended. It was then, it is claimed, that Sri Aurobindo realized the "Supermind." "By the descent of the Overmind, the descent of the Supermind has been assured. . . . Sri Aurobindo ceased to see people and contact could be made with him only through the Mother." [8] His literary activity did not cease, however. In addition to his more systematically developed philosophical works, he wrote numerous letters in reply to inquiries received from all over the world on a variety of subjects. These have been published in four volumes of *Letters of Sri Aurobindo.*

Aurobindo envisaged the Supreme Reality as *Sat-Chit-Ananda.* It is Pure Existence, it is Existence that is both Will and Force, and above all it is blissful Existence. Reality is also personal. He is the Krishna of the Gita, the object of the devotee's devotion and love. He is the God who draws man to himself. The Divine is omnipresent. It includes both Matter and Spirit. Aurobindo likens God and Nature to a boy and a girl at play and in love. "They hide and run from each other when glimpsed so that they may be sought after and chased and captured." [9]

Sri Aurobindo lived and wrote during that period when the theory of evolution was attracting a great deal of attention. While anchoring his system in the Vedanta, he has woven this theory of evolution into his philosophy. Man has come to the present stage of evolution through a process of evolutionary growth, but he still remains incomplete. Man has to grow in consciousness until he reaches the complete and perfect consciousness, not only in his individual but in his collective, that is to say, social, life. In fact, the growth of consciousness is the supreme secret of life, the master key to earthly evolution.[10] The development of Aurobindo's thought is set forth in his massive *The Life Divine*.[11] Evolution involves a prior "involution." There is at the heart of things a Conscious-Force that is evolving to ever-higher forms of being. Just as there is evidence of a physical evolution, so there is an inner evolution, the evolution of the Divine which is at work at the various stages of existence. There is, however, no evolution possible unless that which evolves is already present in the process at every stage. The ascent presupposes a primordial descent into earthly forms. The world is a manifestation of the Eternal Spirit. He has created it out of himself just as a spider creates its web and makes its abode in it. The Divine, thus involved in existence, exercises a constant pressure from lower to higher forms, and from the altitude of the higher lifts upward the lower.

The term "substance," according to Sri Aurobindo, may be applied to existence in the realm of the spirit and of the mind as well as in the material. Thus, he says that there is an ascending series in the scale of substance from matter to spirit. It is marked by a progressive diminution of those properties most characteristic of the physical and an increase of those characteristics of the purely spiritual. Even in the realm of the material, there is an ascending scale that leads from the more dense to the less dense, from the less to the more subtle. And between the most subtle material and the purely spiritual there are grades of ascent from the inconscient to absolute consciousness.[12] Aurobindo thus conceives of reality in terms of eight degrees of being. Using the ancient concept of the Absolute as *Sat-Chit-Ananda*, he traces the ascent (the evolution) to the Divine through the stages from Matter to Life, Psyche and Mind into Supermind, Bliss, Consciousness-Force, and

Pure Existence. In other words, beyond the material plane there is a world based upon a conscious cosmic vital energy—a world of conscious life. This plane is governed by the dominating and determining factor of Mind. Still beyond the level of Mind is the plane of Supermind. The highest stage in the series is pure Conscious-Power or Pure Being. Each plateau of the hill of being gives to our widening experience a higher plane of consciousness and a richer world of existence.[13]

Corresponding to the ascent from the material to the spiritual is the descent (involution) of the spiritual into the material. The upward ascent results from the unceasing pressure downward of the supramaterial planes upon the material compelling it to rise to higher levels. Sri Aurobindo asserts:

> Our material world is the result of all the others (principles), for the other principles have descended into Matter to create the physical universe, and every particle of what we call Matter contains all of them implicit in itself; their secret action . . . is involved in every moment of its existence and every movement of its activity. And as Matter is the last word of the descent, so it is also the first word of the ascent; as the powers of all these planes . . . are involved in the material existence, so they are all capable of evolution out of it. . . . Evolution comes by the unceasing pressure of the supra-material planes on the material compelling it to deliver out of itself their principles and powers which might conceivably otherwise have slept imprisoned in the rigidity of the material formula.[14]

The link between the process of ascent and descent is where Mind and Supermind meet with a veil between them. The rending of the veil is the condition of the "Divine Life" in humanity. By this the Mind can recover its divine light in the all-comprehending Supermind and the soul realize its divine nature.[15]

Physical evolution has brought mankind from lower forms of existence to the present stage of development. That which most fully distinguishes man from other animals is the possession of mental consciousness. But this is not the end of nature's plan for man. Mankind is on the verge of a still higher stage of evolution:

> As there has been established on earth a mental consciousness and power which shapes a race of mental beings and takes up into itself all of earthly nature that is ready for the change, so now there will be established on earth a gnostic consciousness and power which will shape a race of gnostic spiritual beings and take up into itself all of the earth-nature that is ready for this new transformation. It will also receive into itself from above, progressively, from its own domain of perfect light and power and beauty all that is ready to descend from that domain into terrestrial being. For the evolution proceeded in the past by the upsurging, at each critical stage, of a concealed power from its involution in the inconscience, but also by a descent from above, from its own plane, of that power already self-realized in its own higher natural province.[16]

Thus, the next stage in the evolutionary consciousness is the emergence of the "gnostic being." This is our divine destiny. "The gnostic being will have indeed an inmost existence in which he is alone with God, one with the Eternal, self-plunged into the depths of the infinite, in communion with its height and its luminous abysses of secrecy." [17] Ultimately, Aurobindo envisages the emergence of a new humanity beyond the present stage of human evolution. "At first a few will attain to gnostic being in different parts of the world. Gradually the number will increase and small islets of gnostic communities will be established. From within these gnostic communities a Consciousness-Force will emanate, exercising so powerful an influence on the rest of humanity that it too may enter into the destiny that awaits it from eternity." [18] This is the "Life Divine."

This vision of Sri Aurobindo carries him still one step farther. As there has been produced through physical evolution a human body fit to be the vehicle of the human mind, so nature must provide a suitable body in which the Supermind may function. As the spiritual has descended into the material, seeking a fit receptacle or instrument for its manifestation, the body, life, and consciousness of man were provided. But the transformation of the material by the spiritual cannot stop there, for there must be the evolution of a "nobler physical existence" not limited by the ordinary conditions of animal birth, life, and death.

> The ascent of man from the physical to the *supramental* must open out the possibility of a corresponding ascent in the grades of substance to that ideal body which is proper to our supramental being. The invasion of our being by Supermind must render possible a conquest of our physical limitations—the conquest of death, and the experience of an earthly immortality. [19]

The means through which this desired goal is to be brought about is yoga. Aurobindo rejects the common notion that a yogi must renounce the world. All of life can be yoga. This means that every detail of life is so organized as to be consciously directed toward the divine evolution of men.

Integral Yoga

The yoga of Sri Aurobindo—"Integral Yoga"—combines the essential elements of traditional Hindu yogas (*karma-yoga*, "deeds"; *jñānayoga*, "knowledge"; *bhaktiyoga*, "devotion"; and *rājayoga*, "spiritual discipline"), but is more. It is based upon a "subtle metaphysical psychology" developed by Sri Aurobindo. According to him, the individual being is composed of the highest Self, or Spirit (*Ātman*), the soul, the psychic being, and the mental and vital sheaths (or bodies) which enclose the physical body, and, in all but the liberated man, the egoistic self. With the exception of the ego, all these are projections of the Supreme Self, organized in various forms to support its manifestation in the material world.[20] The Self is "in essence one with the Divine or at least it is a portion of the Divine and has all the Divine potentialities." [21] The soul is an aspect of the Self, "a spark of the Divine. . . . This spark is there in all living beings from the lowest to the highest." [22] The psychic being is formed by the soul to support the mind, vital sheath, and body. To grow aware of the psychic being, and to bring it forward so that it controls all the levels of the individual, is one of the principal purposes of the yoga.[23] Screening these psychic powers with their divine potentialities is the ego personality. The ego is built up by nature in the process of evolution. It is the center of imperfect consciousness and imperfect knowledge.

The subtle bodies, or sheaths (*linga-sharira*), sometimes referred to as the etheric body, serve as the center for all psychological changes and link the forces of mind, feeling, and will to the body. The subtle bodies possess seven main centers (*cakras*). According to Sri Aurobindo, the center at the base of the spine governs physical activities down to the subconscient. That over the solar plexus governs the small sense movements. The navel center governs the larger desire movements, the heart center the emotions, the throat center the expressive and externalizing mind. The center between the eyebrows governs the dynamic will, vision, and mental formations. The "thousand-petaled lotus" above the head "commands the higher thinking mind, houses the still higher illumined mind, and at the highest opens to the intuition, through which the Over-mind can have communication or immediate contact with the rest." [24] The opening of the *cakras* or subtle centers to higher forces of consciousness is a central part of the process of Integral Yoga.

"The object of Yoga is to enter into and be possessed by the Divine Presence and Consciousness, to love the Divine for the Divine's sake alone, to be turned in our nature into the nature of the Divine, and in our will and works and life to be the instrument of the Divine." [25]

I hope I have indicated for the average reader the broad outlines of the subtle and unique philosophy of Sri Auro-bindo. Those who would wish to learn more about the in-tricate details of the Integral Yoga are referred to his *The Life Divine, Letters, The Synthesis of Yoga,* and *Essays on the Gita.*[26]

Disciples

Sri Aurobindo's unique philosophy and system of yoga have brought a large number of persons to the ashram in Pondicherry, some as disciples, others as scholars and students, Indians and non-Indians. Among the best known of those who have come from abroad was Margaret Wilson, the daughter of President Woodrow Wilson. After reading several of Sri Aurobindo's works, she became so attracted that she wrote to him asking permission to come to Pondicherry. Upon becoming a member of the ashram in 1938, she was given the name Nistha ("concentration" or "devotion") because her expressed purpose was to devote herself to Divine Realization. Though physically frail, she committed herself to the discipline of the Integral Yoga, and for six years forced upon herself the discipline of the ashram, asking for no special concessions. During the seventh year, she became so critically ill that it was suggested she return to America, where she could get more adequate medical treatment, but she replied, "You see, if I die here my soul will be in the Mother's hand but if I die outside who will take care of my soul?" [27]

Somewhat different was the ashram life of another American disciple of Sri Aurobindo and the Mother. Frederic Bushnell, a Bostonian, suffered a shock when his father, twice the Attorney General of Massachusetts, died in 1949, which sent him "into great thought of soul." Traveling through India, he became converted to Hinduism. "Bushnell died," he said. "In his place now lives Ananta Chaitanya ("infinite consciousness"), in search of divinity." Becoming a member of the Sri Aurobindo Ashram, he acquired an island across the river from the ashram, where he constructed a private temple, cultivates a paddy field that supplies grain for the ashram, and carries on his spiritual discipline under the direction of the Mother.[28]

Contrary to the traditional Hindu ashram practice, where only unmarried disciples were admitted, the Pondicherry Ashram receives married couples who agree to live the life of celibacy. Such a couple is Dr. and Mrs. Jay Holmes Smith. While serving with a mission in India during the British raj he became involved in the independence movement and was expelled from India by the British

Government. Inspired by Sri Aurobindo's *The Synthesis of Yoga*, which he found in the New York Public Library, Dr. Smith and his wife returned to India, became Indian citizens and permanent residents of the ashram.[29]

A non-Indian disciple with possibly the longest period of residence at the ashram was the Englishwoman Dorothy Hodgson, who was given the name Vasavadatta ("one who has given herself") by Sri Aurobindo. Miss Hodgson met the Mother in France, traveled with her to Japan, and then on to Pondicherry in 1920. It is said that no task in the ashram was too menial for her, and her spirit of service was an inspiration to all who knew her.[30]

The number of those who have spent longer or shorter periods at the ashram is impressive. A number of hostels, among them the modern, spacious, and comfortable Golaconda, have been built for the accommodation of residents and visitors. Some who have come as visitors have remained as permanent members of the ashram community. During my visit to Pondicherry I was able to meet and talk with a number of those who had become devoted disciples of "the Master" and "the Mother." A further description of the ashram and its activities will come more appropriately, however, when we tell the story of Mira Richard, the Mother, in Chapter 10.

Sri Aurobindo's Psychic Force

Although Sri Aurobindo never left Pondicherry after his arrival there in 1910 and never left his living quarters after his retirement in 1926, his disciples feel, nevertheless, that he profoundly affected the life of the world. This was through the worldwide spiritual power which they and he called his "Force." Several examples of his use of his Force may be given. Sri Aurobindo, though a recluse, was intensely interested in world affairs. A number of daily newspapers and international journals were constantly at his side. When he became unable to read them for himself he had them read to him. Later, a radio was installed in his room and he spent several hours each day listening to world news. This was all a part of his "work," the influencing of world affairs through the spiritual powers (*siddhi*) which he had gained from his yogic spiritual disciplines (*sādhana*). He once reported to his followers:

As for the Ashram, I have been extremely successful, but while I have tried to work on the world the results have been varied. In Spain, in Madrid, I was splendidly successful. General Miaja was an admirable instrument to work on. Basque was an utter failure. Negus was a good instrument but the people around him, though good warriors, were too ill-organized and ill-equipped. The work in Egypt was not a success. In Ireland and Turkey the success was tremendous. In Ireland I have done exactly what I wanted to do in Bengal.[31]

Sri Aurobindo's use of human instruments in the fulfillment of his divine "Ideal" for the creation of a "New Humanity" is well illustrated by his activities during the Second World War. In spite of the fact that he was greatly misunderstood by the majority of his Indian countrymen, and vilified by some, he used his spiritual Force to ensure the victory of Britain in the dark days of the war. He chose Churchill, whom he greatly admired, as his instrument. Similarly, he directed his Force against Hitler, whom he looked upon as the embodiment of the *asura* ("evil powers"). An American disciple of Sri Aurobindo, whom I have known for many years, told me of one incident in which Sri Aurobindo's psychic Force apparently affected the course of the war. A few years ago an American political historian was visiting Pondicherry. In discussing a recent investigation in which he had been engaged, he spoke of the strange behavior of Hitler at the time of Dunkirk. Although the Allied forces had their backs to the sea and the German panzer units were ready to advance and push them into the channel, Hitler hesitated to act upon the urgent request of his generals to give the command to move forward. He said that his air force could do the job alone. Because of his action, which his own generals considered insane, the Allied forces were able to escape destruction. When asked whether Hitler's strange behavior might not have been the result of Sri Aurobindo's intervention, the historian agreed that this was a plausible explanation.

Narayan Prasad, in his *Life in Sri Aurobindo Ashram*, gives a detailed account of the interest and intervention of Sri Aurobindo in the war. Because he saw that the whole future of humanity hung upon the outcome of the war, he employed his spiritual Force to bring about the victory of the Allies. "Except for five or six hours, day and night, Sri Aurobindo worked for Allied victory. Like a Guardian Angel of the Allied cause he spent most of his time in hearing the news, following the events and watching the effects of his subtle working. To quote his own words: 'My Force . . . is being largely used for helping the right development of the war and for change in the human world.'" Prasad adds that in view of the strong opposition that Sri Aurobindo had given the British while engaged in the independence movement, his support of the Allied cause puzzled the ashramites for a long while, but they came to understand his position and now believe that his intervention in the war saved civilization.[32]

Sri Aurobindo's psychic Force was used, it is believed, not only to influence world affairs, but also to produce change in local situations, such as the cure of illness. He once wrote, "I have tried it in hundreds of cases besides D's (on my own body first and always) and I have no doubt of its efficacy or reality." [33] In explaining the action of his Force in healing a sick person, he indicated that three factors are normally needed: first, the power of the Force itself, that is, its own sheer pressure and direct action on the field of action (the ill person, his condition, his body); second, the instrument (the human agent, such as the doctor or those attending the patient); and third, the instrumentation (the treatment or medicine). But he adds, "I have often used the Force alone, without any human instrument or outer means, but here all depends upon the recipient and his receptivity." [34]

One other instance of his use of his psychic Force by Sri Aurobindo is recalled by his disciples. This occurred at the time of his death when he "withdrew from his body." In India, where embalming was not at that time practiced, decomposition of the body would set in within a few hours. But for ninety hours the body of Sri Aurobindo remained intact.[35] This unusual phenomenon was produced, it is believed, by the supramental Force that Sri Aurobindo exercised upon his own body.

The Deeper Retirement

In mid-November, 1950, it became known to the disciples at the ashram that Sri Aurobindo was not well, but plans for the *darshana* on November 24, the annual event at which Sri Aurobindo appeared publicly before his disciples, went forward. Though he appeared somewhat weaker than usual to those who walked past him, none suspected that the end was near. Various functions planned for disciples and visitors who had gathered from far and wide were carried on according to plan through

December 3, but deep concern was felt when Sri Aurobindo's private physician was called from Calcutta. Early on the morning of December 5, Sri Aurobindo "withdrew from his body." Normally, the funeral and burial would have taken place the same day, but in the afternoon the Mother announced to the press: "The funeral of Sri Aurobindo has not taken place today. His body is charged with such a concentration of Supramental light that there is no sign of decomposition and the body will be kept lying on his bed so long as it remains intact." [36] It was not until December 9 that the body was laid to rest in the marble tomb which had been prepared in the courtyard of the ashram. Some months later, the Mother told of a conversation that had taken place between Sri Aurobindo and herself on December 8: "When I asked him to resuscitate he clearly answered: 'I have left this body purposely. I will not take it back. I shall manifest again in the first supramental body built in a supramental way.'" [37]

It is the faith of the disciples that although he has withdrawn from his physical body, Sri Aurobindo is still present. Many have reported seeing and even conversing with him, especially as they have stood or knelt by his tomb. Their faith has been strengthened by the assurance of the Mother, "He is always with us, aware of what we are doing, of all our thoughts, of all our feelings and all our actions." [38]

There is no temple or other formal place of worship in the ashram, unless it be the *samādh* of Sri Aurobindo. I observed that during the day many persons knelt for a moment at the tomb, and some placed flowers on it as Indians are accustomed to place them on temple altars. But this action was apparently completely voluntary and appeared to be the only form of public "worship" that takes place. Twice a week, on Thursday and Sunday evenings, many of the ashramites gather on the playing field for fifteen minutes of silent meditation. But even this corporate act is but a part of a calisthenics exhibition in which young and old take part. Thus, there is complete freedom of worship, one might say, "from worship," in the ashram. No group is permitted to set up a place of worship or to perform religious ceremonies even on the festival days of the various religions found in India. This does not mean that religion is discouraged or is absent, for throughout the ashram there is a "religious atmosphere." Religion is a private matter, it is believed, and no set forms should be forced on anyone. This is said to be in harmony with the universal spirit of Sri Aurobindo, whose concern was for universal truth.

9

THE SAGE OF ANANDA KUTIR:
Swami Sivananda

On the banks of the holy Ganges River in the foothills of the mighty Himalayas is a spot sacred to all Hindus. It is known as Rishikesh ("The Field of the Rishis"). It gets its name from the fact that for ages rishis ("holy men," "seers") gathered at this place and hallowed it with their footprints. Legend has it that the Ganges is joined here by two other sacred rivers which come up from underground. It was here that saints from time immemorial gathered to engage in those austerities which they hoped would lead to God-realization, or, having reached this goal, to obtain at death final release from the chain of birth and rebirth.

A short distance from the present town of Rishikesh stands the Sivanandashram, headquarters of the Divine Life Society, whose branches are to be found all over the world. The buildings of the ashram climb the mountain from the banks of the Ganges. The lowest building, now the Bookstore, was the original Ananda Kutir ("Hut of Bliss") of the founder. Just above are the General Hospital and the Eye Hospital. A long flight of steps leads to the buildings of the ashram proper—residences for the inmates, a guesthouse, offices, a printing press, and places of worship. Upon our arrival at the ashram, Shamrao and I were greeted cordially by the executive secretary of the Society, Swami Krishnananda, and were shown to our rooms in the guesthouse. Every provision had been made for our comfort, even including toothpaste! Shortly after our arrival a delicious vegetarian lunch was served to us in our rooms. From that time on, one of the monks, Swami Sadananda, became our constant companion and guide. In contrast with other ashrams in Rishikesh we found the Sivanandashram to be a thriving center of activity.

The founder of this ashram and of the Divine Life Society, Kuppuswamy Iyer, later to be known as Swami Sivananda, was born on September 8, 1887, in the village of Pattamadai, in South India. His father, Vengu Iyer, was a government official and a devotee of the god Siva. Srimati Parvati Ammal, his mother, was known for her piety and her compassion for the unfortunate. The qualities of both parents were to find fulfillment in the life of their son. From an early age he showed evidence of the spirit of *tyaga* ("sacrifice and renunciation"), often giving his own food to beggars and stray animals. He led his classes in middle school, high school, and at the Society for the Propagation of the Gospel College, where he earned his degree. At the Medical College at Tanjore he made rapid progress and, upon graduation, entered into private practice at Tiruchi. His literary interest was initiated through the publication of a medical journal, *The Ambrosia*.

Shortly after the death of his father, in 1913, he received an invitation from a medical colleague to transfer his practice to Malaya. The next ten years were spent as the doctor in charge of a hospital maintained by a larger rubber estate near Singapore. The young doctor soon became known both for his professional skill and for his compassion. Though he treated the poor without charge, he soon became fairly well-to-do. He spent his money lavishly on personal clothing, jewelry, and objects made of sandalwood. It is said that "sometimes he purchased various kinds of gold rings and necklaces and wore them all at the same time. He used to wear ten rings on ten fingers!" [1] But a change was to come in his life. A book given to him by a wandering sadhu awakened interest in spiritual matters, and he began the study of religious books and sacred scriptures. In addition to the daily study of the Bhagavad-Gita and other Hindu scriptures he read the Bible and the *Imitation of Christ*. As days passed, he realized more and more that he must renounce the world, so in 1923 he resigned his position in the hospital and returned to India.

The reversal in his way of life was dramatic and complete. Giving away all his possessions, he spent the next year visiting the holy shrines of India, seeking a place for solitary meditation. He who had gloried in fine clothing now wore only two pieces of cotton cloth, which soon became threadbare. Once accustomed to a comfortable home and nourishing food, he often had to sleep on the ground under a tree and eat wild berries and nuts to satisfy his hunger. Toward the end of his year of wandering, a postmaster, with whom he lodged temporarily, suggested that he go to Rishikesh, and provided him the railway fare to Hardwar, the nearest railway station. From Hardwar, the young ascetic walked to Rishikesh. As he was resting by the roadside, a passerby flung a coin to him as an offering. Though he had no money, Kuppuswamy was so determined to have nothing to do with the world that he went away leaving the coin on the ground. Having arrived at Rishikesh, with no fixed abode, he lived for some weeks on the porch of a Dharmasala (a public guesthouse for pilgrims). It was while he was here that a noted guru, Swami Viswananda Saraswati, arrived in Rishikesh and was attracted to Kuppuswamy. After brief instruction, he initiated him into the Sannyasa order and gave him the name Swami Sivananda Saraswati ("The Bliss of Siva of the Order Which Worships Saraswati, the Goddess of Learning"). He now found shelter in a small dilapidated *kutir* ("hut"), deserted and infested with scorpions, which was part of the Swargashram ("Heavenly Retreat").

Swami Sivananda now entered upon a program of strenuous spiritual discipline. He observed silence, fasted for days at a time, and spent more than twelve hours daily in meditation. But along with this intense austerity he resumed his practice of medicine. He visited the huts of the sadhus who were sick, and attended cholera and smallpox patients among the pilgrims who came to Rishikesh. With some money from an insurance policy that had matured he started a charitable dispensary in 1927. This has now grown into a well-organized hospital. The pilgrim path to the famous shrine at Badrinath passed in front of the dispensary, and Swami Sivananda gave small packets of common medicine to pilgrims to be used on their arduous journey. For him, serving his fellowmen was a form of worship. At last, after years of intense and unbroken *sādhana,* he enjoyed the bliss of *Nirvikalpa Samādhi* (the superconscious state where mental modifications cease to exist). He had come to the state of Self-realization, God-realization.

During those days at Swargashram, pilgrims and visitors frequently came to Swami Sivananda for advice and guidance on religious and spiritual matters. As the numbers increased, it occurred to him that others, who could not come to him, might find help in the advice that he had been giving. He decided to write out answers to the many problems and questions that had been put to him and give them wider circulation. But he had no funds with which to buy paper, so he gathered scraps of paper, discarded envelopes, and anything else he could find. Finally a little manuscript was prepared, but there was no money for its publication. It was at this moment that a visitor, impressed by the ascetic appearance of Swami Sivananda, gave him a five-rupee note and begged him to buy milk for himself. Instead of buying milk, Sivananda used it to have his first booklet, entitled *Brahma-Vidya* ("Knowledge of God"), published. This was found to be so helpful that many readers urged him to write others, and offered to bear the cost of their publication. "Thus God willed that the visitor's milk for one man should become the life-giving ambrosia to hundreds and thousands." [2]

As his fame spread, the opportunity came to Swami Sivananda to travel extensively throughout India, lecturing and conducting *sankirtana* (group singing of hymns in praise of the gods). Upon his return in 1932, he left the Swargashram and founded the Sivanandashram. On the banks of the Ganges he found an old hut, dilapidated and unused, which looked like an abandoned cow shed. It had four "rooms." He cleaned the building and occupied it, naming it Ananda Kutir ("Abode of Bliss"). As disciples began to gather around him and required lodging, other cow sheds were found and made habitable. In 1936 the Divine Life Society was founded. From this humble beginning has grown a society with some three hundred branches. As need arose, various departments were opened. The publication of Swami Sivananda's writings led to the establishment of a press. The publication of a monthly journal, *The Divine Life*, was begun in 1938. The Lord Sri Viswanath Mandir ("temple") was constructed in 1943. The doctor-swami had continued his medical services through all the years after his arrival in Rishikesh. The growing demand for medicines led to the establishment in 1945 of the Sivananda Ayurvedic Pharmacy, in which allopathic medicines are prepared from rare Himalayan herbs. This department also has become a thriving industry.

Swami Sivananda had an ecumenical attitude toward religion, and in 1945 he organized the All-World Religious Federation for the purpose of encouraging dialogue between representatives of the various sects and religions. The Sixtieth Anniversary of Swami Sivananda's birth was celebrated with the construction and opening of a number of new buildings in the ashram. The Yoga-Vedanta Forest Academy was established in 1948 to give systematic spiritual training to the number of disciples who had joined the ashram, and to visiting "seekers." An All-India and Ceylon tour in 1950 brought many new adherents to Swami Sivananda and increased the demand for his writings. This resulted in the establishment of the Yoga-Vedanta Forest Academy Press in 1951. The Sivananda Eye Hospital was opened in 1957 in conjunction with the regular hospital. The Silver Jubilee of the Divine Life Society was celebrated in 1961, with a large number of devotees and friends in attendance. Then, on July 14, 1963, after long years filled with devotion and service, Swami Sivananda entered *mahasamadhi*. Since his death the Divine Life Society has been under the presidency of Swami Chidananda, a gifted writer, eloquent speaker, and capable organizer. It is he who has been largely responsible for the rapid spread of the Society into the West.

The Spiritual Guide

The success that attended the publication of his first small booklets encouraged Swami Sivananda to adopt the printed page as the medium of his contribution to the

spiritual life of India and of the world. His writings are
apparently the outcome of a twofold urge: the desire to
awaken, enlighten, aid, and guide all people, and secondly,
to make his ideas and experiences available to men in all
walks of life and in every land. Because of the widespread
use of English in India and abroad he decided to use this
medium in his writings. His literary output, numbering
amazingly some three hundred works, covers the whole
range of human experience and need from essays on "the
Eternal, the Infinite, and the Unutterable" to simple instruction on how to deal with everyday health problems.
A catalog of his writings includes works on metaphysics,
Western philosophy, yoga, religion, psychology, ethics,
education, health, art, drama, poetry, and a variety of other
subjects. It is not my purpose, because of space, to review
this vast body of the swami's writings. A useful interpretation of his message and an analysis of his works have been
given by his successor, Swami Chidananda, in his *Light
Fountain*.[3]

A second major activity of Swami Sivananda was the
guiding of *sādhakas* ("seekers") in their spiritual discipline.
Because of the impairment in his own health as a result of
the severe austerities that he had practiced, Swami Sivananda urged a degree of moderation in *sādhana*. The foundation for spiritual development is laid in ethical culture
and the maintenance of normal physical and mental health.
A seeker ought to observe the rules of health and hygiene,
leading a simple life of moderation and regularity. He
should adhere to the three disciplines of noninjury, truthfulness, and purity—*ahimsā, satyam,* and *brahmacharya.*
Contrary to the teachings of many gurus and swamis,
Swami Sivananda did not demand complete withdrawal
from the world on the part of the seeker. If performed in a
selfless spirit, the seeker's work can be his worship. Al-

though it is true that a devotee may hasten his progress toward his spiritual goal through living a life of celibacy, the householder (*grihastha*) may also enter upon the path of spiritual discipline. Swami Sivananda's message is for all men, whatever their status.

Swami Sivananda's Message

Swami Sivananda's message for the world, disarmingly simple and extremely practical, is well summarized in his motto: "Serve, Love, Meditate, Realize." The impact of his message is also emblazoned on his symbol, a cross with "Serve" at the top, "Love" at the end of the left arm, "Meditate" at the right, and "Realize" at the foot. It is significant that Swami Sivananda put "Service" first. Swami Chidananda writes:

> One factor that stands out distinctly prominent over and above others in his entire teaching, is the stress Swamiji has laid at every turn on the vital importance of selfless service, *Nishkamya Karma Yoga*. Selfless and motiveless service of all creatures, he insists, is the greatest purifying force on earth. It is through such disinterested loving service that that preparatory purification is wrought, so vitally and indispensably essential for the experience of a wider consciousness and a higher life. . . . Done in the spirit of worship, this alone will suffice to take one to the goal of life.[4]

The essential nature of man is his inherent divinity. The goal of his existence is Bliss (*Ānanda*). To achieve Bliss, man must transcend his involvement with his mind and body and with the physical world. Only then can he become one with Brahman, *Sat-Chit-Ananda* ("Absolute Existence, Consciousness, and Bliss"). In order to realize his divinity and become one with Brahman, man must learn to control his animal instincts. This is done through the practice of love (*bhakti*) and nonviolence (*ahimsā*). *Ahimsā* is not just refraining from doing injury to others; it is also the discipline of self-giving love (*bhakti*). *Ahimsā* is the constant striving to cause no harm or pain to any living creature through thought, word, or deed. The opposite of *bhakti* is *krodha* ("anger"). One who practices *ahimsā* does not lose his temper; he bears criticism, rebukes, insults, or assaults without striking back. Ultimate truth can be attained only through the practice of *ahimsā*. Absolute *ahimsā* is impossible, however, for we destroy life, that we may live. For example, the phagocytes in our bloodstream are continually destroying harmful cells or other dangerous foreign materials in our systems. To practice *ahimsā* a man must control his anger. Anger is caused by passion in man's nature, and a passionate man is more apt to become angry than others. To rid himself of anger, he must rid himself of his passions through strict self-control. A further cause of anger is egoism. When one thinks himself superior, he becomes angry when his faults are pointed out to him. Anger causes poisons to enter the bloodstream and upset the body chemistry. A few minutes of violent anger may affect one's health for many days. Constant practice of *ahimsā* is essential to good health as well as to spiritual progress.[5]

In contrast to anger is *bhakti* (self-giving, self-sacrificing love). *Bhakti* has no selfish motive; it is love for love's sake. Through *bhakti* the devotee (*bhakta*) becomes one with the Absolute. He sees the Lord in everyone and everything with which he comes into contact. The whole world is a manifestation of the Lord, and everything in the world is but an aspect of this manifestation. The true *bhakta* sees the Lord in the thief, the prostitute, the scavenger, or even in a murderer. Swami Sivananda tells the story of a *bhakta* who gave his ring voluntarily to a thief who had entered his house to steal, saying: "Take this ring also because it is your duty to steal. Thou art Krishna, keep up this *Lila* ("sport")." Or the story of another *bhakta* who prostrated himself before a prostitute, saying that he saw Mother Kali in her. Therefore he worshiped her.[6]

God, or the Ultimate, is the totality of all existence. He is omnipotent, omniscient, and omnipresent. God, love, bliss, perfection, peace, freedom, immortality—these are all one and the same. God is the only reality in an unreal world. The only way to realize God is to empty oneself of all thoughts of self, of all personal desires. God demands the whole heart of the devotee.

> Forget your own interests, your own longings, your own desires. You will attain the bliss of the Supreme Self. Crucify, sacrifice the lower self, if you wish to have union with God. Empty your egoism. You will be filled with God. Lose your personality. You will find the Divine Life. You will realize God.[7]

Swami Sivananda laid great emphasis upon the importance of meditation in one's spiritual development. Meditation, he said, is the only royal road to the attainment of salvation. It is like a mysterious ladder that reaches from earth to heaven, from error to truth, from darkness to light, from ignorance to knowledge, from mortality to immortality. In meditation, one keeps up an unceasing flow of God-consciousness. But the art of meditation does not come easily. Intense and long practice is necessary. Just as the Ganges flows continually to the sea, thoughts of God should flow continuously toward the Lord. One should engage in meditation in the *brahma muhurta* (the "auspicious moment") in the early-morning hours. A comfortable position in a quiet place, with the mind completely free of anxiety and with all bodily activities completely suspended, is essential for meditation. One should not "strain the brain, one should not struggle or wrestle with the mind." Make no violent effort to control the mind. Even intruding thoughts should not be driven away. Divine thoughts must be permitted to flow gently through the mind. Virtues such as patience, perseverance, mercy, love, forgiveness, and purity must be practiced daily. Regularity in meditation is of supreme importance. There must be alternation between work and meditation. If one will meditate for one or two hours in the *brahma muhurta,* he can work peacefully and successfully throughout the day. His whole system will be charged with spiritual vibrations and he will be guided by a mysterious inner voice.

Realization, or *samādhi,* is union with the Absolute. It is a state of pure consciousness. There is neither physical nor mental consciousness. There is only Existence, or *Sat.* "When the water dries up in a pool, the reflection of the sun in the water also vanishes. When the mind melts into Brahman, when the mind-lake dries up, the reflected *chaitanya* ("absolute consciousness") also vanishes. Individual personality disappears. There remains Existence alone." [8] The worshiper and the worshiped become one, or identical. The meditator has dissolved his personality in the sea of God-consciousness. He has become the instrument of God. *Samādhi* is not a state of inertia. It is a condition of perfect awareness. It is not merely an exhilarating feeling. It is direct, unique, intuitive experience of Truth, of the Ultimate Reality. The state of *samādhi* is maintained even during one's work. He who is established in *samādhi* keeps his body and mind in perfect balance and utilizes them in the service of humanity. In *samādhi,* the purified mind resolves itself into the *Ātman* (Absolute Self), and becomes the *Ātman* itself. With the advent of the knowledge of the

Self, ignorance vanishes. With the disappearance of the root cause—namely, ignorance—egoism also disappears. One can then know the Unknowable, see the Unseen, and obtain access into the Inaccessible.[9] He has obtained *moksha* ("salvation").

Swami Sivananda's Yoga of Synthesis

The path to Self-realization, to salvation, is yoga. Yoga is a science perfected by ancient seers of India, a practical system of self-culture. Swami Sivananda subjected himself to the rigorous practice of yoga, and yoga is at the heart of the program that he devised for developing the spiritual life of his devotees. Contrary to the discipline set by many other gurus, Swami Sivananda insisted that it is not necessary to turn away from life. Yoga is the spiritualization of life. Yoga is primarily a way of life, not something divorced from life. Yoga is not the forsaking of action, but the efficient performance of action. Yoga is not a religion, but an aid to the practice of the basic spiritual truths in all religions. Yoga is not mere physical exercise, the control of bodily functions. The various postures and breath controls are but minor aids to yoga practice. Yoga is for all. It is universal, and may be practiced by anyone anywhere.

To guide his followers both in India and in the West, Swami Sivananda published his *Practical Lessons in Yoga*,[10] possibly the most useful guide available for those in the West who wish to practice yoga. The essential first step on the path to Self-realization is the development of ethical culture. *Ahimsā, satyam, brahmacharya* ("nonviolence," "truthfulness," "chastity") are the very foundation of ethics. "Abstaining from injury in thought, word and deed, mercy to all creatures, gifts, control of anger, freedom from pride and malice, restraint of the senses constitute

praiseworthy behaviour." [11] Food plays an important part
in meditation. Different foods produce different effects on
different compartments of the brain. For purposes of meditation the food should be light, nutritious, and *sattvic*—
those which make the mind pure and calm, such as milk,
cereals, vegetables, fruits, and nuts. Meat and alcohol are
to be avoided. Regular and moderate exercise is essential.
While the exercises of *hatha-yoga* are commended, only
those moderate exercises which cannot be injurious are to
be practiced, and even these should be undertaken gradually. Each of the yogic postures (*āsanas*) is described in
some detail, with an added note concerning their thera-
peutic effect. Similarly, the various types of breath control
(*pranayama*), with their effects, are considered.

In his Yoga of Synthesis, or Integral Yoga, Swami Sivananda finds place for the four traditional yogas: *karma,
bhakti, jñāna,* and *rājā.* His discussion of the Four Yogas
is particularly "practical." *Karmayoga,* he insists, "does not
consist in sitting cross-legged for six hours, or stopping the
beating of the heart, or being buried beneath the ground
for a week or a month; these are mere physical feats. Real
Yoga is the attainment of the highest divine knowledge
through conscious communion with God. . . . Yoga is the
science that teaches the methods of uniting the individual
soul with the Supreme Soul or merging the individual will
in the Cosmic Will." [12] One can realize the goal of life by
four different paths. The one to be chosen depends upon
the person's temperament. *Karmayoga* is for the activist,
but those who follow this path should do work for work's
sake, without selfish motive. A karmayogi should have
complete nonattachment for the fruits of his works, and
should dedicate all his actions at the altar of God in entire
self-surrender. The highest form of *karmayoga* is the selfless service of others. Every act of service may be con-

verted into an act of worship, leading to the goal of Self-realization.

Bhaktiyoga is the path of devotion or the path of love appropriate for those of a devotional temperament. It involves the absolute and unreserved self-surrender to God. True religion does not consist in ritualistic observances, baths, and pilgrimages, but in loving all creatures, for the Lord dwells in the hearts of all. *Bhakti* is the silken, slender thread of love that binds the heart of the devotee to the Lord. Through *bhaktiyoga* the self, or ego, is surrendered forever as an offering to God. The devotee is lost in the consciousness of God. Swami Sivananda outlines the nine "modes" of *bhaktiyoga sādhana*. The first mode is seeking the society of Self-realized saints. The second is the recitation of God's glories. The third is the devotional service of God. The fourth is the faithful and devoted singing of his divine qualities. The fifth is the *japa,* or repetition of his *mantras* with firm faith. The sixth is self-discipline in practicing perfect withdrawal of the senses and the mind from worldly activities. The seventh mode is the practice of seeing the whole world as God. The eighth mode is contentment and cheer, whatever one's lot, and refraining from criticism of others. The ninth mode is to deal with one and all without trick or fraud, to depend upon God and to be indifferent to pleasure and pain.[13]

Jñānayoga is the path to be followed by a person of meditative temperament. Those who would follow the path of *jñānayoga,* or the yoga of wisdom, says Swami Sivananda, should first acquire the four means of salvation: discrimination between the Real and the unreal; indifference or dispassion for sensual objects; calmness of mind, restraint of the senses, faith in God, endurance, one-pointedness of mind; and intense longing for liberation. They should then seek out a Guru who has fully realized the Supreme Self and receive instruction from him. Let them reflect on what they have heard, and practice meditation. Then it will be possible for the jñānī to exclaim in exuberant joy: "The *Ātman* ("Supreme Self") alone is one without a second. The *Ātman* or the Self is the one Reality. I am that *Ātman*. I am *Siva*. I am He." He, the liberated soul, sees the Self alone in all beings and all beings in the Self.[14]

> Jnana ("Supreme Knowledge") is the cessation from thinking of particulars, annihilation of the feeling of separateness or individuality, existing as one unified with all. It is the dissolution of thought in eternal awareness, pure consciousness without objectification, knowing without thinking, merging finitude in Infinity.[15]

Rājayoga should be practiced by one with a disciplined temperament. The student treading the path of *Rājayoga* must ascend the spiritual ladder step by step, stage by stage. *Rājayoga* was systematized by Patanjali in his Yoga Sutras in the second century B.C. as a method of restraining the functions of the mind. Swami Sivananda taught devotees practicing this yoga to follow the eight steps enunciated by Patanjali: *yama*—abstinence from injury, untruth, theft, sensuality, and greed; *niyama*—observance of cleanliness of body and mind, contentment, body-conditioning, study of self, attentiveness, and purity of mind; *āsana*—posture; *pranayama*—breath control; *pratyahara*—withdrawal of the mind from sensual objects; *dhārana*—concentration; *dhyāna*—meditation; *samādhi*—the superconscious state. Each step is described in detail by Swami Sivananda in his *Practical Lessons in Yoga* and in his *Bliss Divine*. The ultimate goal of *rājayoga* is *samādhi*.

> In *Samadhi* all *Sadhana* ("Spiritual Discipline") ends and the Yogi becomes one with the immortal Lord, one with

the Cosmic Spirit. He is immanent and yet transcendent. In Raj Yoga, *Yama* and *Niyama* are the seeds, concentration is the root, self-surrender to the Lord is the shower, meditation is the flower, the superconscious state is the fruit.[16]

To the four traditional yogas, Swami Sivananda added a fifth, *japa yoga*. He taught that there is no yoga greater than *japa*. *Japa* is the repetition of a *mantra* or name of the Lord. *Japa* and *dhyāna* (meditation on the Lord) are inseparable, for name and the object signified by the name are inseparable. When one repeats continually, "Rama Rama" or "Krishna Krishna," the likeness of Rama or Krishna will come into his mind. *Nama-smarana* (remembering the name of the Lord) is a form of worship. *Mantra yoga*, like *nama-smarana*, is an aspect of *japa*. It is the constant recollection of or repetition of a sacred word or phrase by which one is protected or is released from the round of births and deaths. The *japa* of a *mantra* can bring the devotee realization of his highest goal, even though he has no knowledge of the meaning of the *mantra*. The sound vibrations set up by the repetition of a divine name or *mantra* give rise to definite forms. Thus, the repetition of *Om Namah Sivaya* produces the form of Lord Siva and of *Om Namo Narayanaya* that of Vishnu. It is, therefore, said that the name or *mantra* of the god is the god himself. This really means, says Swami Sivananda, that when a particular *mantra* appropriate to a particular god is properly recited, the vibrations so set up create in the higher planes a special form which that god ensouls for the time being.[17] So important did Swami Sivananda consider *japa yoga* that he wrote a separate book on the subject, *Japa Yoga*.[18] In this he discusses the philosophy and benefits of *japa*, lists a number of powerful *mantras*, and describes in great detail the techniques of *japa yoga*. He concludes that the name of the Lord is the sovereign specific for the cure of all ills of mankind. There is an inscrutable, mysterious power in God's name. If uttered with faith and reverence and practice, the Divine Name absolves one of all sin and enables him to obtain salvation, Self-realization (*Sat-Chit-Ananda*).

The Universal Prayer of Swami Sivananda

On a marble column in the courtyard of the ashram has been inscribed in English and in Hindi the Universal Prayer taught by Swami Sivananda. Because of its ecumenical nature, it is used by devotees around the world.

> O adorable Lord of mercy and love,
> Salutations and prostrations unto Thee.
> Thou art omnipotent, omnipresent, omniscient,
> Thou art Existence—Knowledge—Bliss Absolute.
> Thou art the Indweller of all beings.
> Grant us an understanding heart,
> Equal vision, balanced mind,
> Faith, devotion, wisdom.
> Grant us inner spiritual strength to resist temptation
> And to control the mind.
> Free us from egoism, lust, anger, greed and hatred,
> Fill our hearts with divine virtues.
> Let us behold Thee in all these names and forms,
> Let us serve Thee in all these names and forms,
> Let us ever remember Thee,
> Let us ever sing Thy glories,
> Let Thy Name be ever on our lips,
> Let us abide in Thee for ever and ever.
>> Peace. Peace. Peace.

Worship at the Sivanandashram

Corporate worship at the Sivanandashram is normally held mornings and afternoons in the Sri Viswanath Temple and in the evenings in the Bhajan Worship Hall. On Thursdays, the day dedicated for the worship of the Guru, a service is also conducted at the Samadh Shrine, the grave of Swami Sivananda. The *arati* ("fire ceremony") held in the small temple is both elaborate and impressive. On the marble altar are the phallic symbols, the *linga* and the *yoni*, employed in the worship of Siva. On the wall behind the altar hangs a large picture of Swami Sivananda. Thus the worship at the temple is offered both to the deity and to the Guru, who, for the devotee, are one. Extending from the *yoni* to the edge of the altar is a brass trough. A single priest conducts the service. First, in the morning *arati*, milk, and in the afternoon, holy Ganges water, are poured over both the *linga* and the *yoni* as a libation. This milk or water is collected in a bucket at the end of the trough, and is later distributed to the devotees as *prasad* ("sanctified food"). On Thursday mornings the libation consists of a mixture known as *panchamritam* ("five nectars"), composed of mashed banana, honey, butter, sugar syrup, and mashed dates. On Thursday afternoons rose water is used. After the libation, a consecrated powder is scattered over the symbols and they are covered with a saffron-colored cloth. A filigreed arch of silver is then placed over the symbols and covered with a red cloth. A food offering—unleavened bread, fruit, and nuts—on a silver tray is next placed on the altar in front of the symbols. This is later distributed as *prasad* to the devotees. While reciting the 108 divine names of His Holiness Swami Sivananda, the priest scatters leaves from the sacred tulsi plant upon the altar. The *arati* flame is then lighted and swung in graceful curves before the altar and over the *linga* and the *yoni*. After the lamp has been passed among the devotees and each has held his hands over the flame and then touched his forehead, the service comes to a close.

The Bhajan Hall, in which the evening worship service is held, is a large rectangular room. At one end of the hall is a large plaster image of the goddess Sarasvati, and at the other the image of the goddess Durga. In front of the Sarasvati image is a reclining chair on which a large picture of Swami Sivananda has been placed. Behind the Sarasvati image, on the left is a shrine to Krishna and on the right, one to Siva. On the long wall facing the entrance doors hangs another picture of Swami Sivananda, along with pictures of a number of saints, including one of Jesus in the Garden of Gethsemane. During the evening *satsang*, the devotees sit on the floor facing the picture of Swami Sivananda. At the time of our visit, in the absence of Swami Chidananda, Swami Krishnananda sat on the cushion provided for the president of the Divine Life Society. I was invited to sit on a cushion at his right. A small singing band led in the *bhajans* (hymns of devotion to God), and some fifty devotees joined in singing the *bhajans* antiphonally. I noticed that there were among the devotees four non-Indian women dressed in saffron. I had thought that the ashram was for men only, but discovered that I had been mistaken. After the meeting, one of the nuns, an Englishwoman, told me that she had been a resident of the ashram for more than two years. After about an hour of *bhajan*-singing, Swami Krishnananda requested me to speak. I gave a talk that I had prepared for the occasion on the meaning of faith—the four steps to be followed by one seeking a meaningful faith, closing with my under-

standing of the importance of the role of the Spiritual
Guide (the Guru) on one's Spiritual Path. The evening
service of worship then closed with the flame ceremony
before the picture of Swami Sivananda and the images of
Krishna and Siva at the end of the hall. After passing their
hands over the flames and touching their foreheads, the
devotees went quietly to their own rooms.

Swami Chidananda

Dynamic leadership has been given to the Divine Life Society by its current president, Swami Chidananda. Sridhar
Rao was born on September 24, 1916, in the home of a
wealthy landowner in South India. From an early age he
was deeply interested in the Hindu scriptures and determined to become a rishi. In 1936 he was admitted to
Loyola College. It has been said that

> this period of studentship at a predominantly Christian
> College was significant. The glorious ideal of the Lord
> Jesus, the Apostles and the other Christian saints found in
> his heart a synthesis with all that is best and noble in the
> Hindu culture. To him the study of the Bible was no mere
> routine; it was the living Gospel, just as living and real as
> the words of the Vedas, the Upanishads, and the Bhagavad
> Gita. His innate breadth of vision enabled him to see Jesus
> in Krishna, not Jesus instead of Krishna. He was as much
> an adorer of Jesus Christ as he was of Lord Vishnu.[19]

In the spirit of Jesus, "the great physician," Sridhar took a
keen interest in the sick. He had huts built for lepers on
the vast lawns of his home and attended them personally.
Other persons, who were ill, were cared for by him. Even
sick animals were taken care of. His interest in the spiritual
life also developed during his college days. He read the

works of Sri Ramakrishna, Swami Vivekananda, and Swami Sivananda. From time to time he visited the Ramakrishna Center in Madras. Although living in a home of wealth, he undertook a life of strict ascetic discipline. In 1943 he left home for good and became a member of the Sivanand-ashram. He was soon put in charge of the ashram dispensary. His intellectual ability was early recognized and he was called on to deliver lectures, write articles for the ashram magazine, and give spiritual instruction to seekers. When, in 1948, the Yoga-Vedanta Forest Academy was organized he was put in charge. In the same year he was made general secretary of the Divine Life Society. On Gurupoornima Day (the day for the adoration of the guru), Sridhar Rao was initiated into the order of Sannyasa and given the name Swami Chidananda (one who is in the highest consciousness of bliss).

In 1959, Swami Chidananda began the first of his numerous extensive tours outside India. Three years were spent in North and South America, interpreting the message of the Divine Life Society. In 1963, upon the death of Swami Sivananda, he was elected president of the Divine Life Society. In spite of his heavy duties as president, Swami Chidananda has continued tours that have taken him to the principal cities of Asia, Europe, South Africa, Australia, North and South America, as well as throughout India. As a result, 137 affiliated branches have been established in India and 27 overseas. The overseas branches also have satellite centers in smaller cities. To disseminate the teachings of Swami Sivananda and Swami Chidananda a score of the branches publish journals in the language of the country in which they are located. Swamis trained at the Sivanandashram have been sent to work in the larger branches. Here they teach the Vedanta, give instruction on yoga, and deliver numerous lectures. Divine Life Conferences are organized annually in many of the branches and centers.

Under the dynamic leadership of Swami Chidananda, Swami Krishnananda, and others, a wide variety of activities are conducted at the Sivanandashram itself. In addition to treating thousands of patients at the General Hospital and the Eye Hospital, the medical staff has assisted the Leprosy Relief Association in Rishikesh. The output of the Ayurvedic Pharmaceutical Works has been greatly expanded as has that of the Press. Ten books were published during 1969 in addition to a number of smaller booklets and leaflets. *The Divine Life,* the monthly magazine in English, and *Yoga-Vedant,* in Hindi, have wide circulation. The ashram's *gosala* ("dairy") provides milk not only for the inmates but for the many sadhus and other holy men who stop at the ashram on their way to the shrines in the high Himalayas. Similarly, the *annapurna annakshetra,* the ashram's kitchen, has provided food for wandering sadhus and the poor of the community. Thus, throughout the ashram the motto of the Society—"Serve, Love, Meditate, Realize"—is practiced in ways too numerous to be described.[20]

10
FOUR "HOLY MOTHERS"

Since time beyond memory India has venerated the Mother Goddess. Archaeologists, during their excavations in the Indus Valley, have found ring stones of a peculiar shape and female figurines that have been identified as pre-Vedic symbols of the Mother Goddess. The Rig-Veda contains a few references to female deities, but it is in the Tantras that the doctrine of the Mother Goddess is most fully developed. The Supreme Deity is presented in the Tantra as one universal spiritual power (*Shakti*) and is called the Divine Mother (*Devi*). For the purpose of creation and of her own free will she divided herself into the dual aspects of male and female. Of these, Siva is the male principle and the supreme cosmic consciousness (*purusha*) and Shakti is the female principle and the supreme primordial energy (*prakriti*). The Divine Mother pervades the whole world, giving birth to all things and manifesting her majesty both as mind and matter. Siva and Shakti are inseparably connected. The Divine Mother, with her two inseparable aspects of Siva and Shakti, is the true Supreme God (Parabrahma).[1]

In ancient times Shakti has been known and venerated by various names such as Ambika, Uma, Durga, and Kali. There is also evidence that she was worshiped in her virgin aspect as the daughter-virgin, Kanya-Kumari. It is as incarnations of Shakti that the Divine Mother is venerated in various parts of India today. I wish to speak of four of these who have attracted large followings: Sarada Devi, Ma Anandamayee, Godavari Mata, and the Mother of the Pondicherry Ashram.

Sarada Devi

Saradamani, who became the consort of Sri Ramakrishna, was born on December 22, 1853, in the village of Jayrambati, in Bengal, of devout Brahmin parents. She had no formal education, but later taught herself to read. Among her playthings were some dolls, but she was more interested in the little clay images of Kali and Lakshmi, before which she placed flowers and Bilva leaves as a form of worship. When only five years of age, as we saw earlier,[2] she was married to Sri Ramakrishna. Early marriage of girls, even to men many years their senior, was sanctioned by Hindu society. It was said that "a wife could become one in mind with her husband, and participate wholeheartedly in his ideals and aspirations, only if she was brought under the influence of his personality at a tender age, before her individuality was formed and hardened in its distinctiveness by the experiences and contacts of premarital life." [3] After her marriage Saradamani returned to her parents' home. When she was fourteen she spent three months in the company of Ramakrishna during his short visit to his home in Kamarpukur. She was greatly impressed by the various evidences of his spirituality and by his gracious attitude toward her. Four years later she began to hear rumors of the strange behavior of her husband at the Kali temple in Dakshineswar. She heard her neighbors whispering that she had been married to a lunatic and decided that her place must be at the side of her husband. Upon her arrival at Dakshineswar she was kindly received by Ramakrishna and her fears were allayed. It was agreed by both that they, though living together as husband and wife, would adopt the life of celibacy.

Sarada's mother, who came to join her daughter, complained that because of this decision Sarada would "never know the happiness of being addressed as 'Mother.'" To this Ramakrishna replied: "You need not worry about that. Your daughter will have so many children that she will become tired of being addressed day and night as 'Mother.'" [4] By the time of her death many years later this prophecy proved amply true! On Phalaharini-Kalki (1873), the day on which Mother Kali is worshiped, Ramakrishna placed Saradamani on the seat usually reserved for the Kali image, and worshiped her as the Divine Mother, pronouncing the *mantra:* "O Goddess, I prostrate myself before Thee again and again—before Thee, the eternal consort of Shiva." [5] By this ceremony Ramakrishna is said to have invoked in Sarada the presence of the Divine Mother, the same Supreme Energy that manifested itself through his own person. Henceforth, it is believed, her body and mind became the channel for the expression of that Energy. The next thirteen years were spent in the spiritual training given her by Ramakrishna.

In 1885, Ramakrishna developed cancer of the throat, and steadily grew worse. On August 15 of the following year, realizing that his end was near, Ramakrishna assured Sarada Devi, as she was now called, that she would be all right and that his young disciples would take care of her as they had of him. He died the next day. After the cremation of his body, Sarada was removing her jewelry, as Hindu widows do, when Ramakrishna appeared to her in a vision, it is said, and told her not to do so, assuring her that he had not gone away but had only passed from one room to another. Confident of his continual presence with her, the Holy Mother, as she was known to her devotees, committed herself to teaching and guiding the young disciples who had been left in her care. Intermittently, she went to Kamarpukur, Ramakrishna's birthplace where, unfortunately, she was shunned by his relatives, and to Jayrambati, where she was imposed upon by her own relatives. Until 1909, she lived in the homes of her devotees, or in rented quarters, but then a building was constructed in Calcutta which served both as her home and residence for the disciples, and as an office for the Ramakrishna movement.

Many months were also spent in visits to pilgrimage places sacred to the Hindus, instructing and initiating disciples, and in her own spiritual activities. While at Bodh Gaya she was impressed with the monastery that had been constructed there. Later she reported: "I went to see the monastery of Bodh Gaya. It was filled with various articles, and the monks did not suffer for want of funds. After seeing this I often wept before the Master (i.e., Ramakrishna) and prayed, 'O Lord, my children (the monastic disciples of Ramakrishna) have no place wherein to lay their heads. They have very little to eat. They trudge from door to door for a morsel of food. May they have a place like this.' Subsequently the Belur Math was established through the grace of the Master." [6] The Holy Mother paid frequent visits to Belur while the monastery was being constructed and counseled with Vivekananda and the other early disciples concerning the development of the Ramakrishna Order and Mission. It is said that she made two important contributions to this development: first, through her life of service she demonstrated the central idea that an aspirant's spiritual potentialities are unfolded by service of Ramakrishna through dedicated work done in his name and for the advancement of his mission on earth, and, second, she bore witness to the fact that the Master is a living presence, for she had visions of and instructions from him in all the critical situations which confronted the movement.[7]

Just as the young disciples had looked upon their Master, Ramakrishna, as an incarnation of the Divine, so they came to regard Sarada Devi as the Holy Mother, the divine power of Shakti in human form. During the Durgapuja they worshiped the Mother in place of the consecrated image. The powers that the Master had created through his austerities were mediated through the Holy Mother. Devotees came to seek her grace both for spiritual development and for the cure of physical ills, bowing at her feet as they presented their various personal problems. Miraculous powers were attributed to her. She could transform the life of those who committed themselves to her—a drunkard was cured of his desire for drink, an immoral woman was transformed, a revengeful wife overcame her desire to harm her husband. The Holy Mother, it was said, appeared to devotees, and even to strangers—among them an atheist—in dreams and visions. On one occasion, when the Durgapuja was taking place during the rainy season, the Holy Mother did *japa* (repeating a divine name) each time before the ceremony and not a drop of rain fell upon the worshipers assembled in an open courtyard. Yet Sarada Devi did not emphasize the miraculous, nor did she encourage her devotees to seek mystic experiences.

Like Ramakrishna himself, Sarada Devi used simple illustrations and familiar stories in instructing her followers. Although her teachings presupposed all the important doctrines of the Vedanta, she never entered into abstract discussion of these doctrines. Rather, in her "Conversations" [8] with her devotees she stressed the importance of the worship of God and gave them instructions in methods of worship. She laid special emphasis upon *japa*, the continuous repetition of the sacred *mantras* that had been given at the time of initiation. And like Ramakrishna, she emphasized the importance of altruistic works. The true spiritual life was not a life of retreat from the world, she said, but a life of active involvement in the normal life of the world. One could worship as he worked, and work itself could be worship.

The Holy Mother entered into *mahasamadhi* on July 20, 1920, at her home in Calcutta, and her body was cremated on the banks of the Ganges at the Math at Belur.[9]

Sri Ma Anandamayee

Of the "holy" personages whom I met personally, two were women. The more influential of these was Sri Ma Anandamayee—"Mother Joyous." One of her followers remarked, "Mother is a very simple, spiritual, and honest lady. She is a happy and joyous person." I found myself in agreement with his description of this very unusual woman, believed by many of her devotees to be an avatara of Shakti, the Creative (Female) Power of the Absolute. Though she is worshiped by many, she does not demand it. During the worship service that I attended she sat quietly with eyes closed, as though unaware of the adoration being shown her. Unlike some others of the God-realized persons of India, she is quite approachable. When I went to see her she was seated on a low platform in a small unpretentious room. She greeted me with a smile and inquired through an interpreter where I had come from. I replied that I had come from America to see her. She said, "You have come to see yourself." (This could be interpreted either that the Divine is present in each of us, or that she, as a divine person, is present in all.) In response to further conversation along this line I observed that each of us wishes to discover his own self—his own identity. To this she replied, "It may take a long time, or it may be instantaneous." She meant that long years of *sādhana* ("spiritual discipline") might be required to attain Self-realization, or through the *kripa* ("grace") of the guru it could occur instantaneously. When I asked her, "What message have you for the people of America?" she replied, in Bengali, "All are one." Then she said, in English, "All one!" Turning with a smile to the interpreter, she asked, "Is that right?" He assured her, " 'All one!' is correct English." She laughed like a happy schoolgirl, and as I left she placed a garland around my neck.

Nirmala Bhattachari was born on April 30, 1896, of devout Brahmin parents in a small village in Bengal. One or two years of very irregular attendance at a poorly equipped lower primary school, the only educational institution available to her, was the only schooling she ever had. Yet her philosophical discourses astonish learned scholars, and maharajas, High Court Judges, professional men, and college professors come to her for spiritual guidance. In accord with Hindu practice she was married at the age of twelve to Srijut Ramani Mohan Chakravarty, who was some years her senior, and went to live with his family. It had been noticed that even as a child Nirmala was often absentminded, little interested in matters that normally concern small girls. This trait developed after marriage into frequent fits of apparent insensibility to external surroundings, sometimes involving the repetition of hymns or *mantras* in a language which those around her did not understand. Still, at other times she appeared quite normal and performed the duties expected of her to the satisfaction of her husband and his family.[10] When these spells became more frequent her young husband concluded that she was no ordinary person and soon "ceased to look upon her as wife proper. Thus in spite of marriage and staying with her husband, she continued a *kanya kumari* ("virgin"), under which living form the followers of *Shakti Tantra* have worshipped the Divine." [11] Bolanath, as her husband was familiarly known, later himself became a brahmachari (a "spiritual bachelor"), and later still a sannyasin (one who has renounced all earthly possession and ties).

But before that, Bolanath had reason to be concerned about his wife's behavior. Various "supernatural phenomena began to manifest in her." While chanting the names of certain deities, she would fall into a trance. At the age of eighteen she left home and went to Bajitpur, a small village in East Bengal, where she stayed for five or six years. Toward the close of this period she was heard to recite strange *mantras* and was seen to assume various yogic postures. But for the last year and a half of her stay she lost her voice entirely, and remained silent for a further period of a year and a half after returning to her husband's home, in 1923. Fearing that she might be possessed of some evil spirit, Bolanath called sadhus ("holy men") and exorcists to see her, but their efforts to restore her to "normalcy" were of no avail. He was forced to conclude that she was indeed more than human.

Nirmala's saintly character began to attract attention as Bolanath's employment as a gardener caused them to move from place to place. Soon many from all walks of life came to listen to her spiritual discourses or to seek her guidance in personal and religious matters. It was one of these followers, Hara Kumar, who first called her Mother. Although he was considered somewhat eccentric by those around him, his action in calling Nirmala "Mother" and

bowing at her feet became an example for others who began to come to her. In 1924, Jyotish Chandra Ray, a government official, became an ardent disciple of Mataji
("Mother"), and it was he who gave her the name "Ma
Anandamayee" ("Mother Joyous").[12] Later, he retired
from government service and, known as Bhaiji ("Elder
Brother"), became one of Ma Anandamayee's most devoted followers.

In 1932, Ma Anandamayee, Bolanath—now known as
Pitaji ("Father")—and Bhaiji left Bengal and established
an ashram in Dehra Dun, in the foothills of the Himalayas.
Sometime later a second ashram, which has become the
center of the cult, was established in the holy city of
Varanasi. Since then ashrams have been established in
honor of Ma Anandamayee from the east coast to the west,
and from the Himalayas in the north to the Vindhyas in the
south. Sixteen centers, in addition to the headquarters at
Bhadaini, Varanasi, carry on activities in her name. A well-
equipped hospital, high schools for boys and girls, an
orphanage, a charitable dispensary, and a milk distribution
center are among the institutions under her guidance.[13] Ma
Anandamayee travels constantly between these various
centers, although she is well into her seventies, meeting her
devotees and instructing them in the faith. Although she
has never left the shores of India, she also has followers
scattered throughout the world. In a commemorative volume, *Mother as Seen by Her Devotees*, there are chapters
by American, British, German, and French devotees,
among others.

Many efforts have been made to identify or describe Ma
Anandamayee[14] but with little success. A statement by
Ethel Merston well illustrates this:

It is impossible to describe her with a subjective mind—to
each one she means something different according to how

our limited ego-minds allow us to glimpse the whole that is such an ego-less Being. To some she is Love personified, to others God Himself, All-powerful, to yet others she is Wisdom, All-knowledge. In the stories told of her, some see divine miracles and they worship her, praying that she may exercise her powers on their behalf; others, again, are attracted by the radiance of her smile and the rippling, infectious laugh, free as a child's.[15]

I myself would fall within the last of these groups; I must confess that I have rarely met a more winsome personality than Ma Anandamayee!

My contact with Ma Anandamayee, which I have mentioned earlier, was at her center in Dehra Dun, in the Himalayan foothills. A kind of camp meeting or "Week of Self-Denial" was in progress. Hundreds of devotees had gathered and were living in tents surrounding a large tent. The day opened with a prayer service at 5:30 in the morning and closed with a fellowship hour at 9:30 at night. Between these hours there were lectures by learned pundits and a message by Ma Anandamayee, a period of silent meditation (or worship) before Ma Anandamayee, and a midday meal, the only meal of the day. On the first and last days this consisted of only water from the holy Ganges River and on the other days of rice with a few vegetables, except the fourth day when the menu consisted of fruit and milk. The purpose of this regimen was said to be to attain growth in one's spiritual life through disciplining one's mind, senses, and instincts through fasting and meditation. In spite of the rigors and seriousness of the occasion, the devotees seemed happy and cheerful, having perhaps caught the spirit of Mother Joyous.

Ma Anandamayee's teachings are deceptively simple. An examination of her teachings in such works as *Words of Sri Anandamayi*,[16] *Matri Vani*,[17] *Ananda Varta* ("Joyous

Words")—the quarterly magazine of the ashram—and the commemorative volume to which reference has been made will show that she is able to put the abstract concepts of Vedanta, with which she is apparently quite familiar, into the simple language of the common man. Her teaching is generally spontaneous: a question by a devotee concerning some spiritual or personal matter is answered by a telling illustration or story. One is reminded of the teaching method used by Jesus of Nazareth.

Sri Godavari Mataji

"You will soon assume the responsibility of looking after everything here. All this belongs to you." With these words, addressed to a small girl only ten years of age, Upasani Baba Maharaj foretold the strange career of one who came to be known as Her Holiness Sati Godavari Mataji. Possibly this prophecy of Upasani Baba did not greatly surprise the child's father, Vasudevrao, for had not even her miraculous birth been foretold? Godavari's paternal grandfather, Sri Bhaskarrao, became a staunch devotee of Gajanana Maharaj, a great saint living in their native village, Shegaon, in Berar province. Once when Sri Bhaskarrao was greatly dejected because he had only one living child, the Maharaj is said to have told him: "Do not worry; you still have one son and through him I shall give you the rarest of gifts. I shall take birth in your family again and lead hundreds of pure souls like you to the portals of liberation." [18] Godavari was born in 1914. When she was still quite young her mother had a vision in which a luminous figure, presumably a goddess, entered the room, then bent down over Godavari and whispered something in her ear. Serious by nature, Godavari as a child had little interest in her usual toys but made, instead, images of the gods and then worshiped them. She never attended school, but a very retentive memory enabled her to acquire a large store of Hindu religious lore.

In 1924, Godavari's father, who had heard much about Upasani Baba, sent his wife and daughter to the ashram in Sakuri. It was at this time that Upasani Baba made the declaration about her future. For some reason that is not clear, Godavari's mother left her at the ashram. Possibly this was in order that the Maharaj could direct her spiritual discipline. Again, for some reason that has not been recorded, Upasani Baba had her married, though barely ten years of age, to a young man, Vishnupant Chandorkar. But Godavari did not live with him, even for a day, for he left immediately to complete his studies in Bombay, and she was left in the ashram. Four years later, her husband appeared unexpectedly and declared that he wished to dedicate his wife to Upasani Baba so that she could continue her spiritual discipline and lead an ascetic life. Upasani Baba objected to this at first, but then indicated that after Godavari had been dedicated to the god Siva, her marriage to her husband thus being annulled, she might be dedicated to him. Vishnupant followed these instructions, prostrated himself at the feet of Godavari as Mother, and left the ashram. Godavari, for her part, dedicated herself to the service of her guru, Upasani Baba, and made rapid progress in her spiritual discipline under his guidance.

In July, 1928, a significant incident occurred. On Gurupoornima, the day on which special honor is paid to one's guru, Upasani Baba removed from his own neck a rosary that had belonged originally to Sai Baba and put it around Godavari's neck. This act signified her spiritual status as the Holy Mother. Upasani Baba now worshiped her with appropriate rites and ordered the devotees to perform an *arati* in her honor. To devotees who wished to prostrate themselves before him he said: "Do not bow to me. Bow to her, for she is the supreme Shakti. Her very *darshana* (the vision of her) will wash away hundreds of sins." [19] Gradually, Upasani Baba delegated to Godavari Mataji more and more of the responsibility for the management of the ashram and permitted her to make a number of progressive changes in its routine. When Upasani Baba died in 1941 the devotees understood that "Baba's immortal essence had been absorbed by the Mother and that his mantle as Guru had fallen upon her." [20]

During the years a number of other kanyas ("virgins") had also been dedicated to Upasani Baba, and Godavari Mataji had assumed the responsibility of training them. It was now her duty to guide them, and others who have since joined the Kanya Kumari Sthan ("Ashram for Virgin Maidens"), in their spiritual discipline. An essential part of this is *nama japa* (repetition of a divine name). The divine name to be repeated or *mantras* given to the *sadhaka* ("disciple") at the time of initiation are thought to have great potency. Mataji teaches that of all instruments of purification, the use of *japa* is most efficacious. Constant repetition of the Divine Name stills the mind and makes it aware of a hidden Light. Thereafter, deep meditation becomes possible. Along with guidance in their private *sādhanas* the kanyas are taught to recite the Hindu scriptures in their original Sanskrit. When this is done in unison by a number of the kanyas, with appropriate gestures, it is most impressive. Nowhere else in all India did I witness such a service.

The devotees of Godavari Mata record a number of incidents in their lives which they attribute to her miraculous intervention. Sometimes, by mere sight and touch, it is said, her devotees are healed of physical and moral difficulties. Many have discovered that her prophetic word has come to pass. A devotee of the Mother had to deceive her family, who were loyal to another guru, whenever she came to see Godavari Mata. She was skeptical when she was told, "Maybe these prejudices will disappear from your family in a short time, and then you will be in no need of such subterfuges," but shortly after, the family not only abandoned their opposition but themselves became devotees of the Mother.[21] A young disciple, to whom Godavari Mata had promised an autographed photo of herself, went swimming in the Ganges. He was caught in a whirlpool and carried under by the strong current. Watchers on the banks were powerless to save him. His death was reported to Mataji, who replied: "He has not been drowned. He will come back. He *must* come back . . . , for I have promised to give him my photograph." Shortly after, he *did* come back. Miraculously, a log had floated near him and, clinging to it, he had been saved.[22] Another devotee was cured of a severe heart attack at midnight when she crawled out of bed and prostrated herself at the altar that she had dedicated to Godavari Mata. Geeta Tai, a young devotee, had been bedridden for many years, paralyzed from her waist down. But a radical transformation has taken place in her physical condition. She is now able to sit up, stand, and walk a few steps. Shamrao and I saw her with Godavari Mata during our visit to the ashram. Both the doctor who has been attending her and Geeta Tai "attribute the healing to the Divine Miracle which is inherent in Mother's spirituality." Dr. Hanumantharao, a physician at the ashram, who has been treating her homeopathically, and with whom we talked, believes that through medical treatment alone this remarkable recovery could not have taken place. Less spectacular, but no less impressive, are the transformations reported in the moral character of her devotees. During our visit to the Sthan we were able to talk with a number of devotees who reported the

changes wrought in their lives through the grace of Godavari Mata. One of these, a wealthy retired cement manu-
facturer whom we met on the train, has erected a cottage
at the ashram so that he can spend periods of meditation in
the presence of the Mother. He told of the influence that
she had had not only upon his personal life, but also upon
his business practices.

Even those who are not devotees must be impressed with
Godavari Mata's quiet influence as they come into her presence. It was our privilege to spend a few moments with
her during our visit to the Kanya Kumari Sthan. In contrast
to the other saints whom we met personally, she appears
somewhat shy and retiring. Yet there is a certain dignity
and poise that indicate inner strength and confidence.
As she talked with us, through an interpreter, there was that
"sweetness and light" which has been attributed to her by
others. Her "motherly" concern was demonstrated in her
inquiry about my experiences in India and in her gracious
invitation to lunch and hospitality should we find it possible to stay longer in the ashram. Apparently she guides the
lives of her devotees with a firm, but loving, hand.

Unlike Sathya Sai Baba, Meher Baba, and others, Godavari Mata has written no books, nor does she engage in
deeply philosophical discourses. She does not go into
trances, nor does she conduct herself with any eccentrici-
ties of speech or manner. She does not advocate withdrawal from the world. Life, she teaches, should be joyous
and meaningful. Action and service in the world are the
normal expressions of one's spirituality. The guidance
given by Krishna to Arjuna in the Bhagavad-Gita is to be
followed. Yet, there must be periods of retirement from
active life for spiritual renewal. When I asked Dr. Tipnis,
our guide, what contribution the Kanya Kumari Sthan was
making to the social welfare of India, he replied that

through providing a quiet retreat in the presence of the Mother, busy, often frustrated and harassed businessmen are prepared to make a significant spiritual contribution to the life of the nation. The Mother, he declared, is well aware of the problems of our technological age, and she advocates the use of science for the improvement of men's physical conditions. But she feels that men generally "act like bears (she said this in reference to the death of President Kennedy, which she felt very much)" and she urges that men "become men, not beasts." She believes that it is her mission to help bring this about.

Although visitors to the Kanya Kumari Sthan, devotees and others, are apparently free to worship as they please, the devotional life of the inmates is carefully regulated. The Sthan employs ritual as a vital part of its spiritual discipline. All the kanyas are carefully instructed in the intricacies of the various ceremonies that are performed in strict adherence to the *shastraic* mandates. Among the many rituals observed by the Sthan, the *arati*, the *yajña*, and the initiation of the kanyas appear to be the outstanding ones. We were privileged to observe the first two of these. At the Sthan the *arati* is performed four times a day. It consists of the chanting, by the kanyas, of hymns of adoration of Upasani Baba and Godavari Mata, accompanied by the swinging of lights in front of the image and the Mother. Godavari Mata is seated beside the cage in which Upasani Baba enclosed himself, and in which his image now rests.

The *yajña* is an elaborate form of a Vedic sacrifice that was performed to ward off danger by propitiating the deities. Oblations are offered to the sacred fire of Agni, who conveys them to the Lord. The *yajña* creates a climate for Divine visitation, and devotees report visions of deities emerging from the flames to receive the offerings. At the

Kanya Kumari Sthan the *yajña* is performed in the Yajna Mandir ("Temple of Sacrifice"), which is an area some dozen feet below the level of the rest of the ashram. It is covered by a separate roof and is enclosed by a grating through which spectators may view the proceedings. In the center of the *mandir* is a fire pit into which a kanya drops spoonfuls of *ghī* ("clarified butter") while reciting in a low tone.

At the opposite end of the *mandir* from where we stood, there was an altar supporting a picture of the goddess Durga, of whom, for some, Godavari Mata is an incarnation. The rest of the kanyas stood around the walls of the *mandir*, facing the altar. After a considerable quantity of *ghī* had been offered, a tray of oil lamps was brought forward by a tall, fair kanya, and the lights were gracefully waved in front of the altar while the kanyas chanted hymns to the accompaniment of clanging cymbals. The lamps were then carried around the circle and each kanya passed her hands over the flames and then touched her forehead and breast. Next, flowers were distributed to the kanyas, who passed single file before the altar and dropped flower petals on it. The kanyas encircled the fire pit and passed in front of the altar three times, and then ascended from the Yajna Mandir to pass the flames around among the devotees standing outside the *mandir*. Led by the kanyas, all the devotees walked in procession around the ashram, passing in front of the Temple of Kanya Kumari and other shrines in the ashram compound.

The initiation ceremony, in which young novitiates who have proved their worth are finally admitted by Godavari Mata into mature kanyahood, lasts, we were told, for three strenuous days. An imposing ritual, created by Upasani Baba, is used. On the last day the girls are dedicated by their parents and accepted by the Mother. The young virgin-brides are thus symbolically married to the Lord, incarnate in their spiritual preceptor, Godavari Mata. They were now committed completely to the service of God and mankind.

As we went to take leave of Godavari Mata we found her seated in the hut in which her own guru, Upasani Baba Maharaj, had passed his last years and where he had died. She responded to our expressions of appreciation with a smile and a nod of her head—a gracious benediction.

The Mother of Pondicherry

Is it possible that a Frenchwoman in European dress could be the incarnation of the Supreme Being, whom the Hindus know as Brahman? Is it possible for the Divine Mother to take a European body? These questions greatly troubled the devotees of Sri Aurobindo. One of them, who calls himself Pasupati, stated his doubts to Sri Aurobindo, who replied: "To recognize the Divine Mother at once by looking at her other form is not possible for you just at present. You have now to start with a will to believe, to appreciate that when Sri Aurobindo firmly declares her as the Divine Mother it must be so; his own words are proof enough." To another doubter he wrote: "Mother has taken the body because a work of a physical nature (i.e., a change in the physical world) has to be done." [23]

Mira Richard, the Mother, was born in Paris on February 21, 1878, of an affluent family. Her interest in spiritual matters began early, for even at the age of four she began the discipline of meditation. Later, when about twelve, she felt that she could communicate with the trees and small animals which she found in the forest of Fontainebleau, near Paris, where she would go for solitary walks and meditation. Thus, from early childhood little Mira felt that she was different from others. She believed that she was surrounded by a vast consciousness-force and that a bright, mysterious Light hung over her head. When she was about thirteen, for a whole year, as she lay in her bed at night, it seemed to her that she came out of her body and rose above the house and the town. She saw herself clad in a magnificent golden robe, which, as she rose, spread in a wide circle around her, covering the whole town. Men, women, and children gathered from all sides under the spreading robe, imploring for help in their suffering and sorrows. As they touched the robe they were healed. Often, beside her, she saw the image of a benevolent old man who encouraged her. Later, she realized that this was the personification of him who is called "the man of sorrows." [24]

In her early twenties Mira went to Algeria to study occultism from a famous occultist, Monsieur Theon. One day, she awoke from deep meditation to see a large cobra, with expanded hood, immediately in front of her. Using her will-force to the utmost, she calmed the snake and escaped unharmed. During her return to France a striking incident occurred. A violent storm arose and the passengers and crew became greatly concerned. Mira recounts:

> Theon looked at me and said, "Go and stop it." The captain was astonished; he did not understand what it meant, but I understood. I went to my cabin, lay down there, and leaving my body went freely to the open sea. There I found innumerable formless beings were madly jumping about and creating havoc over the waters. I approached them and very humbly and sweetly appealed to them to stop this mischief, saying, "What can you gain by torturing these poor people? Please calm down and save their lives." I went on remonstrating and appealing to them for half an hour, after which they refrained from their activities. The troubled sea became calm. I then went back to my body

and came out of my cabin. When I went on deck I found all people gathered there happily engaged in jovial talks.[25]

Very little is known about her life from this time until her arrival in Pondicherry in 1914, except through incidental references in her diary. The first entry in this spiritual diary is for November 2, 1912, and the last was made on November 24, 1931. Those who read the *Prayers and Meditations of the Mother* are reminded somewhat of the *Confessions* of Augustine. In her first entry she wrote:

Although my whole being is in theory consecrated to Thee, O sublime Master, who art the life, the light and the love in all things, I still find it hard to carry out this consecration in detail. . . . I shall make my confession to Thee as well as it may be, not because I can tell Thee anything— for Thou art Thyself everything. . . . How many times a day, still, I act without my action being consecrated to Thee! I at once become aware of it by an indefinable uneasiness which is translated in the sensibility of my body by a pang in my heart.[26]

Mira was married to Paul Richard. They had one daughter. From time to time, in her dreams, she had seen the form of one whom she recognized as her true guru. So, in March, 1914, she set out with her husband for India, where she hoped to find this guru. They were led to Pondicherry. Upon meeting Sri Aurobindo, she recognized him as the guru of her visions, accepted him as her guru, and placed herself under his spiritual guidance. With the help of the Richards, Sri Aurobindo inaugurated the publication of the quarterly journals, *Arya* in English and *Revue de Grande Synthèse* in French. Unfortunately, the First World War broke out at this time and the Richards had to return to France. Later, they went to Japan together, but not long after this their marriage was dissolved. Now followed a period of poverty and depression for Mira. Yet the entries in her diary reveal her deep awareness of the presence of the Divine in all her vicissitudes and of her utmost trust and faith in God. The close of the war made it possible for her to return to India, and in April, 1920, she was back in Pondicherry to remain permanently. Sri Aurobindo received her as the Divine Mother.

In his work *The Mother*, Sri Aurobindo considers at length the person and mission of the Mother. He and she are one, the Divine and the Shakti. The Divine and the Shakti, God and the Mother, Existence and Consciousness-Force, Narayana and Lakshmi, Purusha and Prakriti, Ihsvara and Ishvari—these pairs denote the same identity in difference. The Divine Mother is truly "the divine Consciousness-Force that dominates all existence, one and yet so many-sided that to follow her movement is impossible even for the quickest mind and for the freest and most vast intelligence." [27] There are four Shaktis (powers and personalities) of the Mother. Sri Aurobindo names these Maheshwari, Mahakali, Mahalakshmi, and Mahasaraswati. In the words of Sri Aurobindo:

Four great Aspects of the Mother, four of her leading Powers and Personalities have stood in front in her guidance of this Universe and in her dealings with the terrestrial play. One is her personality of calm wideness and comprehending wisdom and tranquil benignity and inexhaustible compassion and sovereign and surpassing majesty and all-ruling greatness. Another embodies her power of splendid strength and irresistible passion, her warrior mood, her overwhelming will, her impetuous swiftness and world-shaking force. A third is vivid and sweet and wonderful with her deep secret of beauty and harmony and fine rhythm. Fourth is intimate knowledge and careful and flawless work and quiet and exact perfection in all things.[28]

In another work, *Sri Aurobindo on Himself and the Mother*, we find recorded more than three hundred pages of questions about the Mother put to Sri Aurobindo by devotees and his answers. These deal with the divinity of the Mother, her powers and personalities, the reality and significance of bright lights that are at times seen to surround her person, and of visions of her that have been seen by her devotees, the necessity of complete surrender of oneself to her if one would receive her grace and her spiritual guidance, the various ways in which the "Mother's Force" has been manifested in the universe and in the lives of her devotees, the possibility of being aware of the Mother's presence though one may be far distant from her, the power of the Mother through her Consciousness-Force to lift one into higher realms of consciousness, and the necessity of worshiping the Mother by members of the ashram.[29]

The devotees of the Mother believe that it is possible for them to communicate mentally their needs, spiritual or physical, to her, that wherever they may be, near or far away, she is aware of their need, and that through her Consciousness-Force she sends the help needed. The Mother substantiates this belief:

My consciousness can be felt in the material vital, then on the mental plane, everywhere. . . . Each time there comes a call, each time there is a need for me to know so that I may send out a force, an inspiration, protection or any other thing, a sort of message comes to me all of a sudden and I do the needful. . . . With those whom I have accepted as disciples, to whom I have said "yes," there . . . is an emanation of me. This emanation warns me whenever it is necessary and tells me what is happening. Indeed, I receive intimations constantly but all are not recorded in my active memory. I would be flooded; the physical consciousness acts like a filter.[30]

One of the ashram inmates with whom I talked assured me that the Mother not only is aware of events in the lives of her devotees but is supernaturally aware of events taking place around the world, and that through her Consciousness-Force she is directing world forces toward the goals that she and Sri Aurobindo have for mankind.

When the Mother came to Pondicherry in 1920 the ashram was very small, but under her guidance it has grown into a large and impressive institution. Sri Aurobindo was then living in a house that constituted the entire ashram. The Mother was given a room on the upper floor. Sri Aurobindo's four or five disciples lived in other parts of the house. The ashram today is a practically self-sufficient community within the old town of Pondicherry. There are some fifteen hundred inmates living in about two hundred buildings in a 25-acre area owned by the ashram. Some seven hundred workers, not members of the ashram, come from outside for employment in the various ashram enterprises. These enterprises are called services. Each has its own director who is immediately responsible to the Mother for the operation of his department. The inmates of the ashram, in addition to their spiritual disciplines (*sādhanas*), are each engaged in one of these departments. Life in the ashram is communal. There is a common dining hall in which all take their meals. All personal needs, clothing, even soap and toothpaste, are provided from a community store, called Prosperity. Until recent years the Mother herself personally distributed with her blessing the articles required.

I found the ashram a veritable beehive of activity. All materials for constructing, furnishing, and maintaining the various buildings are manufactured in the numerous shops of the ashram. The needs of the dining hall are supplied from the bakery, flour mill, oil mill, dairy, poultry yards, and fields operated by the several departments. Cloth is made and clothing is prepared in the Weaving Service and Cottage Industries. Extensive workshops maintain the autos, trucks, and machinery of the ashram. The Ashram Press turns out a flood of books, a magazine, *Mother India,* and other literature. A library and hospital provide their services to the community. The extensive activity of the ashram at Pondicherry is in marked contrast to the quiet of the simple life at the Kanya Kumari Sthan at Sakuri. Apparently the Mother has attempted, with a large measure of success, to yoke Western materialism with Eastern spirituality. In her own words: "To work for the Divine is to pray with the body." [31]

Two concerns that have been dear to the heart of the Mother are education and physical exercise. The center of education inaugurated by the Mother in 1951, under the name of "The Sri Aurobindo International University Centre," had a small beginning during the lifetime of Sri Aurobindo. Shortly after her arrival in Pondicherry the Mother organized a small school in which she herself taught French. Teachers were selected from among the members of the ashram. In later years teachers from overseas as well as from India have been added to the faculties, making the institution truly international. Education, according to the Mother, should touch all aspects of life: physical, vital, mental, psychic, and spiritual. Physical culture is necessary and beneficial for all ages, and the formation of regular habits of exercise is an essential part of education. Until she reached an advanced age the Mother herself was a tennis enthusiast. The training of the vital is more difficult. The control of responses to the senses and the direction of inner urges through self-analysis and the correction of all defects is essential. Education should be exciting and challenging, not dull and burdensome. The student's imagination, inquisitiveness, and creativity should be stimulated through interesting, practical exercises. Along with one's growth in secular knowledge there must be development in spiritual knowledge. The ultimate purpose of education is to know God. Psychic training is essential for the progressive transformation of personality. Through this the ego-sense will vanish and one will enter into the infinite superconsciousness. In the future there will be a further dimension, the supramental training. "Its work will begin from above downwards, passing through different strata of being, reaching down to the physical, culminating in a divine body. That will be the superman, precursor of a new race on earth." [32]

Near the center of the ashram is the playing field. It is an enclosed area about the size of a football field. Here the Mother has encouraged participation in various types of games and physical exercises, some Indian, some Western. Until recent years, she herself spent much time at the playing field. In a very interesting way physical exercises and spiritual exercises have been combined here. In all the ashram there is no temple or place of formal worship. The only gathering of a religious nature takes place on the playing field on Thursday and Sunday evenings. Preceding the "meditations" there are drills by various athletic groups, the last consisting of older men. At 7:45 P.M. this group is brought to attention facing a wall on which is painted the map of southern Asia in green, with the symbol of Sri Aurobindo in its center. Others who come for the meditations also stand facing the wall. Formerly, the Mother took her place in front of the wall and stood facing the assembly in silence for five minutes. On the occasion of my visit only her chair marked the place of her presence. After the five-minute period of silence, mats were spread and all sat on the ground. All lights were extinguished except one illuminating the map. On certain occasions, even after her retirement, the Mother speaks to the assembled company over a public-address system from a microphone in her room, but on this night only a recorded message and a hymn were broadcast. Complete silence followed for a period after which the lights went on again. Athletes and drill teams then took up their activities once more on the playing field-cum-sanctuary!

As impressive as has been the development of the Sri Aurobindo Ashram under the guidance of the Mother, even more ambitious is the plan for Auroville ("The City of the Dawn"). "Auroville has its origin in a dream of the Mother in which she said: 'There should be somewhere upon the earth a place that no nation could claim as its sole property, a place where all human beings of good will, sincere in their aspiration, could live freely as citizens of the world.' " [33] The site chosen for the new city, about ten miles from Pondicherry, is a place of beauty, with three lakes on one side and the sea on another. The basic pattern of the township is circular. There will be four zones: residential, industrial, cultural, and international. In the center of Auroville will be the Matrimandir ("The Temple of the Mother"). The residential zone will consist of houses of various architectural designs, set amid parks, flowing fountains, and flower gardens. The homes will be grouped in settlements with picturesque names such as Peace, Repose, Promise, Hope, Aspiration. Nine settlements have already been opened. In the industrial zone, Auroville Foods, a large flour mill, has already gone into production, as has Auto-Electronics, for producing electronic equipment. A printing press is also in operation. Licenses have been granted, or plans approved, for such industries as woodworking, carpets, leather manufacturing, paints, cement, ceramics, and textiles. The main features of the cultural zone will be the World University, a museum, an Institute of Film Technology and Production, a World Communications Center, an auditorium, and a sports stadium. The international zone will house permanent pavilions of various countries and Indian States.

At the inauguration ceremony on February 28, 1968, the Mother announced the Charter of Auroville:

> Auroville belongs to nobody in particular. Auroville belongs to humanity as a whole. But to live in Auroville one must be willing to serve the perfect Consciousness. Auroville will be the place of unending education, of constant progress, and a youth that never ages. Auroville wants to be the bridge between the past and the future. Taking advantage of all discoveries from without and from within, Auroville will boldly spring toward future realisations. Auroville will be the site of a material and spiritual research for a living embodiment of an actual human unity.[34]

In November, 1966, the General Assembly of UNESCO gave its unanimous approval to the plan for Auroville in a resolution which stated in part: "Appreciating that one of the aims of 'Auroville' will be to bring together in close juxtaposition the values and ideals of different civilizations and cultures, [the General Conference] expresses the belief that the project will contribute to international understanding and promotion of peace and commends it to those interested in UNESCO's ideals." [35] Led by Japan, a number of countries have already indicated their intention of participating in the project.

Whether the Mother will live to see the fulfillment of her dream in Auroville is uncertain, but what is certain is the fact that when Auroville does come into being as a living reality it will bear the indelible marks of a most remarkable personality.

11

CHELAS:
American Disciples
of the Masters

The personality cults of contemporary Hinduism that have been described in preceding chapters have their devotees in America as well. Five of them have centers or branches in this country and four have devotees who, as yet, have formed no such organizations. It is the purpose of this chapter to investigate briefly the history of these cults in the United States and the activities of their members.

The Vedanta Societies

The first of the cults that we have described to establish branches in the United States was the Ramakrishna Order. In 1893 a Parliament of Religions was held at the World's Columbian Exposition in Chicago. Friends in India raised the money to pay for the passage of Swami Vivekananda, one of the young disciples of Sri Ramakrishna. He arrived too early, his money ran out, and he lost the address of his hosts in Chicago. It was at this moment that he was rescued by a well-to-do woman who gained him admission to the Parliament. When his turn to speak came he captivated his audience as he described the life and teachings of his Master, Sri Ramakrishna.

The newspapers gave his message wide publicity and invitations to lecture came to him from all over the country. He decided to stay in the United States for some time longer. He proved to be a brilliant speaker and large audiences heard him expound the Vedanta philosophy. He toured extensively, lecturing and holding private classes. In 1894 he decided to make New York his headquarters, and there he founded the first Vedanta Society. He returned to India in 1897 and participated in the founding of the Ramakrishna Mission and in the establishment of centers of the Order and Mission in various parts of India. He was back in America in 1899. The following year was spent chiefly in the development of small groups and the training of devotees in the major cities of the North. To carry on the work of the Vedanta Society in New York another direct disciple of Sri Ramakrishna was called from India, and from that time onward the Ramakrishna Order has sent an increasing number of monks to America as teachers. Each of these has come to this country upon the invitation of some group of Americans, who wished to learn more about the Vedanta philosophy. They are guest-teachers, it is said, and not missionaries. Although the Vedanta Societies of America are under the spiritual guidance of the Ramakrishna Order, whose headquarters are at Belur, Calcutta, each center is an independent, self-supporting unit. Nearly all of them have their own boards of trustees, made up of American citizens.[1]

A descriptive brochure gives the following information:

Public lectures and classes, and interviews for private instruction, form the general activities of the Vedanta Societies. The times and numbers of lectures and classes vary in each center, but most centers have a public lecture on Sundays. Through the lectures, the public is acquainted with the principles of the Vedanta philosophy and their application to everyday life. Those who wish to practice meditation are invited to take individual instruction from the swami in charge.

The classes are held for the study of the religious literature of India, including the Upanishads, the Bhagavad-Gita, the writings of Shankara, and Patanjali's yoga aphorisms. In some of these centers, there are resident students, living under the supervision of the swami, who trains them in the practice of meditation, worship, and service; two centers have monasteries attached to them, and one has a convent. All of the swamis in charge of the centers are ordained monks of the Ramakrishna Order.[2]

In January, 1938, a magazine was started under the auspices of Swami Ashokananda of the San Francisco Center and Swami Prabhavananda of the Los Angeles Center. For the first three years it was called *The Voice of India;* it then became *Vedanta and the West.* It has appeared bimonthly since that time, published by the Vedanta Press in Hollywood, California. The gifted editor is Swami Prabhavananda.

The Vedanta Society of California, organized by Swami Prabhavananda in 1930, has attracted the support of quite a number of distinguished writers whose pens have further spread the teachings of Vedanta. Among these have been Aldous Huxley, Gerald Heard, Gerald Sykes, John Van Druten, and Christopher Isherwood. John Yale edited *What Vedanta Means to Me,* a symposium by sixteen writers. Christopher Isherwood has written *An Approach to Vedanta* and *Ramakrishna and His Disciples,* and has edited *Vedanta for the Western World* and *Vedanta for Modern Man.*[3]

In the East, three Swamis of the Ramakrishna Order have set forth the Vedanta philosophy through their works: Swami Akhilananda in *Hindu Psychology: Its Meaning for the West, The Hindu View of Christ,* and *Mental Health and Hindu Psychology;* Swami Nikhilananda in *Hinduism: Its Meaning for the Liberation of the Spirit,* and as editor and translator, *Ramakrishna: Prophet of New India* and *The Upanishads;* and Swami Yatiswarananda in *Adventure in Vedanta.* All three of them are very able exponents of the teachings of the Ramakrishna Order.[4]

In 1969 the activities of the Vedanta Societies were carried on in eleven Vedanta Centers, scattered from San Francisco to Boston, in two monasteries and two convents under the direction of twenty ordained monks of the Ramakrishna Order.[5] The Vivekananda Vedanta Society of Chicago, a branch of the Ramakrishna Math and Mission, has recently undertaken the project of developing a monastery and retreat center in honor of Swami Vivekananda on an 81-acre tract of land in Ganges Town City in Michigan. This monastery and retreat center will, it is said, provide a beautiful and serene spot to which both Americans and Indians may go for relaxation, reflection, and contemplation. In addition to the monastery and retreat center, there will be fifty self-contained units for devotees who wish to seek the contemplative life. The Vivekananda Monastery and Retreat will be open to everyone, regardless of creed or religion, who seeks to further spiritual and cultural values. It is estimated that the entire project will cost $500,000.[6]

The Sri Aurobindo Societies

I have been unable to discover by whom, or when, the teachings of Sri Aurobindo were first introduced into America. It must have been fairly early in this century.

In the late 1920's Margaret Wilson, daughter of President Wilson, found a copy of *Essays on the Gita* in the Public Library in New York City. She is said to have heard of Sri Aurobindo at a meeting at which Dhangopal Mukherjee was present.[7] Also, in the late 1920's an American couple, the Macpheeters, spent some time at the ashram in Pondicherry.[8] Some years later Dr. Jay Holmes Smith read *Among the Great* and *The Synthesis of Yoga* in the New York Public Library and was so impressed with the teaching of Sri Aurobindo that, with his wife, he went to India and became a member of the Sri Aurobindo Ashram.

Among the first to give systematic lectures in the United States on the teachings of Sri Aurobindo, it appears, were Dr. Frederic Spiegelberg, Dr. Judith Tyberg, and Dr. Haridas Chaudhuri. Dr. Spiegelberg became deeply impressed with the philosophy of Sri Aurobindo through reading *The Life Divine*, in 1947, and had a personal interview with him in Pondicherry in 1949. Through his efforts, courses on Sri Aurobindo were introduced into the Department of Asian Studies at Stanford University. When the American Academy of Asian Studies, in San Francisco, wished to have a disciple of Sri Aurobindo for its Chair of Indian Philosophy, Dr. Spiegelberg invited Dr. Haridas Chaudhuri to fill the post. Dr. Chaudhuri was among the earliest to receive a doctorate on Sri Aurobindo's philosophy from the University of Calcutta.[9] In June, 1951, the Cultural Integration Fellowship was founded in San Francisco by Dr. Chaudhuri in "accordance with Sri Aurobindo's vision of East-West cultural integration as the basis of human unity and the consummation of human evolution in Life Divine on earth."[10] It was incorporated as a nonprofit cultural, religious, and educational organization, and in

1956 obtained tax-exempt status both from the Federal Government and the State of California. The California Institute of Asian Studies was founded in San Francisco in 1968, also by Dr. Chaudhuri, as an outgrowth of the Cultural Integration Fellowship. It is a graduate school conferring the M.A. and Ph.D. degrees for students doing original research in Asian culture or in comparative studies East and West. In both of these institutions, lectures on the life and work of Sri Aurobindo find a large place.

Dr. Judith Tyberg went to India in 1947 on a scholarship for research as a Sanskrit Scholar at the Varanasi Hindu University. She was searching for the inner spiritual meaning of the Vedas, the basis of India's wisdom. There she became acquainted with Sri Aurobindo's *Hymns to the Mystic Fire,* and determined to seek permission to visit the ashram in Pondicherry. From her first meeting with the Mother she was deeply impressed. She had the opportunity of seeing Sri Aurobindo first in November of 1947 and for the last time in 1950. Upon her return to America she began lecturing on Sri Aurobindo among educational and religious groups, and founded The East-West Cultural Center in 1953. The Center grew, and in 1963 it moved to its present headquarters in Los Angeles. It has now become an important center for disseminating the teachings of Sri Aurobindo and the Mother.[11]

Centers of the Sri Aurobindo Society have been established in a number of the larger cities of the United States. In 1953 the Mother permitted Mrs. Moore Montgomery to found, and become the president of, The Sri Aurobindo International Center Foundation in New York. Here a large amount of memorabilia and other information about Sri Aurobindo has been gathered. Mrs. Nick

Duncan's Crescent Moon Ranch with its spiritual activities received the Mother's blessing in 1966, and became the Sri Aurobindo Center in Sedona, Arizona. Mrs. Ida Patterson was made the director of the Sri Aurobindo Society in Minneapolis. A society has also been established in the Southeast, at Memphis, Tennessee. In 1962 a young American artist, Sam Spanier, had an interview with the Mother. She requested him to become a link between the East and the West. A center was established at Matagiri ("the Mother's Mountain") at Mount Tremper, New York. Although there is at present no press in the United States that publishes books by or about Sri Aurobindo exclusively, Matagiri, which distributes the works published in Pondicherry, plans to establish such a press. No doubt there are Sri Aurobindo Societies of which I have no information in other American cities as well.

The development of Auroville, the "Universal City" near Pondicherry, has furthered interest in the teachings and work of Sri Aurobindo and the Mother. A group known as Friends of Auroville in America has been formed to implement the Resolutions on Auroville adopted by UNESCO inviting the assistance of all the member states in the development of Auroville. Mrs. Seyril Schochen Rubin has been especially designated by the Mother, along with Mrs. Patterson, to present Auroville to the American public.

A variety of activities are carried on at the East-West Cultural Center in Los Angeles, whose purposes are said to be:

> To teach and help integrate the cultural and spiritual values of East and West in order to create a greater world unity, and a more progressive spiritual activity in the fields of education, the living arts, philosophy, and religion. The

teachings of Sri Aurobindo, the integrator of East and West, are the inspiration of the Center. His Vision of a divine life on earth and his saying "The knowledge that unites is the true knowledge," are the guiding torchlights.[12]

Study groups in which the writings of Sri Aurobindo are read and discussed, Sanskrit classes, yoga classes, instruction in meditation and the use of the *mantra* are conducted throughout the week. Special lectures are given on Sunday afternoons. The Auroville Group, composed of those interested in understanding and forwarding in some practical manner the construction of Auroville, also meets at the Center. A school for "selected and gifted children" is conducted by Dr. Judith Tyberg. Lessons in Indian classical music are provided. An Oriental library is available to those who wish to read or do research in the writings of Sri Aurobindo, the Mother, and other Eastern authors. Books from the East by many of the contemporary Spiritual Masters are sold at the Center. "Incense, colorful cards with spiritual messages, beautiful art gifts from India, Mantra and Meditation records and tapes are also available." [13]

The activities of the Cultural Integration Fellowship, in San Francisco, are somewhat similar, though apparently not as specifically related to the teachings of Sri Aurobindo as those of the East-West Cultural Center. There is a lecture each Sunday morning, as well as special events such as the observation of Eastern festivals, discussion groups in the afternoons, and lessons in Eastern chants and devotional songs in the evening. Classes are held every evening for such subjects as techniques of meditation and Self-realization, *hatha* and *kundalini yoga,* and the theory and practice of Indian musical instruments. A radio program, *The Meeting of East and West,* is given over a local station on Wednesday evenings. Each Saturday evening group meditation is held at the San Francisco Ashram. The Book Store of the Fellowship stocks a large selection of books by Sri Aurobindo and Mother Mira, by Dr. Haridas Chaudhuri and other disciples of Sri Aurobindo, as well as those by other outstanding Spiritual Masters. Tape recordings of the talks and lectures by Dr. Chaudhuri are also available. Closely associated with the Cultural Integration Fellowship is the California Institute of Asian Studies, with a large and impressive faculty. Programs leading to the Master of Arts and Doctor of Philosophy degrees in area studies, comparative studies East and West, and studies in integral psychology are offered. As would be expected, courses on the life and work of Sri Aurobindo are included.

The influence of Sri Aurobindo is fairly widespread in the United States. Books by or about him are to be found in college and university libraries and are available from several American publishers. Brief, or more extended, references are made to his philosophic system in the departments of religion in a number of universities. But there is as yet no central organization for coordinating the activities of the Sri Aurobindo Societies and Centers in the United States, though plans for forming such an organization are under consideration.

The Radhasoami Satsang

Two sections of the Radhasoami Satsang have branches in the United States, the Radha Soami Foundation, Beas, which acknowledges Master Charan Singh as the successor of Master Sawan Singh, and the Ruhani Satsang, founded in 1951 in Delhi by Master Kirpal Singh, whose members assert that he is the true successor. As far as I have been able to determine, there is no large following of either the Radhasoami Satsang, Dayalbagh, or the Radhasoami Satsang, Soamibagh, in the United States.

Shortly after the turn of the present century, Ker Singh Sasmus, a devoted disciple of Master Sawan Singh, accepted a position with the Canadian Pacific Steamship Lines as interpreter for the large number of Indians who were then migrating to the lumber camps in Canada. He was later asked to serve in the same capacity with the Canadian-Pacific Railroad. His duties with the latter took him also to the State of Washington. Probably because he was from India and the "mystic East," those who were seeking a spiritual path approached him with their questions. One day two "sincere and ardent seekers," Dr. and Mrs. Brock of Port Angeles, Washington, asked him, "Who is the saintly-looking man with the white turban and white beard who appears to us above your head?" Ker Singh then told them about Master Sawan Singh, and explained *Sant Mat* ("Religion of the Saints") to them in some detail. They were greatly impressed, for this seemed an answer to their prayers. They wished to be initiated into the Radha Soami Satsang, but were unable to go to India for this purpose. Ker Singh wrote to Master Sawan Singh and was given permission by him to initiate them as disciples. This was in 1911.[14]

A number of seekers were attracted by the teaching of the Brocks, and after the return of Ker Singh to India, Dr. and Mrs. Brock were authorized by Master Sawan Singh to give *nām* ("initiation") on his behalf. They rendered this service to seekers for over twenty years. In each case it was necessary for Master Sawan Singh to receive the applicant and approve his initiation before *nām* was administered. Since it was not always possible for initiates to go to Port Angeles, the Brocks began to travel widely along the West Coast, as far as Southern California, to give *nām* to accepted applicants and to answer the questions of new seekers. Among those who were initiated by the Brocks was Dr. Julian Johnson, who later went to India and spent a long while at Beas. His *With a Great Master in India* is considered one of the most authoritative works on the Radhasoami movement. He received initiation in 1931. Later that same year Harvey Myers heard a lecture by Dr. Johnson that gave the answers he had been seeking in his search for ultimate truth. He too was initiated by the Brocks in 1931.[15]

After the Brocks had served as Master Sawan Singh's representatives in America for many years, Harvey Myers, on the recommendation of Dr. Johnson, was appointed as his representative in Southern California. Harvey Myers served as the Master's representative for thirty-three years, and until 1948 as his sole representative. In 1951, Master Sawan Singh died and was succeeded by Master Charan Singh as spiritual head of the Radha Soami Satsang, Beas. In the early 1950's James Replogle was appointed by Master Charan Singh as his representative for the Eastern United States, with his headquarters in Chicago. In 1960, the North American Sangat was founded, with Harvey Myers in charge. Also in 1960, Colonel E. R. Berg, of Minneapolis, was appointed a representative at large, with responsibilities for the Midwest and Southwest. In 1964, Master Charan Singh further expanded the representative structure by appointing Henry F. Weekley as his representative in the Northeast, with headquarters in Washington, D.C., and Claude Duel, in St. Petersburg, Florida, for the Southeast. James Replogle died in 1965 and his responsibilities were transferred to Henry Weekley. Upon the death of Harvey Myers, in 1967, Roland de Vries, with his headquarters in Riverside,

California, was appointed representative for the West. Meanwhile, Gordon E. Limbrick, of Victoria, B.C., had been appointed Canadian representative and Dr. Walter Schidle, of Jalisco, the representative for Mexico.

These details have been given somewhat extensively in order to indicate the steps by which the organization of the North American Sangat has developed and to suggest the possible reason for the rapid expansion of the Radhasoami movement in America. The Sangat publishes a bimonthly magazine, the *R. S. Greetings*, which carries news of the activities of the members. A recent issue lists the locations and the dates and hours of meetings of fourteen *satsangs* east of the Rockies and twenty-six to the west. Three *satsangs* in Canada and one each in Mexico and in Hawaii are also listed.

In the spring of 1970 the members of the American Sangat had the opportunity of meeting Master Charan Singh in person. As a part of a world tour he spent two and a half months in America. Arriving from Mexico, brief stops were made en route to Washington, D.C. At San Antonio a hundred disciples greeted the Master and at Dallas there were two hundred. More extensive visits were made to Washington, Detroit, Chicago, Minneapolis, San Francisco, and Los Angeles. Some days were also spent at centers in Canada. *Satsangs* and other meetings were held in a leading hotel in each city. The attendance of disciples and "seekers" varied, it is reported, from four or five hundred in Washington to fourteen or fifteen hundred in Los Angeles. Nearly three hundred seekers were initiated during the tour, 178 of these in Los Angeles.

Master Charan Singh was greatly impressed by the enthusiasm and receptivity of his American followers. The reason, he explained, is that "people are hungry for

spirituality and they realize now that material achieve-
ments have not led them to any happiness or peace of
mind, and strangely enough they are not very rigid in
their Christian beliefs. They have started thinking openly
and trying to come out from the traditional beliefs, and
it is very easy to reach them through the Bible." [16] This
last comment is especially interesting, since Master
Charan Singh has written and spoken rather extensively
on the Christian Bible, giving his own mystical interpretation of its meaning.[17] The mornings, during his tour,
were given to private interviews and to question-and-
answer sessions with his followers and with inquirers. In
the afternoons, lectures were given on *Sant Mat* ("Religion of the Masters") and in the evenings formal *satsangs*
were held. Prof. Janak Puri, who accompanied Master
Charan Singh on his world tour, lectured on such themes
as the need for spirituality, the *Path* and *Sant Mat*, the
evils in the use of addictives and hallucinogenic drugs,
and the influence of the Master upon the life of the
satsangi.

Master Charan Singh himself spoke in the evening *satsangs* on the mystical interpretation of The Gospel According to John and Matthew. One of his disciples has
summarized the lectures on The Gospel According to
Matthew as they were given in Chicago:

> Maharaj Ji accomplished the impossible feat of placing the
> living Shabd into the Bible text. . . . Following the path
> of Sant Mat does not make one a less devout Christian; in-
> stead, one is able to follow the real teachings of Christ, as
> He gave them and not as others have interpreted them.
> There is no difference between the teachings of Christ and
> those of other Saints. Rather, Christ, like all the Saints,
> advocated the need of a living Master. Christ is always
> present in the human form on this earth, by one name or

another, to help the true seekers of God. So, the teachings
of Sant Mat do not differ from the teachings of Lord Jesus
Christ. The difference lies only in one's understanding and
interpretation of them. . . . To put a living interest of the
soul-life and its real needs into an unprepared and indifferent type of soil and its real needs is indeed a herculean
effort. (To illustrate this point Master Charan Singh explained the "Parable of the Soils," Matt., ch. 13.) Jesus also
spoke of that problem when he said, "Only my sheep hear
my voice and follow me." A Saint collects only those souls
which the Father has given him. . . . Maharaj Ji summed
up His Soul-liberating Message of the Shabd in the cres-
cendo of ONENESS, of all the Law and the Prophets, as
quoted from the Bible, where Jesus said, "Love the Lord
thy God with all thy heart, and with all thy soul, and with
all thy mind." This is the first and great commandment.
And the second is like unto it, "Thou shalt love thy neighbor as thyself." (Matt. 22:37–39.) Maharaj Ji said that in
order to love God with body, mind and soul, we have to
concentrate all the attention from the body up to the eye
center, which is the seat of the mind and soul knotted
together in the body. . . . It is only when all the energies
are concentrated at the eye center that we can love with all
our entire being—that of body, mind and soul." [18]

There is very little ritual in the Radha Soami Satsang
as it is held in America. Reverence is paid to the photograph of the Living Master. *Simran* ("repetition," "remembrance") forms an important part of the Satsang. This
may involve remembrance of the Master and his teachings, or the repetition of certain phrases or names, as, for
example, the five holy names of the Rulers who preside
over the five Regions in the Radha Soami cosmology.
Bhajans are sung honoring the Master or describing the
beauty of the Path. A lecture on some aspect of the Radha
Soami teaching is given by the Master's representative,

or by some other mature satsangi. A fellowship hour follows the *satsang*.

The Ruhani Satsang

The second section of the Radha Soami Satsang, Beas, which has members in the United States is the Ruhani Satsang, founded by a disciple of Master Sawan Singh, Kirpal Singh. As a youth Kirpal Singh prayed that he would be led to a True Master. When he was seventeen years of age a "Radiant Form," that of Master Sawan Singh, was revealed to him. He mistook this form, which appeared to him from time to time, to be that of Guru Nanak. In 1924, seven years after the first appearance, he met Sawan Singh in person at Dera Baba Jaimal Singh, Beas. "He instantly recognized him to be the same personality who, in his Radiant Form, had been his guide and preceptor in higher spiritual planes. 'Why has your holiness taken so long in guiding me to your feet?' he asked. The white-bearded sage smiled. 'This is the opportune time for our physical meeting.'" [19] Thus began a guru-chela relationship which lasted for twenty-four years, until the death of Master Sawan Singh in 1948. It is believed by the followers of Master Kirpal Singh that just prior to his death Master Sawan Singh passed on his "Spiritual Heritage" to their Master.[20] In 1951, on the behest of his Master he founded the Ruhani Satsang, the "Fellowship of the Spirit," or "Science of Spirituality." Sawan Ashram has been built by the Sangat in Delhi.

I have not visited this ashram, for I had not learned of the Ruhani Satsang at the time of my visit to Delhi. In fact, I was not informed by the leaders of the other sections of the Radha Soami Satsang, with their centers in

Agra and Beas, that there was still another section or division of the Satsang. Apparently each section claims to be the true successor to the original founder, Soamiji Maharaj. Concerning his own succession, Kirpal Singh reports:

> On the morning of 12th October, 1947, at 7 o'clock He (i.e., Master Sawan Singh) called me. When I was present in His august presence, he said: "Kirpal Singh! I have allotted all other work but have not entrusted my task of Naam—initiation and spiritual work—to anyone. That I confer to you today so that this holy and sacred Science may flourish." [21]

In fulfillment of this commission, it is said that Master Kirpal Singh has "initiated approximately 90,000 souls in India and abroad into the Mysteries of the Beyond." [22] The Ruhani Satsang carries on an extensive publishing program. Kirpal Singh himself has written more than twenty works. His largest work is *Gurmat Siddhant* ("The Path of the Masters"), first published in 1935 in two volumes of some two thousand pages. He has made two world tours, one in 1955, the other in 1963. His followers expect that he will soon make a third world tour. This will enable him to be seen by his followers in Europe, Africa, and the Americas. His work is directed in the United States by four official representatives, and in Canada by two.

The Meher Baba Lovers

Meher Baba made the first of his numerous visits to the West in September, 1931. Early in 1928 he had sent one of his disciples, Rustom Irani, to England for the purpose of bringing back some English boys to be enrolled in a school that he had opened in Meherabad. Although the effort ended in failure, Rustom Irani made contact with a few persons who expressed interest in Meher Baba. One of these, Meredith Starr, went to India and spent six months with Meher Baba. Upon his return he opened a retreat center in Devonshire which was to become Meher Baba's headquarters in England. In New York, Malcolm and Jean Adriel Schloss directed a metaphysical center in connection with their bookshop. A copy of Malcolm Schloss's book of mystical poems, *Songs to Celebrate the Sun,* came into the hands of Meredith Starr, who sent a young disciple of Meher Baba named Milo to America to invite the Schlosses to come to Devonshire. Before they could make the trip, however, they received word from Meredith Starr asking them to arrange accommodation for a visit by Meher Baba and his party to the United States.

A spacious gray stone house at Harmon-on-Hudson was secured. Meher Baba and his party arrived in December, 1931, and conducted a series of interviews with numerous friends of the Schlosses who had been invited to meet him. One of these was Princess Norina Matchabelli. Born in Italy, in 1914 she had married Prince Georges Matchabelli. Coming to the United States in 1924, her husband established the Prince Matchabelli Perfumery. Another friend of the Schlosses was Elizabeth Chapin Patterson, who, during the First World War, had served in the American Red Cross, often as an ambulance driver. At the end of the war she entered the insurance brokerage field and was quite successful. She married Kenneth Patterson in 1929, but continued her insurance career. Both Norina Matchabelli and Elizabeth Patterson were captivated by Meher Baba and became his ardent devotees. Together they made their first trip to India in 1933. Later they were to spend long periods with Meher Baba in India and on his numerous journeys abroad.

During this first visit to the United States, which lasted for a month, Meher Baba had won Malcolm and Jean Schloss and a number of others to discipleship. Less than a year later he was back in America. Again, Malcolm and Jean Schloss were requested to make arrangements for the visit. After three days spent in New York giving interviews to the newspapers and meeting devotees, the party proceeded to the center at Harmon-on-Hudson. It had been expected that Meher Baba would make an extended visit and plans were made for entertaining a large number of inquirers, but after only two days he suddenly announced that he would like to go to California. This caused great disappointment, because the New York papers had carried numerous articles about the "Silent Messiah" and it had been expected that many would want to meet him. In Hollywood a number of meetings were hastily arranged and many hundreds came to see him. His chief concern, however, seemed to be to meet as many of the motion-picture stars as possible. In the midst of plans for numerous appearances in San Francisco, Meher Baba announced that he must go to China for a short visit, promising that he would return. But the ways of Meher Baba were a puzzle even to his closest followers, for, from China he sailed for India, leaving his American disciples the task of canceling all the engagements that had been made for him! [23]

In December, 1934, he returned to the United States for his third visit. After a brief stay in New York, a month was spent in Hollywood. In 1936 he invited a small group of his Western disciples to come to India, pledging them to spend five years with him. Elaborate plans were made for their stay in a newly constructed ashram. Five women and one man went from America and four women and two men from England. Among the Americans were Malcolm and Jean Schloss, Norina Matchabelli, Elizabeth Patterson, and Estelle Gayley, who had become a disciple. To the surprise of all, they were sent back to their homes in July of the following year!

Norina Matchabelli and Elizabeth Patterson returned to India in 1937 and stayed with Meher Baba until 1941. In that year Meher Baba sent them back to America to establish a center that he could use as his headquarters in America. A large tract of virgin land near Myrtle Beach, South Carolina, was secured. In 1949 some buildings were constructed and other plans made for Meher Baba's anticipated visit, which took place in April, 1952. A month spent at the Center was crowded with interviews and other activities. A number of new disciples were won. On May 20, Meher Baba sent some of the *mandali* ahead to make arrangements for his arrival at Meher Mount, Ojai, California, which was to become a Western center. The next day the rest of the party started out in two cars. But they were never to reach their destination, for four days later the car in which Meher Baba was riding was involved in a head-on collision with another car and he, along with others in the car, was severely injured.[24] When he was able to be moved he returned to Myrtle Beach, where he stayed until the middle of July. The injuries received in the accident were to trouble him to the end of his life, seventeen years later.

In 1956, Meher Baba made his fifth, but brief, visit to the United States. Seven days were spent in New York, six at Myrtle Beach, and five in California. A few months after his return to India, Baba was involved in another motor accident. He was seriously injured, and it appeared unlikely that he could ever travel abroad again. But in

May, 1958, he was back at the Myrtle Beach Center for his sixth visit to America. Invitations had been sent to his European and American devotees to meet him at the Center for a *sahavas*. About 225 "Baba Lovers" spent two weeks with him there. In addition to private interviews given to his followers and to some visitors the time was given to the instruction of his followers. Each day several "discourses" were read to the gathering. They covered such subjects as the meaning of *sahavas*, the intimate companionship that the Master shares with his disciples; the nature of Love, the mystical relation between the Lover and the Beloved; the Split-Ego, the real "I" which mistakenly identifies itself with the false "I"; obedience; real birth and real death; and a number of others. One of the more unusual discourses was entitled "I am the Son of God the Father and God the Mother in One." In the Beyond state, explained Meher Baba, God is both God the Father and God the Mother simultaneously. In past periods the Avataras of God have all been male, Beloved Sons who represent the strength and wisdom of God. In the Beyond state, God did not have occasion to play the part of God the Mother. But there is in God a tender side of his nature which suffers. Meher Baba has undergone for the sake of his devotees intense suffering as a result of his two accidents. Thus, he is also the well-beloved Son of God the Mother. In this incarnation of the Avatara, God has had the occasion to play the part of both Father and Mother.[25]

Although this visit to America marked the end of his journeys outside India, it was not the last contact that he was to have with his Western devotees. Early in 1962 a notice was sent to his followers in the West, as well as to those in the East, that he would give *darshana* to his "Lovers" for seven days from November 1. One hundred and thirty-seven devotees came from Europe, America, Australia, and New Zealand, about three thousand from the East. This meeting with Meher Baba came to be known as the East-West Gathering. In October, 1968, Meher Baba issued another invitation to his Western disciples to gather for a *darshana* in May and June of 1969. "The 1962 East-West Gathering was nothing compared with what this Gathering will be," he said. "The Darshan will be strictly for My Lovers." [26] Elaborate plans were made both in India and in the West for this significant event, for Meher Baba had said that "it would be the last Darshan given in Silence, the last before He speaks His world-renewing word." [27] Special air flights were arranged from America, Europe, and Australia. But on January 31 he "dropped his body," his silence unbroken. Early in February, Adi Irani, secretary to Meher Baba, telegraphed the Western disciples, "Despite Baba's physical absence those lovers who desire to visit Guruprasad Poona to honour Baba's invitation for Darshan up to Tenth June can still come." [28] In response to this invitation one hundred and eighty-six Americans went for a "last *darshana.*" The details of the moving experiences that they had are described in a special number of *The Awakener*. Although Meher Baba had "dropped his body," many asserted that they were aware of his living spiritual presence with them. Even today, "Baba Lovers" insist that he is not "dead," but that he is everywhere present directing them step by step in their daily lives.

There is no central organization of the devotees of Meher Baba in the United States. He had insisted on numerous occasions that he had not come to establish a new religion, sect, or other organization, but to "awaken" the adherents of the various religions to his "Universal Love" for them and to win their love to himself. The quarterly magazine, *The Awakener,* serves as a link between Baba's devotees by publishing reports of their activities across the country. Books by or about Meher Baba are published by an organization known as Sufism Reoriented, located in San Francisco.[29] Meher Baba Centers have been established in a number of American cities, four in California, three in New York, two in Florida, one in Virginia. Perhaps the best known and most active of the centers is that at Myrtle Beach, South Carolina, where two of Baba's earliest disciples, Elizabeth Patterson and Kitty Davy, are in charge.[30]

The Meher Baba movement has won large acceptance among college and university students, and groups of "Meher Baba Lovers" meet regularly on a score of American campuses across the country. It is interesting to note that these students have had a particular concern for the problems related to drug addiction and that a number of the members of the groups are former addicts. Apparently, although most of the other cults in America appeal largely to middle-aged and older adults, the Meher Baba and Hare Krishna cults have made their strongest appeal to youth.

The Divine Life Society

The first official representative of Swami Sivananda and the Divine Life Society to come to America was Swami Chidananda, an intimate disciple of the swami and, later, his successor as president of the Society. In 1959 he was sent by Swami Sivananda on a tour of Europe, South America, and the United States. It is reported that "the tall, slender, saffron-robed monk charmed everyone with his magnetic personality, humility and simplicity." [31] As a result of his visit to the United States a number of disciples were won and several centers of the Society were established. In 1968, Swami Chidananda set out on another extended tour, which took him to Africa, Greece, France, Germany, England, and Holland, in each of which countries there are several Divine Life Society Centers. He arrived in New York in April, 1969. At the Sivananda Yoga-Vedanta Center he gave a series of talks "to packed audiences." The next ten months were spent in visiting other Divine Life Society Centers in the United States and Canada. In August he dedicated a new branch at Harriman, New York. As a result of Swami Chidananda's visit the Divine Life Society now has well-established branches in a number of American cities.[32]

Outstanding among these American branches are the Sivananda Yoga-Vedanta Center in New York City, under the leadership of Swami Shivapremananda; the Integral Yoga Institute in Yonkers, New York, with Swami Satchidananda as its head; the Sivananda Yoga-Vedanta Center, in San Francisco; and the Sivananda Yoga Vedanta Church, in South Milwaukee, with Mrs. Victoria Coanda as its founder-president. The activities carried on in these and other Sivananda branches are many and varied. The daily program of the Harriman, New York, branch includes the reading of the Hindu scriptures, such as the Bhagavad-Gita, the Upanishads, and Patanjali's Yoga Sutras, and the reading of the life stories of great Spiritual Masters, the chanting of *mantras* and the practice of *hatha-yoga, pranayama,* and meditation. The branch also functions as a spiritual retreat and a center where teachers of Yoga and Vedanta may come to further their training.[33] This branch has also held three-day seminars in other cities, such as Columbus and Cincinnati, Ohio. The program at the New York branch is even more extensive. Five classes, devoted to physical, mental, and spiritual culture, are held daily. The branch has its own building in Manhattan in which public lectures, the celebration of special festivals, classic dance recitals, and similar activities are held. There are regular *satsangs,* the singing of *kirtans* and *bhajans,* the chanting of *mantras,* and meditation. Swami Sivapremananda gives lectures on Yoga and Vedanta in various places both in the city and outside on behalf of the Center.[34] The branch in San Francisco conducts a number of Vedanta and Yoga classes, holds regular *satsangs,* arranges special lectures and distributes leaflets containing the teachings of Swami Sivananda. On certain festival occasions food is distributed to the poor. This branch also has a free lending library.[35] The program at the Sivananda Yoga Vedanta Church, in Milwaukee, is apparently not quite so extensive, but somewhat similar to programs in the other branches.

In 1959, Swami Vishnudevananda, another disciple of Swami Sivananda's, came to the West. Since that time he is said to have established forty Yoga-Vedanta centers in the United States and Canada. He has founded two Sivananda ashrams, one on Paradise Island, in the Bahamas, the second at Val Morin, in Quebec. These two ashrams have become important centers for training in the practice of yoga, during the winter at Paradise Island and during the summer at Val Morin. A recent development has been the organization of the True World Order, whose "aims are based upon the ancient science of Yoga and Vedanta Philosophy. It is the belief of the True World Order that much of mankind's misery can be attributed to a lack of tranquility, peace of mind and self-control, particularly among the political leaders of the world. The aims of the True World Order are to be implemented by training political, religious, social and economic leaders in the Yogic way of life, and by bringing up a new genera-

tion of potential leaders in the spirit of Yoga." [36] The
headquarters of TWO are at the Sivananda Yoga-Vedanta
Ashram, Val Morin, Quebec. A monthly journal, *Yoga
Life International*,[37] contains articles by Swami Sivananda, Swami Chidananda, and other leaders of the Divine Life Society, as well as articles on a variety of
subjects written by American and Canadian members of
the Society. Although many of the writers are concerned
with Yoga and Vedanta, others deal with a variety of
subjects such as health, drugs, diet, reincarnation in
Christianity, the first man on the moon, and so on. The
first Yoga World Brotherhood Convention, held at Val
Morin in 1969, brought persons interested in Yoga from
all over the world. Under the dynamic leadership of
Swami Vishnudevananda the message of Swami Sivananda is being widely disseminated. Branches of the Society in Chicago, Washington, D.C., New Haven, Detroit,
Fort Lauderdale, Orlando, Daytona Beach, Los Angeles,
and Albuquerque, and in eight Canadian cities are under
his direction. Toward the end of 1970, Swami Vishnudevananda began a world tour on behalf of the True
World Order in his two-engine plane, piloted by himself.
A "flying swami" is something new in Hinduism!

The Hare Krishna Movement

A short while ago I was sitting cross-legged on the floor,
talking to a young man who had graduated a year earlier
from the university where I have been teaching. Immediately after graduation he had abandoned his cap and
gown and put on the Western equivalent of the garb of
the Hindu sadhu ("holy man"). A saffron-colored cloth
was thrown over the right shoulder, crossed under the left
arm and then wound around his waist. His feet were

bare and his head was shaved, except for a small tuft of hair at the back. As we talked he fingered the string of beads around his neck. With enthusiasm and deep earnestness he told me of the ecstatic experiences he had had during the past year. He was not a hippie, high on drugs. In fact, he expressed deep concern for the plight of drug addicts. He has been initiated into one of the fastest growing cults in America, the International Society for Krishna Consciousness—ISKCON. Founded in July, 1966, by A. C. Bhaktivedanta Swami Prabhupada, it now has more than thirty temples in cities scattered across the country. Young devotees in saffron robes chanting *"Hare Krishna, Hare Krishna"* have become a familiar sight from coast to coast. ISKCON has made its appeal to youth especially. From American college and university campuses more than a thousand men and women have renounced the ordinary pursuits of life and have taken up their abode in the temples as brahmacharis. The movement is spreading overseas, as well, and there are now ISKCON centers in England, Holland, Germany, France, Australia, and Japan. Although I heard nothing of the movement during my visit to India in 1968, as the result of a recent visit of the founder a number of centers have been opened. Young American devotees, who accompanied the swami, created quite a sensation on the streets of Calcutta, Delhi, and Bombay as they danced and chanted *"Hare Krishna, Hare Krishna."*

A. C. Bhaktivedanta Swami Prabhupada is quite a remarkable man. He was born Abhay Charan De on September 1, 1896, in Calcutta. He was graduated from the University of Calcutta in 1920, having majored in philosophy, economics, and English. Shortly after, he became the manager of a large chemical concern in Bengal. The turning point in his life occurred in 1922 when he met

Sri Srimad Bhaktisiddhanta Sarasvati Gosvami Maharaja, the founder of numerous Gaudiya Vaishnava Maths in India and Europe. Abhay Charan De was formally initiated in 1933, and given the name by which he is now known. Shortly before his death in 1936, Sri Srimad Bhaktisiddhanta ordered his disciple Swami Bhaktivedanta to spread "Krishna Consciousness" to the West through the English language. Apparently, he did not take this command seriously until some years later when, in a commentary on the Bhagavad-Gita, written by Srila Bhaktivinode Thakur, he read that a disciple cannot separate the commands of a Spiritual Master from his life. Having accepted a Master, one must obey his commands. So in 1959 he was initiated into the order of *sannyasa* and dedicated himself entirely to the religious life. In 1965, at the advanced age of seventy, he arrived in New York to fulfill the mission committed unto him. Young Americans were soon attracted to him, and the International Society for Krishna Consciousness was formed.[38]

Concerning the mission and program of the International Society of Krishna Consciousness it is said that

> by books, literature and records, the Society is dedicated to awakening the worldwide public to the normal, ecstatic state of Krishna consciousness, so that all may regain their eternal position of favorably serving the will of Krishna. *Sankirtana*—congregational chanting—is carried to the people: in public parks, schools, on television, in the theater, on the streets. Krishna consciousness is not an idler's philosophy. Rather, by chanting and by engagement in the service of Krishna, anyone who takes part will experience the state of *samadhi*, ecstatic absorption in God consciousness, twenty-four hours a day! Since the philosophy of Krishna consciousness is nonsectarian, any man, Hindu or Christian, will become better in his faith by chanting the

holy name of God and by hearing the *Bhagavad-gita*.
Without knowledge and realization and loving service to
the one Supreme God, there can be no religion.[39]

It is claimed by the devotees of Swami Bhaktivedanta
that he is in direct "disciplic" succession to Krishna Chaitanya, a Vaishnava saint who was born in 1486. It was
believed by Chaitanya's disciples that he was none other
than an incarnation of Krishna, and they and their successors have known him as Lord Chaitanya. Chaitanya
traveled widely across India popularizing the reading of
the Bhagavad-Gita and the ecstatic practice of *bhakti*.
Large crowds followed him as he sang, chanted, and
danced in praise of Krishna. His exposition of the Gita,
the Vedanta Sutra, and the Upanishads brought him great
renown. In contrast to most of the pandits of his day
who taught the impersonality of the Absolute, Chaitanya
insisted that Krishna was the Supreme Personality of
Godhead. Undoubtedly, he did much to popularize the
worship of the Divine as personal. Chaitanya is said to
have introduced the practice of publicly chanting the
mahamantra, "*Hare Krishna, Hare Krishna, Krishna,
Hare, Hare, Hare Rama, Hare Rama, Rama, Rama, Hare,
Hare.*" Chaitanya predicted that "the chanting of *Hare
Krishna* will be heard in every town and village of the
world." To carry out his mission he selected six of his
closest disciples—the Six Gosvamis—and gave them special training. They formed the nucleus of the order which
has perpetuated the teachings and practices of Chaitanya
to the present day.[40]

ISKCON is, in a sense, the representation of the Chaitanya Order in the West. The initiated devotees live a
communal life in the centers, or "temples." All the centers, with the exception of New Vrindavana, are located

in cities. New Vrindavana is a rural ashram situated in an isolated section of West Virginia. Here, surrounding the temple, are farmlands and the cottages of devotees. In memory of Krishna's life among the cowherds and the Hindu reverence of the cow, cows are given special attention. To live as an initiated student in an ISKCON temple one takes the four vows: no meat-eating, no illicit sex, no intoxicants, and no gambling. Contrary to the practice in most Hindu ashrams, Swami Bhaktivedanta has encouraged the enrollment of the *grihastha*, the "householder," the married man with his wife and family. There is no prohibition against the brahmachari marrying and raising his family in the center. At present unmarried young women may live in the center, but this practice is not to become permanent. The *sankirtana*, the chanting of the *Hare Krishna mantra*, is said to be the "heart and soul" of the Krishna Consciousness movement, and all other activities are subsidiary. *Sankirtana* is carried on several times daily in the thirty centers, and *sankirtana* parties chant the *Hare Krishna mantra* on the streets and in public places "for the benefit of all citizens." The *sankirtana* chanting is to the accompaniment of the *mardanga* (a drum with two heads), the *karatals* (hand cymbals), and tambourine. To chant, or even to hear, the *Hare Krishna mantra*, because it is a "pure transcendental sound vibration," produces the ecstatic experience of Krishna Consciousness.

Classes in the "transcendental science of God consciousness, or *bhaktiyoga*," are held regularly in the ISKCON centers, and the public is cordially invited to attend. In addition to the *sankirtana* and *bhaktiyoga* classes, *arati*, the worship of the deity and of the Spiritual Master, is conducted before the altar in the shrine room of the temple. Every Sunday, in each of the ISKCON centers, a vegetarian meal, prepared in Indian style, is served to members who do not reside in the center and to guests or visitors who may drop in. Residents of San Francisco observe the yearly Rathayatra festival in which a large cart bearing the Jagannath deity is wheeled to the sea to be immersed. During the Rathayatra celebration of 1970, more than twenty thousand people, it is said, followed the great eight-thousand-pound carts, and thousands were fed plates of *prasada* ("sanctified food") at the seaside.

The centers, or temples, of ISKCON play a very important role in the spiritual life of the devotees. The center is generally a house which has been purchased and modified to meet the needs of the devotees. Some are quite large and pretentious. The upper floor is adapted to the needs of the married couples, bachelors, and single women. The lower floor is altered so as to provide for a large shrine room, dining room, and other facilities for members and visitors. At one end of the shrine room an elaborate altar is arranged. Images of Sri Krishna and of other deities and pictures of various saints are placed on the altar. Usually, one or more pictures of Chaitanya and his disciples are hung above the altar and about the room. Incense, candles, and objects used in worship are placed on the altar or nearby. This description of the daily worship services appears in *Back to Godhead:*

> The Deities are regularly worshipped by a performance called *aratrika,* which is an offering of foodstuffs, incense, flowers, a waving handkerchief, a fan and a lamp. In the ISKCON temples the Deities are worshipped with *aratrika* early in the morning, at 4 A.M. Then at 8 A.M. the altar is decorated and breakfast offered. At 11:30 there is again an offering of foodstuffs. At 5 P.M. the temple is opened after the Deities have rested from one to four. Then there is

another *aratrika* ceremony. In the morning fruit and milk are offered to the Deities, and at noon *dahl* and *chapatis* and many other varieties of foodstuffs are offered. At dusk there is *aratrika* and at 9 P.M. an offering of puris, vegetables, milk and sweetmeats, and after this final *aratrika* the Deities finally rest.[41]

The instruction of the devotees and inquirers forms another important function of the temple. Regular classes, which follow a prescribed curriculum, are held. After studying and working in a temple for a year, the student may be awarded the title of *bhakti-shastri* ("ordained minister"), with further responsibilities and with advancement of service. He may finally take the "renounced order," called *sannyasa*, and receive the title "Swami." [42] The aim of the chanting in public, the worship services, and the instruction is to lead people to Krishna Consciousness, the recovery of the memory of God which they have lost. This, the members of ISKCON contend, is "performing the greatest service and highest welfare work for suffering humanity."

Scattered Devotees

Our investigation of those Hindu cults which have large followings in India would indicate that only those with strong central organizations have had effective missionary activities outside that country. It may be said that the Meher Baba movement and the International Society for Krishna Consciousness are exceptions. In a sense this is true, for neither has a strong Western-type organization. But the *mandali*—the small core of intimate disciples of Meher Baba in Meherabad—has been very effective in spreading the influence of Meher Baba abroad, and the International Society for Krishna Consciousness is an outgrowth of the five-hundred-year-old Chaitanya Order which has centers outside India. Further, Meher Baba visited America on several occasions and Swami Bhaktivedanta has lived here for a number of years. Both are charismatic personalities and have exerted a strong personal influence upon all who have met them.

Sai Baba and Upasani Baba are apparently largely unknown in America. Ma Anandamayee, Godavari Mata, and Sathya Sai Baba, though still alive, have never visited America, nor have they sent outstanding representatives to acquaint Americans with their teachings. Thus, their devotees in the United States are few in number in comparison with those of the other Masters whom we have mentioned above. Although Ma Anandamayee's name is known to some students of Eastern religions in America, I have not been able to discover that she has many adherents in this country. There are at least a half dozen followers of Godavari Mata here at the present time. The disciples of Sathya Sai Baba, though more numerous, are widely scattered.

Some years ago Indra Devi, who has a Spiritual Life Center at Rancho El Cuchuma in Tecata, Mexico, visited India and met Sathya Sai Baba. She wrote to a number of her friends in the United States about this Master who had so profoundly affected her life. One of these was Muriel J. Engle, of Santa Barbara, California. Arrangements were made for Indra Devi to give a series of lectures on Sathya Sai Baba at the University of California Campus at Santa Barbara in 1967. Moving pictures that she had made at Prasanthi Nilayam introduced to an American audience the strange Master who has captured the hearts of so many. Later, Muriel Engle went to India to meet Sathya Sai Baba in person. Of this experience and of her contact with the Master she writes:

He is sage, father, mother, child. With wisdom and devotion he has evidenced his love, has attended to our every physical want and spiritual need, has taught us—turned no one aside. With humor and joy, he has delighted in our pleasure. Physical problems are of no great concern now; the cares and anxieties I leave in His hands. With His benediction, I leave—serene, loved and worthy. How do I know? I cannot tell you what has happened, except that He has said that this is so. "I am with you always—do not fear." Have you sung the hymn? "And beyond the dim unknown standeth God within the shadow keeping watch above His own." Never have I stood so close to God.[43]

Charles Penn, a disciple also in California, speaks of having conversations with Sathya Sai Baba, though separated by thousands of miles. He, too, has gone to India to meet his Spiritual Master in person.[44] Hilda Charlton is a member of a group of Sathya Sai devotees which meets in New York City. She tells of their awareness of Baba's presence with them as they remember him in prayer. She reports several cases of physical healing that have resulted from prayers offered to him.[45]

Elsie Elbright's experience was as dramatic. She and her husband had been searchers for truth for many years, but with little success. Finally, one day in desperation they prayed "for the Highest Living Master to come and take us to our goal." Two days later a friend handed them a book. The moment they touched it they "felt a strong vibration." The book was a life of Sathya Sai Baba. After they had read it, a "great serene peace" filled them, and they knew that their prayers had been answered. Shortly after this another friend whom they had not seen for some weeks brought them a small folded paper. When opened, it contained some ashes. These, she explained, had been brought from Sai Baba. They were instructed to put some on their tongues each night. This was something new to them, but it was the beginning of "the Blessings and Miracles" which happened in their lives. One day as Elsie was in her room "there came a streak of Light" and she fell on her knees. She "was filled with gratefulness. For, the great Sathya Sai Baba, 12,000 miles away, had given her God-realization, which precedes Self-realization." Although she was unable to see him with her eyes, she says, he made himself known to her and her husband in various ways. After this startling experience the Elbrights decided that they must go to Prasanthi Nilayam. They were with their new-found Master in January, 1968.[46]

It is interesting to note that the phenomena said to have been experienced by these devotees of Sathya Sai Baba in America are similar to those of his disciples in India.

12
AT THE LOTUS FEET
OF A MASTER

In India, when a chela meets his Spiritual Master he bows and touches his feet, and while being instructed by the Master, sits at his feet. As we have seen, large numbers in India have sought the "Lotus Feet" of such Masters as Sathya Sai Baba, Meher Baba, and Ma Anandamayee. But why, one may ask, have so many Americans also chosen to "sit at the feet" of a Spiritual Master from faraway India? Why have Americans who have thought of themselves as individualists, sometimes "rugged individualists," who have prized their freedom to make their own decisions, to live their own lives, to do their own thing, been willing to sacrifice these options and to surrender themselves "body and soul" to a "Master" whose absolute authority is generally unquestioned? In this land where national surveys and opinion polls are so popular, no comprehensive survey or poll has been taken, so far as I am aware, of the factors that influence Americans to join the cults in increasing numbers. A phenomenon so complex as that which we have been describing defies simple and easy explanations. I have found that it is much easier to record what I have observed happening than to explain why it has happened. I can only give certain impressions gained from attending the meetings of the cults, talking with their members, and reading their literature.

It seems to me, in the first place, that one must distinguish between the appeal of Vedanta—as taught by Vivekananda, Sri Aurobindo and Swami Sivananda—and the incarnational faiths of Meher Baba, Radhasoami, and Swami Bhaktivedanta. Further, a distinction may be made between that which has appealed to youth and that which appeals to those of more mature years. With a few exceptions, of course, Vedanta has apparently had a greater appeal to the middle-aged or older adult who is seeking for something that he has not found in earlier religious experiences. The cults with faith in a personal incarnation, an avatara, on the other hand, appeal especially to youth, many of whom have had little or no personal religious experience. The Radhasoami Satsang, however, which also has an incarnational philosophy, draws its membership more largely from among the older generation than from the younger. The reason for this, perhaps, is that its practices are not activistic enough to attract youth.

Vedanta and the Christian Faith

I know of no better literary sources to suggest to one who attempts to understand the appeal of the Vedanta philosophy than to point him to the experiences of the American Vedantists recorded in *Vedanta for the Western World*, edited by Christopher Isherwood, and *What Vedanta Means to Me*, edited by John Yale.[1] Most of those who have been drawn to Vedanta have been members, at least nominally, of one of the Christian denominations. But they have found difficulties with their parental faith. It is too exclusive and dogmatic, they say; its doctrine that history moves progressively toward a final culmination which will

continue eternally seems contrary to recorded fact; its dealing with the problem of evil is inadequate; the God who
permits such differences to exist between man and man in
capacity, opportunity, and inclination cannot be the Absolute; and the "conversion experience" claimed by many
has been too often apparently more imagined than real.
These difficulties have been removed for them by Vedanta.
Vedanta is not dogmatic. All religious practices are equally
valid routes to the knowledge of God, Vedanta teaches, if
engaged in with sincerity. The cyclical theory of history,
prominent in Greek thought but abandoned by Christian
theology, fits the facts of experience and is now supported
by contemporary historians such as Arnold Toynbee. The
doctrines of *karma* and reincarnation, taught by Vedanta,
help one to understand the existence of evil and the apparent inequalities in life. Spiritual perfection does not come
in any sudden or miraculous manner. It may require many
rebirths of the soul, the *Ātman*, before it reaches the final
goal of union with the Godhead, which is impersonal.

The dualism of Christianity and of Western philosophy
has been abandoned by Vedanta. "Vedanta," says John
Yale, "is not only a spiritual religion, but is one that is
compatible with modern knowledge. Divisiveness in outlook is as dated in today's world as the flat-earth theory." [2]
This point of view is echoed by the Nobel Prize-winning
physicist Erwin Schrödinger in his *My View of the World*.
His world view, derived, he says, from Vedanta, is that
there is only a single consciousness of which all things are
but different aspects. "The external world and consciousness are one and the same thing, in so far as both are constituted by the same primitive elements." In giving his
reason for the necessity of "abandoning the dualism of
thought and existence, or mind and matter," he insists that
"the condition for our doing so is that we think of *every-*

thing that happens as taking place in our *experience* of the world, without ascribing to it any material substratum as the object *of which* it is an experience; a substratum which would in fact be wholly and entirely superfluous." [3] This is indeed a startling statement from one who is himself constantly dealing with the "material," but it is a point of view being held by an increasing number of scientists, influenced, though perhaps unconsciously, by Vedanta.

Of the fact that Vedanta presents a real challenge to orthodox Christianity there can be no doubt. "The main fight, make no mistake," says the Christian theologian Nels Ferré, "is between the Christian faith in its inner classical meaning and the new Orientalized versions whether they come via Neoplatonism or in modern forms. . . . The supernatural, personalistic, classical Christian faith is now being undermined by an ultimately nondualistic, impersonal, or transpersonal faith." [4] This observation is supported by Edmund D. Soper, a historian of religion, in his *The Inevitable Choice: Vedanta Philosophy or Christian Gospel*: "Vedanta . . . has been attracting the interest, capturing the imagination, and securing the adherence and loyalty of large numbers of the intelligentsia of Western Europe and America. And even when Vedanta has not been embraced as the one true philosophy of life, it has entered, sometimes almost unconsciously, the minds and influenced the thinking of many who have been thus turned away from their loyalty to their ancestral faith and who are led to doubt the validity of the Christian claim that the revelation of God in Jesus Christ is the one completely adequate message for mankind." [5]

Jacob Needleman, in his *The New Religions,* suggests that another appeal of cults such as Vedanta has been due to the fact that by its emphasis upon the fallen nature of man and his utter dependence upon God, Protestantism has tended to produce an "underestimation of human possibilities." [6] "Vedanta," asserts Christopher Isherwood, "does not emphasize the vileness of man's mortal nature or the enormity of sin. It dwells, rather, on the greatness of man's eternal nature." [7] "The basic tenet of Vedanta is that the Ground of all being is God. There is nothing but God. I am God; you are God; the pulsations seen as matter are God." Such an affirmation as this has been welcome news to the "deflated ego" of those who had been taught from childhood to sing, "Would He [i.e., Jesus] devote that sacred head for such a *worm* as I?" Surely man who has been able to harness the forces of nature and project himself to the moon is not as debased as conservative Protestant theology has asserted. If he can but dispell his ignorance concerning his true nature, as Vedanta teaches, his potentialities are unlimited. Ultimately, he can attain Self-realization, which is, in fact, God-realization, Divinity.

The Social Gospel

Paradoxically, "liberal" Protestants in America, in contrast to the conservative "fundamentalist" just described, have created problems of another sort for certain members of the church. In their effort to "apply the Christian gospel" and to do their part in "bringing in the Kingdom of God on earth," some denominations have laid particular stress on the "social gospel." They have developed "social creeds" for the guidance of their members, and a number of them have engaged in extensive social welfare work. But in recent years, disenchantment has set in for many members of these churches. They apparently feel that this kind of activity is not the primary function of religion. Here, again, the personality cults have made their appeal. In these movements the ideal of a social religion is subordinated to an emphasis on the individual's spiritual development. So far as I am aware, not one of them is engaged in what might be called social welfare work. Nor do they have as their primary goal the transformation of the structures of society. They have little direct concern for the great issues of our day: war and peace, social justice and racial equality, pollution, poverty, and population control. Perhaps it has been the very sense of frustration in dealing with these problems which has caused some to turn to the apparently less demanding involvement in the practice of meditation and yoga, chanting, listening to the Spiritual Sound Current, and demonstrating spiritual love for one another.

Youth and the Cults

And what of American youth? Why are so many of them joining the cults, especially the Meher Baba Lovers and ISKCON, in increasing numbers? Paradoxically, some of the very youth who have revolted against authority figures and who have "kicked the Establishment" have surrendered themselves, apparently, completely to the autocratic and absolute authority of a newly discovered guru, swami, or avatara! Marcus Bach suggests that we can understand this "switch" only in the context of their experiences—drugs, rock festivals, campus violence, Vietnam, the draft, the police, and sex—and their estimate of an older generation viewed across the credibility and communication gaps, a generation that appears to them to be pseudoreligious, culturally faked, economically frustrated, pharmaceutically drug-crazed, dying in its own environmental poisons.[8] To them it appears that the institutions of the American and Western culture are "phony," materialistic, destructive, while those of the East are "real," "spiritual," "redemptive."

To many, the cults open doors to new and fascinating ventures in the search for meaning and purpose in life.

Perhaps many of the same factors that have led American youth to join the Jesus Revolution have also had their influence upon those who have become members of the Hindu cults. In a lead article, *Time* observes:

The Jesus revolution rejects not only the material values of conventional America but the prevailing wisdom of American theology. Success often means an impersonal and despiritualized life that increasingly finds release in sexploration, status, alcohol and conspicuous consumption. Christianity—or at least the brand of it preached in prestige seminaries, pulpits and church offices over recent decades —has emphasized an immanent God of nature and social movement, not the new movement's transcendental, personal God who comes to earth in the person of Jesus, in the lives of individuals, in miracles. The Jesus revolution, in short, is one that denies the virtues of the Secular City and heaps scorn on the message that God was ever dead. . . . This is the generation that has burned out many of its lights and lives before it is old enough to vote. . . . As Thomas Faber writes in *Tales for the Son of My Unborn Child*: "The freedom from work, from restraint, from accountability, wondrous in its inception, became banal and counterfeit. Without rules there was no way to say no, and worse, no way to say yes." The search for a "yes" led thousands to the Oriental and the mystical, the occult and even Satanism before they drew once again on familiar roots.[9]

Many youthful converts to the Jesus Revolution see Jesus as a marvelous father-figure. They are searching for authority, love and understanding—ingredients missing at home. Many of the young people in the Hindu cults with whom I have talked give essentially the same reply when asked why they have become members of these new faiths. This is especially true of the youthful disciples of Meher Baba and Swami Bhaktivedanta. The permissiveness that characterizes our society—in the home, the school, and often in the church—has left many youth uncertain about values and with a sense of insecurity as they face the future. The cults seek to provide both certainty and security through their authoritative leadership and through the love and fellowship of other dedicated and committed devotees.

A New Fellowship for the Lonely

The cult movement in America is apparently an urban phenomenon. So far as I have been able to discover, no centers have been formed in rural areas or small towns. The majority of the middle-aged or older adherents with whom I have talked, or about whom I have read, were formerly members of one of the "main line" Christian denominations. Although I have no published data to support the assumption, I am led to believe that many of those who have joined the cults were members of larger urban congregations, where the impersonality of the "computer age" has often penetrated. Although members may not be regarded as "mere numbers," they often feel lost and lonely in a large congregation where they are not personally known to the pastor and officials. They have been given no significant responsibilities and have little sense of really "belonging." The cults, on the other hand, surround the seeker with friendliness, welcome, and acceptance. If he joins, he is soon assigned tasks which seem significant and which integrate him into the fellowship of the group.

A similar observation may be made about the youth who have become devotees of a Spiritual Master. They have apparently come from campuses of the larger colleges and universities where the religious influence has been minimal or nonexistent. They too have had the experience of lostness and loneliness. Groups of Meher Baba Lovers have found such students fertile soil for their mission. Although the Hare Krishna movement has not as yet formed groups on college campuses, it, too, has had a strong appeal for students from the larger, more secularized, institutions. Most of the young people who have joined the personality cults were probably raised in "Christian" homes and were members of a Christian church, but contacts with both have become weak. To many, the church back home seems irrelevant and meaningless. I have come to the conclusion, therefore, that many of those, whether young or older, who join a personality cult—a spiritual movement centered in a charismatic founder—have done so because they are seeking incorporation into a significant fellowship under the leadership of a spiritual guide who will give meaning and direction to their lives. They have found life in our day so impersonal, so uncertain, and even so hazardous, that they are fearful of venturing into the unknown without such a fellowship and such a guide.

The Search for New Techniques and Methods

Ours is an age that seeks for new techniques and methods for doing things. We are prepared to follow any expert or specialist who promises to help us. We will abandon older techniques and methods, although they have worked reasonably well, when something new is offered us as being better. This is precisely where the cults are making their appeal. They may not openly condemn the old as outworn and worthless; rather, by their techniques they propose to "make Christians better Christians," to assist seekers to reach their spiritual goal more quickly. It is true that the earlier "fundamentalists" often gave specific instructions concerning "what one must do to be saved." But later "liberalism" does not give earnest seekers such guidance. The cults that we have described were founded by charismatic personalities who, it is believed, revealed specific divine patterns of life and of worship for their followers. Thus, the Vedanta Societies, the Sivananda Divine Life Societies, and the Aurobindo Societies teach their members the techniques of meditation and yoga; the Radhasoami Satsang emphasizes the importance of listening to the Spiritual Sound Current, the Meher Baba Lovers practice "Baba's Love" in their meetings, and the devotees of the Hare Krishna movement attain Krishna Consciousness through the performance of *sankirtana*—chanting the name of Krishna.

Hindu-Christian Syncretism

The use that Master Charan Singh makes of the New Testament illustrates yet another appeal of the cults, the syncretistic nature of their message. The founders of all the cults introduced in earlier chapters, with the possible exception of Sai Baba and Upasani Baba, were acquainted with the Christian religion. Consciously or unconsciously they have embodied aspects of the Christian faith in their own teachings. Sathya Sai Baba freely uses parables from the New Testament. Meher Baba spoke of himself as the "Christ" for this age. Kirpal Singh quotes extensively from Jewish and Christian scriptures, and Charan Singh interprets the Gospels in a mystical fashion that he insists is the true and original interpretation. The swamis of the Vedanta Society make constant use of Christian terminology in presenting the message of Vedanta. One issue of ISK-CON's *Back to Godhead* devotes several pages to Old and New Testament quotations that are said to support the practice of chanting the name of God.[10] This extensive use of Judeo-Christian concepts opens the way for adherents of the Christian faith to move more easily into the fellowship of the cults. I have, in fact, met several devotees who assured me that they were still "good Methodists" or "good Episcopalians"! The transition from the old to the new is made less difficult when they are assured that there is no real conflict—that the teachings of the Masters merely go deeper into the spiritual understanding of the Scriptures than those given by their former teachers.

The Aura of the Orient

There are some Americans who are undoubtedly attracted to the Eastern cults by their novelty, mystery, and esoteric teachings. The impressive serenity of the turbaned swami, the personal charm of the bearded guru, the nimbus surrounding the avatara, all make their appeal to Americans who are inveterate hero-worshipers.

The fragrance of incense, the quiet serenity of the sanctuary, the attractive arrangement of the altar, the silent meditation, or the soft chanting of a *mantra* charm those of an aesthetic temperament. Some who are constantly seeking the new or bizarre in our "cafeteria-oriented age" move from one cult to another, "tasting" the teachings and practices of each, yet never fully satisfied.

In the final analysis, only those who have joined one of the personality cults and have become devotees "sitting at the feet" of a Spiritual Master can tell us what motivated them to do so, but Charles Braden, long a student of religious movements in America, is probably correct when he asserts that "in general the cults represent the earnest attempt of millions of people to find the fulfillment of deep and legitimate needs of the human spirit, which most of them seem not to have found in the established churches." [11]

Missionary Activities

Finally, the cults are aggressively missionary. Their members believe that they have made a significant spiritual discovery and are committed to the task of sharing it with others. They go about this task with enthusiasm and determination. They give generously of their time and money to inform others concerning the teachings of their Masters and to testify to the satisfactions to be found while sitting at their feet. The cults are aware of the power of the printed page and have produced books by the hundreds. Attractive magazines or journals are circulated widely. Use is made of the mass media. The Masters, or their representatives, are encouraged and assisted to visit America, and wide television, radio, and newspaper coverage is secured for their messages. Conventions bring members and invited guests together for religious and social fellowship. Although other Americans may find opportunities for service through their fraternal and civic clubs, the members of the cults channel their energies and enthusiasm through devotion to their Spiritual Masters and through the propagation of their teachings. Their spirit is optimistic and contagious. With a message that apparently meets men in areas of spiritual need, widespread publicity, effective organization, and missionary zeal, one should not be surprised to learn that the cults are gaining new adherents in increasing numbers. Hinduism is striking its roots deep into American soil.

NOTES

1. WHAT IT IS ALL ABOUT

1. A chant said to have been introduced by Chaitanya (1485–1527), a Hindu saint, whose followers are to be found in large numbers in India today. *Hare* ("Lord" or "God"), usually *Hari*, is a title given to Krishna and Rama, incarnations of the Hindu god Vishnu. It is also applied to Siva, the third member of the Hindu Trimurti. It was the belief of Chaitanya and his followers that the Lord granted salvation to those who chanted his name continuously.

2. The American writers who were probably the first and among the most influential in introducing Hinduism to America were the New England transcendentalists Ralph Waldo Emerson, Bronson Alcott, and Henry David Thoreau. See Frederic I. Carpenter, *Emerson and Asia* (Harvard University Press, 1930), and Arthur Christy, *The Orient in American Transcendentalism* (Columbia University Press, 1932). The Theosophical Society, founded in New York by Helena Petrovna Blavatsky, embodied many elements of Hinduism, especially after the movement came under the leadership of Annie Besant. See Charles S. Braden, *These Also Believe* (The Macmillan Company, 1949). It was the philosophical rather than the cultic aspect of Hinduism, however, which was of concern to these earlier writers. It was Swami Vivekananda, who organized the Vedanta Society in America in New York in 1894, and Swami Yogananda, who established the Self-Realization Fellowship in California in 1935, who introduced to America the cults that

venerate Hindu gods and saints. See Christopher Isherwood (ed.), *Vedanta for the Western World* (The Viking Press, Inc., 1960), p. 26, and Paramhansa Yogananda, *Autobiography of a Yogi* (Philosophical Library, Inc., 1947), p. 366.

3. The growth of "personality cults" in India, Japan, Africa, and the United States in recent decades is an interesting phenomenon. The number of adherents in most of these groups is not large enough to constitute distinct sects, but they generally manifest the chief characteristic of a cult—"devoted attachment to, or extravagant admiration for, a person." Coverage of the extensive literature on the subject of the "messianic movements" in Africa has been given by Robert C. Mitchell *et al.*, in *A Comprehensive Bibliography of Modern African Religious Movements* (Northwestern University Press, 1966). See also: D. B. Barret, *Schism and Renewal in Africa: An Analysis of 2,000 Contemporary Religious Movements* (Nairobi: Oxford University Press, 1968); Beyerhaus, *Messianische Kirchen, Sekten, und Bewegungen in heutigen Afrika* (Leiden: E. J. Brill, 1965); B. Sundkler, *Begegnungen mit Messianischen Bewegung in Afrika* (Stuttgart: Ev. Missionsverlag, 1967); *Journal of Religion in Africa* (E. J. Brill). For an introduction to the "New Religions of Japan," see: Raymond Hammer, *Japan's Religious Ferment* (Oxford University Press, 1962); H. N. McFarland, *The Rush Hour of the Gods* (The Macmillan Company, 1967); Clark B. Offner and Henry Van Straelen, *Modern Japanese Religions* (Twayne Publishers, Inc., 1963); Harry Thomsen, *The New Religions of Japan* (Tokyo: Charles E. Tuttle, 1963). Numerous works have been produced on individual personality cults in America, such as Christian Science, but for a general introduction the following are useful: Marcus L. Bach, *They Have Found a Faith* (The Bobbs-Merrill Company, Inc., 1946) and *Strangers at the Door* (Abingdon Press, 1971); Charles S. Braden, *These Also Believe;* Richard R. Mathison, *Faiths, Cults, and Sects of America* (The Bobbs-Merrill Company, Inc., 1960); Jan K. van Baalen, *The Chaos of Cults* (Wm. B. Eerdmans Publishing Company, 1962); Jacob Needleman, *The New Religions* (Doubleday & Company, Inc., 1970). Although the founders and adherents of the contemporary personality cults in Hinduism have published a flood of books about their own cults, few of them are available as yet in

America. But see J. N. Farquhar, *Modern Religious Movements in India* (London: Macmillan & Co., Ltd., 1924; reprinted, Lawrence Verry, Inc., 1967), and *The Cultural Heritage of India*, ed. by Haridas Bhattacharyya, Vol. IV (Calcutta: Rama-krishna Mission Institute of Culture, 1956), for brief descriptions of the earlier of the "contemporary" cults. Other works available in America are listed in our "Notes."

4. Satis Chandra Chatterjee, "Hindu Religious Thought," in Kenneth W. Morgan, *The Religion of the Hindus* (The Ronald Press Co., 1953), pp. 238–239, *passim*.

5. *Ibid.*, pp. 239–240, *passim*.

6. *Ibid.*, pp. 240–243, *passim*.

7. Carl Michalson, *Japanese Contributions to Christian Theology* (The Westminster Press, 1960), p. 9.

8. Nels F. S. Ferré, Foreword, in Surjit Singh, *Christology and Personality* (The Westminster Press, 1961), p. 14.

2. THE FAKIR: *Sri Sai Baba of Shirdi*

1. Nagesh Vasudev Gunaji, *Shri Sai Satcharita* (Bombay: Nirnaya Sagar Press, 1965), p. 20.

2. *Ibid.*, pp. xxv–xxvii, *passim*.

3. *Ibid.*, pp. 42–43. See also Brahmananath Nadre, *The Living Force of Sri Saibaba* (Poona: Swananda Mudranalaya, 1965), pp. 15–24, *passim*.

4. Swami Prabhavananda, *The Spiritual Heritage of India* (Doubleday & Company, Inc., 1963), pp. 155–156.

5. Bharatan Kumarappa, "The Hindu Conception of the Deity," *The Religious Quest of India* (Calcutta: Y.M.C.A. Press, 1925).

6. K. V. Gajendragadkar, "The Maharastra Saints and Their Teachings," in Bhattacharyya (ed.), *The Cultural Heritage of India*, Vol. IV, p. 368.

7. Sarvepalli Radhakrishnan (ed.), *The Bhagavadgita* (London: George Allen & Unwin, Ltd., 1958), pp. 180–181.

8. Gunaji, *Satcharita*, pp. 216–217.

9. *Ibid.*, pp. 239–240.

10. *Ibid.*, p. xxvii.

11. Radhakrishnan (ed.), *Bhagavadgita*, pp. 153–155.

12. Sri Rupa Gosvami, *Bhakti-Rasamrta-Sindhu* (Vrindaban: Institute of Philosophy, 1965), p. 399.

13. Swami Saradananda, *Sri Ramakrishna the Great Master* (Madras: Sri Ramakrishna Math, 1952), p. 95.

14. Gunaji, *Satcharita*, p. 232.

15. Arthur Osborne, *The Incredible Sai Baba* (Bombay: Orient Longmans, Private, Ltd., 1957), p. 100.

16. Recorded at the worship service in Jabalpur, India, Sept. 5, 1968.

17. Osborne, *Sai Baba*, p. 100.

18. Recorded at Centenary Celebration, Shirdi, India, Sept. 24, 1968.

3. THE SAINT WHO SUFFERED:
Sri Upasani Baba Maharaj

1. B. V. Narasimha and S. Subbarao, *Sage of Sakuri* (Bombay: New Bharat Printing Press, 1966), pp. 8–9.

2. *Ibid.*, p. 12.

3. See the *Yoga Sutra* in Sarvepalli Radhakrishnan and C. A. Moore (eds.), *A Source Book in Indian Philosophy* (Princeton University Press, 1957), pp. 462–478.

4. Gosvami, *Bhakti-Rasamrta-Sindhu*, pp. 125–131, *passim*.

5. Narasimha and Subbarao, *Sage*, p. 39.

6. Upasani Baba, *Upasani Vak Sudha* (Sakuri: R. G. Vakil, 1934), 3:i, 6. Quoted in S. N. Tipnis, *Contribution of Upasani Baba to Indian Culture* (Bombay: New Bharat Printing Press, 1966), p. 87.

7. Tipnis, *Contribution*, p. 102.

8. *Ibid.*, pp. 122–124.

9. Narasimha and Subbarao, *Sage*, p. 199.

10. *Upasani Vak Sudha*, 2:xix, 324.

11. *Ibid.*, 1:xx, 339.

12. Madhav Nath, *Sad Guru Upasani Maharaj Yancha Charitra* (Bombay: R. S. Irani, 1923), p. 132. See Tipnis *Contribution*, p. 232.

13. *Ibid.*, p. 231.

14. *Ibid.*, p. 227.

4. THE HIGHEST OF THE HIGH: *Meher Baba*

1. Warren C. Healy, *Who Is Meher Baba?* (Ahmadnagar: Meher Publications, 1967), p. 2.

2. Charles B. Purdom, *The God-Man* (London: George Allen & Unwin, Ltd., 1964), p. 398.

3. Healy, *Who Is Meher Baba?* p. 3.

4. Purdom, *The God-Man*, pp. 15–23, *passim*.

5. Healy, *Who Is Meher Baba?* p. 5.

6. W. Le Page, *Avatar Meher Baba* (Rose Bay NSW: M.G.A. Publications, n.d.), p. 2.

7. Purdom, *The God-Man*, p. 9.

8. *Ibid.*, p. 137.

9. *Ibid.*, p. 139.

10. *Ibid.*, p. 140.

11. For details, see *ibid.*, pp. 163–197, *passim*.

12. *Ibid.*, p. 189.

13. *Ibid.*, p. 207.

14. Meher Baba, *The Highest of the High* (Seattle, Wash.: W. C. Healy Press, 1954), pp. 1–3, *passim*.

15. Purdom, *The God-Man*, p. 218.

16. Meher Baba, *Listen, Humanity,* narrated and edited by Don E. Stevens (Dodd, Mead & Company, Inc., 1957), pp. 9–90, *passim*.

17. Purdom, *The God-Man*, pp. 219–294, *passim*.

18. Warren C. Healy (ed.), *Meher Baba's Call* (Seattle, Wash.: W. C. Healy Press, n.d.), pp. 1–4, *passim*.

19. Purdom, *The God-Man*, p. 314.

20. Francis Brabazon, *The East-West Gathering* (Queensland, Australia: Woombye, n.d.).

21. Meher Baba, *Discourses* (Ahmadnagar: Meher Publications, 1938–1954).

22. See, for example, Ivy O. Duce and Don E. Stevens (eds.), *God Speaks* (Dodd, Mead & Company, Inc., 1955), which describes with charts Meher Baba's teachings on the Evolution of Consciousness.

23. Ivy O. Duce and Don E. Stevens (eds.), *Discourses by Meher Baba* (Tokyo: Komiyama Printing Co., 1968).

24. Purdom, *The God-Man*, pp. 381–389, *passim*.

25. Duce and Stevens (eds.), *Discourses*, 3:22–27, *passim*.

26. Purdom, *The God-Man*, p. 390.

27. Duce and Stevens (eds.), *God Speaks*, pp. 141–142.

28. Duce and Stevens (eds.), *Discourses*, 1:43–64, *passim*.

29. *Ibid.*, 1:56.

30. *Ibid.*, 1:57.

31. *Ibid.*, 1:58.

32. Duce and Stevens (eds.), *God Speaks*, pp. 8–9.

33. Duce and Stevens (eds.), *Discourses*, 1:59–60.

34. *Ibid.*, 1:35–36.

35. Duce and Stevens (eds.), *God Speaks*, pp. 40–52, *passim*.

36. These are discussed in detail, with accompanying charts, in *God Speaks* and *Discourses by Meher Baba*.

37. K. K. Ramakrishnan (ed.), *Meher Baba on Love* (Poona: Meher Era Publications, 1968), p. 9.

38. *Ibid.*, p. 17.

39. *Ibid.*, pp. 49–50.

40. Unpublished worship service used by Meher Baba Lovers, Emory University, released by Meher Publications, Ahmadnagar, 1962.

5. THE DIVINE MAGICIAN: *The Miraculous Life of Sathya Sai Baba*

1. N. Kasturi (ed.), *At the Lotus Feet of Bhagavan Sri Sathya Sai Baba* (Prasanthi Nilayam, 1968).

2. N. Kasturi (ed.), *Sathya Sai Speaks*, 5 vols. (Prasanthi Nilayam: Sanathana Sarathi, 1965–1968), Vol. I, pp. 1–2.

3. N. Kasturi, *Sathyam Shivam Sundaram: The Life of Bhagavan Sri Sathya Sai Baba* (Prasanthi Nilayam: Sanathana Sarathi, 1968), p. 84.

4. A. V. Suryanarayana, *Paradise Regained: The Divine Life of Sri Sathya Sayi Baba* (Guntur, n.d.), pp. viii–xiii, *passim*.

5. Kasturi, *Sathyam*, p. 5. See also *Newsweek*, Nov. 17, 1969, p. 113.

6. Suryanarayana, *Paradise*, p. xiii.

7. Kasturi (ed.), *At the Lotus Feet*, p. 100.

8. Suryanarayana, *Paradise*, p. 35.

9. *Newsweek*, Nov. 17, 1969, p. 113.

10. *Ibid.*, p. 116.

11. Kasturi, *Sathyam*, p. 98.

12. *Ibid.*, p. 95.

13. *Ibid.*, pp. 74–84, *passim.*

14. Kasturi (ed.), *At the Lotus Feet*, p. 65.

15. This work, edited by N. Kasturi, and a number of *Vahinis* ("Discourses") by Sathya Sai Baba, such as *Prema Vahini* ("The Love Discourse") and *Upanishad Vahini* ("Discourse on the Upanishad"), are all published by Sanathana Sarathi, Prasanthi Nilayam.

16. Kasturi, *Sathyam*, p. 31.

17. "The Discourse on Duty," "The Discourse on Truth," etc.

18. Kasturi, *Sathya Sai Speaks*, Vol. II, p. 269.

19. See Kasturi, *Sathyam*, p. 31.

20. Kasturi (ed.), *At the Lotus Feet*, p. 98.

21. *Ibid.*

22. Suryanarayana, *Paradise*, p. xiii.

6. THE SOUND THAT LIBERATES:
The Radhasoami Satsang

1. *The Dayalbagh Herald*, Vol. 40, No. 13 (Agra: Dayalbagh Press), p. 8.

2. Sivaprasad Bhattacharyya, "Religion Practices of the Hindus," in Morgan, *The Religion of the Hindus*, p. 168.

3. *Ibid.*, p. 169.

4. *Ibid.*, pp. 171–172.

5. Sahabji Maharaj, *Yathartha Prakasa, Part I* (Agra: Dayalbagh Press, 1954), pp. 40–43, *passim.*

6. Bhattacharyya, "Religious Practices," p. 172.

7. *Souvenir in Commemoration of the First Century of the Radhasoami Satsang*—1861–1961 (Dayalbagh: Radhasoami Satsang Saba, 1962), p. 7.

8. *Ibid.*, p. 28.

9. *Ibid.*, p. 21.

10. *Ibid.*, p. 23.

11. *Ibid.*, p. 24.

12. *Ibid.*

13. *Ibid.*, p. 31.

14. *Ibid.*, p. 40.

15. *Ibid.*, p. 63.

16. *Ibid.*, p. 173.

17. *Ibid.*, p. 174.

18. Published in 1964 at Dayalbagh by Radhasoami Satsang Saba.

19. Katherine Wason, *The Living Master* (Delhi: National Printing Works, 1966), pp. 59–70, *passim*.

20. *Ibid.*, p. 77.

21. *Ibid.*, p. 78.

22. Maharaj Sawan Singh, *Spiritual Gems* (Beas: Radha Soami Satsang Beas, 1948).

23. Wason, *The Living Master*, pp. 258–260, *passim*.

24. Sardar Jagat Singh, *The Science of the Soul* (Beas: Radha Soami Satsang Beas, 1951).

25. Wason, *The Living Master*, p. 81.

26. *Ibid.*, p. 52.

27. Maharaj Charan Singh, *Spiritual Discourses; Divine Light; St. John the Great Mystic; The Path; Light on Sant Mat; Master Answers* (all published by the Radha Soami Satsang, Beas). These and other books are available from Seva Trust, Oak Park, Ill.

28. S. D. Maheshwari, *Teachings of the Radhasoami Faith* (Agra: Radhasoami Satsang, Soamibagh, 1960); Myron H. Phelps, *Notes on Discourses by Babuji Maharaj on the Radhasoami Faith* (Agra: Radhasoami Satsang, Soamibagh, 1947).

29. S. D. Maheshwari, *A Brief Description of the Radhasoami Faith* (Delhi: Amrit Electric Press, 1960), pp. 23–31, *passim*.

30. Each of the three Satsangs has published its own English translation of the *Sar Bachan*.

31. This outline of the Radhasoami Faith has been gleaned from the *Sar Bachan* and from the *Discourses* of the several Sant Sat-Gurus, noted above.

32. Sahabji Maharaj, *Radhasoami Mat Darsana* (Dayalbagh: Dayalbagh Press, 1960), pp. 23–24.

7. THE PRIEST OF KALI: *Sri Ramakrishna*

1. Christopher Isherwood, *Ramakrishna and His Disciples* (Calcutta: Advaita Ashrama, 1965), p. 24. The story of the life

of Ramakrishna is given in detail in this and two other works: *The Gospel of Sri Ramakrishna,* by "M" (Mahendra Nath Gupta) (Ramakrishna-Vivekananda Centre, 1942), and *Ramakrishna the Great Master,* by Swami Saradananda (Madras: Sri Ramakrishna Math, 1952). A very extensive bibliography of works in English is to be found in Isherwood.

2. Gupta, *The Gospel,* pp. 5–13, *passim.*

3. Swami Vivekananda, *My Master* (Calcutta: Surajit C. Das, 1965), p. 27.

4. Isherwood, *Ramakrishna,* p. 65.

5. Gupta, *The Gospel,* p. 15.

6. *Ibid.,* p. 28.

7. *Ibid.,* p. 29.

8. *Ibid.,* p. 30.

9. Vivekananda, *My Master,* p. 44.

10. Isherwood, *Ramakrishna,* p. 166.

11. *Ibid.,* p. 167.

12. *Ibid.,* p. 297.

13. *Ibid.,* p. 303.

14. Saradananda, *Great Master,* pp. 692–723, *passim.*

15. Swami Gambhirananda, *History of the Ramakrishna Mission and Math* (Calcutta: Advaita Ashram, 1957) and *Annual Report of the Ramakrishna Mission and Math* (Belur, 1967).

16. Isherwood (ed.), *Vedanta for the Western World,* pp. 1–15, *passim.*

8. THE LIFE DIVINE: *The Vision of Sri Aurobindo*

1. Herbert Jai Singh, *Sri Aurobindo, His Life and Religious Thought* (Bangalore: The Bangalore Press, 1962), p. 1.

2. Sri Aurobindo (Ghose), *Sri Aurobindo on Himself and the Mother* (Pondicherry: Sri Aurobindo Ashram Press, 1953), pp. 9 ff.

3. K. R. Srinivasa Iyengar, *Sri Aurobindo* (Calcutta: Arya Publishing House, 1950).

4. *Ibid.,* pp. 107–108.

5. Sri Aurobindo, "Uttarpara Speech," *Speeches* (Pondicherry: Sri Aurobindo Ashram Press, 1952), pp. 56–57.

6. Sri Aurobindo, *Collected Poems and Plays* (Pondicherry: Sri Aurobindo Ashram Press, 1942), 1:121.

7. Iyengar, *Sri Aurobindo,* p. 205.

8. R. R. Diwakar, *Mahayogi* (Bombay: Bharatiya Vidya Bhavan, 1954), p. 205.

9. Sri Aurobindo, *Thoughts and Glimpses* (Pondicherry: Sri Aurobindo Ashram Press, 1932), p. 14.

10. N. K. Gupta, *The Message of Sri Aurobindo and the Ashram* (Pondicherry: Sri Aurobindo Ashram Press, 1951), p. 2.

11. Sri Aurobindo, *The Life Divine* (Pondicherry: Sri Aurobindo Ashram Press, 1960).

12. *Ibid.,* pp. 304–305.

13. *Ibid.,* pp. 313–323, *passim.*

14. *Ibid.,* pp. 308–309.

15. Herbert Jai Singh, *Sri Aurobindo,* p. 11.

16. Sri Aurobindo, *The Life Divine,* p. 859.

17. *Ibid.,* p. 935.

18. *Ibid.,* p. 916.

19. *Ibid.,* pp. 311–312.

20. Morwenna Donnelly, *Founding the Life Divine* (Hawthorn Books, Inc., n.d.), pp. 69–70.

21. Sri Aurobindo, *Letters,* Vol. I, p. 159.

22. *Ibid.,* p. 144.

23. Donnelly, *Founding,* p. 71.

24. *Ibid.,* pp. 73–74.

25. Sri Aurobindo, *Letters,* Vol. II, p. 3.

26. Published by E. P. Dutton & Company, Inc., New York. See also Donnelly, *Founding.* Valuable summaries of *The Life Divine* and of *The Synthesis of Yoga* can be found in Chapters XIV and XVI of Iyengar's *Sri Aurobindo.* Obviously, an introductory study such as the present could not, under necessary limitations of space, present, even in summary form, the contents of the 1272 pages of *The Life Divine* and the even longer *Synthesis of Yoga!*

27. Narayan Prasad, *Life in Sri Aurobindo Ashram* (Pondicherry: Sri Aurobindo Ashram Press, 1965), p. 241.

28. *Life* magazine, Dec. 23, 1957, pp. 98–99.

29. Prasad, *Life,* p. 363.

30. *Ibid.*

31. *Ibid.,* p. 287.

32. *Ibid.,* pp. 285–305, *passim.*

33. Sri Aurobindo, *On Himself and the Mother,* p. 282.

34. *Ibid.*, p. 283.
35. Prasad, *Life*, p. 332.
36. *Ibid.*, p. 331.
37. *Ibid.*, p. 332.
38. *Ibid.*, p. 337.

9. THE SAGE OF ANANDA KUTIR: *Swami Sivananda*

1. The Divine Life Society, *Handbook of Information* (Sivanandanagar: Yoga-Vedanta Forest Academy Press, 1967), p. 8.
2. Swami Chidananda, *Light Fountain* (Sivanandanagar: Yoga-Vedanta Forest Academy Press, 1967), p. 163.
3. *Ibid.*, pp. 126–150, *passim.*
4. *Ibid.*, pp. 188–189, *passim.*
5. Swami Sivananda, *Bliss Divine* (Sivanandanagar: Yoga-Vedanta Forest Academy Press, 1965), pp. 1–16, *passim.*
6. *Ibid.*, pp. 24–31, *passim.*
7. *Ibid.*, pp. 180–181, *passim.*
8. *Ibid.*, p. 415.
9. *Ibid.*, p. 420.
10. Swami Sivananda, *Practical Lessons in Yoga* (Sivanandanagar: Yoga-Vedanta Forest Academy Press, 1967).
11. *Ibid.*, p. 7.
12. *Ibid.*, p. 57.
13. *Ibid.*, p. 78.
14. *Ibid.*, p. 99.
15. *Ibid.*, p. 106.
16. *Ibid.*, p. 98.
17. Swami Sivananda, *Japa Yoga* (Sivanandanagar: Yoga-Vedanta Forest Academy Press, 1967), p. 12.
18. *Ibid.* Swami Sivananda also discusses the importance of *japa yoga* in his *Bliss Divine*, pp. 232–240, and in his *Elixir Divine* (Sivanandanagar: Yoga-Vedanta Forest Academy Press, 1969), pp. 80–82.
19. Divine Life Society, *Handbook of Information*, p. 16.
20. For details, see *ibid.*, pp. 38–71, and "Annual Report Number" of *The Divine Life*, magazine of the Divine Life Society, July, 1970.

10. FOUR "HOLY MOTHERS"

1. Chatterjee, "Hindu Religious Thought," in Morgan, *The Religion of the Hindus*, pp. 257–259, *passim.*

2. Cf. p. 125, above.

3. Swami Tapasyananda, *Sri Sarada Devi the Holy Mother* (Madras: Sri Ramakrishna Math, 1958), p. 15.

4. *Ibid.,* p. 35.

5. Saradananda, *Great Master,* p. 292.

6. Tapasyananda, *Sri Sarada Devi,* p. 229.

7. *Ibid.,* pp. 273–274.

8. *Ibid.,* pp. 297–560, *passim.* See also Swami Gambhirananda, *The Message of Holy Mother* (Calcutta: Advaita Ashram, 1962), and Swami Suddhasatwananda, *Thus Spake the Holy Mother* (Madras: Sri Ramakrishna Math, 1965).

9. Suddhasatwananda, *Thus Spake,* p. xiii.

10. *Mother as Seen by Her Devotees* (Varanasi: Shree Shree Anandamayee Sangha, 1967), p. 24.

11. *Ibid.*

12. Jyotish Chandra Ray, *Mother as Revealed to Me* (Varanasi: Shree Shree Anandamayee Sangha, 1962), p. 20.

13. K. Bose (ed.), *Annual Report* (Varanasi: Shree Shree Anandamayee Sangha, 1966), *passim.*

14. See, for example, Gopinath Kaviraj, Introduction, *Mother as Seen by Her Devotees*, pp. i–xxix.

15. *Ibid.,* p. 57.

16. Brahmachari Kamal Bhattacharjee (recorder), *Words of Sri Anandamayi Ma* (Varanasi: Shree Shree Anandamayee Sangha, 1961).

17. Gurupriya Debi (recorder), *Matri Vani* (Varanasi: Shree Shree Anandamayee Sangha, 1963).

18. Mani Sahukar, *Sweetness and Light: An Exposition of Sati Godavari Mataji's Philosophy and Way of Life* (Bombay: Bharatiya Vidya Bhavan, 1966), p. 9. This section on Godavari Mata and the Kanya Kumari Sthan is based on *Sweetness and Light; Sage of Sakuri,* by B. V. Narasimha and S. Subbarao, pp. 163–176; and *Contribution of Upasani Baba to Indian Culture,* by S. N. Tipnis, pp. 41–45.

19. Sahukar, *Sweetness and Light,* p. 17.

20. *Ibid.*, p. 18.

21. *Ibid.*, p. 47.

22. *Ibid.*, p. 50.

23. Pasupati (Phanibhusan Nath), *On the Mother Divine* (Calcutta: Temple Press, 1968), pp. 4–5.

24. *Ibid.*, p. 16.

25. *Ibid.*, p. 13.

26. Quoted in Pasupati, *On the Mother Divine*, p. 18.

27. Sri Aurobindo, *The Mother* (Pondicherry: Sri Aurobindo Ashram Press, 1937), pp. 35–36, *passim.*

28. *Ibid.*, pp. 48–50, *passim.*

29. Sri Aurobindo, *Sri Aurobindo on Himself and the Mother* (Pondicherry: Sri Aurobindo Ashram Press, 1953), pp. 43–772, *passim.*

30. *Bulletin of Physical Education* (Pondicherry: Sri Aurobindo Ashram Press), Feb., 1958, p. 75.

31. Pasupati, *On the Mother Divine*, p. 31. For a detailed description of the ashram institutions and activities, see Narayan Prasad, *Life in Sri Aurobindo Ashram* and *Sri Aurobindo Ashram* (Pondicherry: Sri Aurobindo Ashram Press, 1968).

32. Pasupati, *On the Mother Divine*, p. 46.

33. Prasad, *Life*, p. 382.

34. *Ibid.*, p. 390.

35. *Ibid.*, p. 386.

11. CHELAS: *American Disciples of the Masters*

1. The Vedanta Society, *Vedanta in America* (Hollywood: Vedanta Press, n.d.), p. 4.

2. *Ibid.*

3. John Yale (ed.), *What Vedanta Means to Me: A Symposium* (Doubleday & Company, Inc., 1960); Christopher Isherwood, *An Approach to Vedanta* (Hollywood: Vedanta Press, 1963), *Ramakrishna and His Disciples*, and as editor, *Vedanta for the Western World* and *Vedanta for Modern Man* (Harper & Brothers, 1951).

4. Swami Akhilananda, *Hindu Psychology: Its Meaning for the West* (London: Routledge & Kegan Paul, Ltd., 1948), *The*

Hindu View of Christ (Philosophical Library, Inc., 1949), *Mental Health and Hindu Psychology* (Harper & Brothers, 1951); Swami Nikhilananda, *Hinduism: Its Meaning for the Liberation of the Spirit* (Harper & Brothers, 1958), *Man in Search of Immortality* (London: George Allen & Unwin, Ltd., 1968), and as ed. and tr., *Ramakrishna: Prophet of New India* (Harper & Brothers, 1948) and *The Upanishads* (Harper & Row, Publishers, Inc., 1964); and Swami Yatiswarananda, *Adventures in Vedanta* (London: Rider & Co., 1961).

5. Laurie B. Whitman (ed.), *Yearbook of American Churches* (Council Press, 1969).

6. *India News* (Washington, D.C.: Information Service, Embassy of India), 10:4, p. 4.

7. Prasad, *Life,* pp. 238–239.

8. *Ibid.,* p. 269.

9. *Ibid.,* p. 364.

10. Haridas Chaudhuri, in a personal letter to the author dated March 2, 1971.

11. Prasad, *Life,* pp. 368–369.

12. East-West Cultural Center, *Newsletter,* April, 1971.

13. *Ibid.*

14. Unpublished report of the Secretary, Radha Soami Satsang, Beas, n.d.

15. Roland de Vries, in a personal letter to the author dated Feb. 2, 1971.

16. The Seva Trust, *R. S. Greetings* (Waukegan, Ill.: Dery Press), June, 1970, p. 29.

17. See, for example, Maharaj Charan Singh *St. John, the Great Mystic* (Beas: The Radha Soami Foundation, n.d.).

18. *R. S. Greetings,* June, 1970, pp. 32–37, *passim.*

19. Sawan Ashram, *Glimpses from Life* (Delhi, n.d.), p. 2.

20. Sawan Ashram, *Ruhani Satsang* (Delhi, 1970), p. 1.

21. Kirpal Singh, *Hazur Baba Sawan Singh Ji Maharaj* (Delhi: Kirpal Printing Press, 1968), p. 11.

22. Kirpal Singh, *Ruhani Satsang* (Delhi: Kirpal Printing Press, 1970), p. 27.

23. Jean Adriel, *The Avatar* (Santa Monica, Calif.: F. Rowny Press, 1947).

24. Purdom, *The God-Man,* pp. 202–204.

25. *Ibid.,* pp. 297–340, *passim.*

26. The Universal Spiritual League of America, *The Awakener* (Berkeley: Craftsman Press), Vol. 13, Nos. 1–2, p. 1.

27. *Ibid.*

28. *Ibid.*

29. Sufism Reoriented Center, 1290 Sutter St., San Francisco, Calif.

30. For addresses of these centers, see *The Awakener*.

31. Quoted from a leaflet published by the Divine Life Society, Sivanandanagar, India.

32. Swami Krishnananda (ed.), *The Divine Life* (Sivanandanagar: Yoga-Vedanta Forest Academy Press, n.d.), 31:11, p. 454.

33. *Ibid.*, p. 485.

34. *Ibid.*, 30:11, pp. 467–468.

35. *Ibid.*, 32:9, p. 384.

36. Sivananda Yoga Vedanta Center, *Yoga Life International* (Val Morin, Quebec: Sivananda Yoga Vedanta Center), 1:5, p. 1.

37. *Ibid.*

38. A. C. Bhaktivedanta Swami, *On Chanting the Hare Krishna Mantra* (Boston, Mass.: ISKCON Press, n.d.).

39. International Society for Krishna Consciousness, *Back to Godhead* (Boston: ISKCON Press), No. 37, p. 2.

40. A. C. Bhaktivedanta Swami, *The Teachings of Lord Chaitanya* (Tokyo: Dai Nippon Printing Co., 1968), pp. xxvii–xxxvi, *passim*.

41. *Back to Godhead*, No. 38, pp. 26–27.

42. Bhaktivedanta, *On Chanting Hare Krishna*, p. 10.

43. Bhagavan Sri Sathya Sai Seva Samithi, *At the Lotus Feet* (Bombay: States' People Press, 1968), p. 13.

44. *Ibid.*, pp. 3–6.

45. *Ibid.*, pp. 21–22.

46. *Ibid.*, p. 71.

12. AT THE LOTUS FEET OF A MASTER

1. Isherwood (ed.), *Vedanta for the Western World* (The Viking Press, 1960), John Yale (ed.), *What Vedanta Means to Me* (Doubleday & Company, Inc., 1960).

2. Yale (ed.), *What Vedanta Means to Me*, p. 16.

3. Erwin Schrödinger, *My View of the World* (Cambridge University Press, 1964), p. 67.

4. Ferré, Foreword, in Surjit Singh, *Christology and Personality*, p. 14.

5. Edmund D. Soper, *The Inevitable Choice: Vedanta Philosophy or Christian Gospel* (Abingdon Press, 1957), p. 5.

6. Needleman, *The New Religions*, p. 27.

7. Yale (ed.), *What Vedanta Means to Me*, p. 54.

8. Bach, *Strangers at the Door*, p. 162.

9. *Time* (TIME Inc.), June 21, 1971, pp. 56, 59.

10. *Back to Godhead*, No. 37, pp. 21–27.

11. Braden, *These Also Believe*, p. xi.

INDEX